The Crimir
Old and New

CU00985448

JURY POWER FROM EARLY TIMES TO THE PRESENT DAY

John Hostettler

John Hostettler is a solicitor, legal biographer and historian whose subjects have included Sir James Fitzjames Stephen, Sir Edward Coke, Sir Matthew Hale, Thomas Erskine and Lord Halsbury. He has written widely for the legal press, including as a regular contributor to the weekly journal *Justice of the Peace*. A former magistrate, he played a leading role in the abolition of flogging in British colonial prisons. He has also served as chair of Social Security Appeals Tribunals. He holds the degrees of BA, MA, LLB (Hons), LLM and PhD (London) and is a member of the Royal Society of Literature.

The Criminal Jury Old and New
Jury Power from Early Times to the Present Day

Published 2004 by
WATERSIDE PRESS
Domum Road
Winchester S023 9NN

Telephone 01962 855567; UK Local-rate call 0845 2300 733
E-mail enquiries@ watersidepress.co.uk
Online bookstore www.watersidepress.co.uk

ISBN Paperback 1 904 380 11 5

Cataloguing-in-publication data A catalogue record for this book can be obtained from the British Library

Printing and binding Antony Rowe Ltd, Eastbourne

Cover design Waterside Press.

Other books by John Hostettler

The Politics of Criminal Law: Reform in the Nineteenth Century (1992) Barry Rose
Thomas Wakely: An Improbable Radical (1993) Barry Rose
The Politics of Punishment (1994) Barry Rose
Politics and Law in the Life of Sir James Fitzjames Stephen (1995) Barry Rose
Thomas Erskine and Trial by Jury (1996) Barry Rose
Sir Edward Carson: A Dream Too Far (1997) Barry Rose
Sir Edward Coke: A Force for Freedom (1997) Barry Rose
At the Mercy of the State: A Study in Judicial Tyranny (1998) Barry Rose
Lord Halsbury (1998) Barry Rose
The Red Gown: The Life and Works of Sir Matthew Hale (2002) Barry Rose
Law and Terror in Stalin's Russia (2003) Barry Rose

With Brian P. Block:

Hanging in the Balance: A History of the Abolition of Capital Punishment in Britain (1997) Waterside Press
Voting in Britain: A History of the Parliamentary Franchise (2001) Barry Rose
Famous Cases: Nine Trials that Changed the Law (2002) Waterside Press

The Criminal Jury Old and New
Jury Power from Early Times to the Present Day

CONTENTS

WATERSIDE PRESS
WINCHESTER

Acknowledgements

I am indebted to Dr Richard Vogler, Senior Lecturer in Law at the University of Sussex, for his helpful advice and guidance during the writing of this book. His keen interest and comments have been invaluable. Any errors that remain are entirely my own.

I also wish to thank the staff of the British Library and the London Library, the Sussex University Library and the Public Record Office for their courtesy and help throughout the research undertaken for the writing of this book

John Hostettler

October 2004

Glossary and Key Historical References

Accusing jury The Assize of Clarendon (below) provided that from each hundred 12 men of good repute and no criminal record - and four lawful men of every *vill* (i.e. each township or village) - were to report people in the locality accused or notoriously suspected of serious crimes. Over time, they were also known as the 'presenting jury' or 'grand jury' (below).

Actus reus The physical aspects within the definition of a criminal offence.

Assizes Originally regional criminal courts dealing with the most serious crimes. They were abolished by the Courts Act 1971 and replaced by the Crown Court in 1972.

Assize of Clarendon In 1166 the Assize established the accusing jury (above). People accused or notoriously suspected of serious crimes were taken before the sheriff in the shire (county) court or brought before the itinerant royal judges when they visited the area. In either case they faced being sent to trial by ordeal. (*Chapter 2*)

Benefit of clergy Device concocted by the Church whereby a convicted prisoner would be set free if he or she could read the first verse of Psalm 51 (the so-called 'neck verse'). The benefit was not available to women until 1624 and treason was never 'clergyable'. In Tudor times it was provided that the benefit could not be claimed more than once, leading to branding for the purposes of future identification. Abolished by statute in 1827.

Blood feud Vengeful violence by the family of a victim of crime - against the alleged perpetrator - particularly in Anglo-Saxon times. In tight communities this might work well, but feuds were often 'self-feeding' and could lead to warfare and anarchy. Kings tried to prevent them by an alternative arrangement known as *wergild* (below).

'Bloody Assize' In 1685 the Duke of Monmouth unsuccessfully attempted a rebellion in the West Country. Lord Chief Justice Jeffreys presided at the Assizes in the major towns of the area where alleged rebels were prosecuted. He constantly browbeat accused and witnesses alike and sentenced large numbers of people to death without a fair trial. (*Chapter 5*)

Canon law See Civil law (below).

Challenge for cause All or any potential members of a jury may be challenged for cause, i.e. objected to by the defence on the basis of a sound reason. This might include that he or she is not qualified to serve or is suspected of partiality. Challenges are tried and determined by the judge. Challenge for cause should be contrasted with 'peremptory challenge' (below).

Civil law In the context of this book, Roman law as opposed to the common law of England.

Commonwealth The period of Oliver Cromwell's rule of England from 1649 - when the country was declared to be a republic - to 1653. (*Chapter 4*)

Compurgators People who swore to the innocence and character of an accused person in order to secure his or her release. Abolished by the Assize of Clarendon (above) in 1166.

Constructive treason A doctrine - invented by the judges - that a conspiracy to do some act in regard to the King which might endanger his life was itself treason, even though not defined as such until the Treason Act 1795.

Court of Common Pleas Higher court dealing with actions between subject and subject as distinct from monarch and subject which occurred in the Court of King's (or Queen's) Bench.

Criminal Justice Act 1855 Statute that first introduced either-way offences, since when most such cases were (and are) dealt with in local magistrates' courts rather than at the Crown Court (formerly Assizes and Quarter Sessions) before a judge and jury. (*Chapter 8*)

Dame Alice Lisle As part of the 'Bloody Assize' (above), Dame Alice Lisle, widow of Judge Lisle, was charged with concealing a rebel at her home. After ruthless 'cross-examination' by Judge Jeffreys he told the jury to find her guilty and she was beheaded. (*Chapter 5*)

De bono et malo In the earliest days of jury trial prisoners were said to put themselves into the hands of the community 'for good and ill'.

De odio et alia To avoid trial by battle an accused could claim an allegation had been made 'from hate and spite' - and buy from the King a writ to have a jury decide that issue.

Either-way case A case that may be tried in the Crown Court by a jury or before magistrates subject to a preliminary procedure known as mode of trial. Today there are some 30 main types of either-way offence, comprising around 700 individual crimes from simple theft to offences involving violence and certain sexual offences.

England's 'Bloody Code' Byword for the 200 or so offences that became punishable by death under a series of statutes from 1723 onwards. (See *Chapter 6*)

Ex officio By virtue of office.

Ex officio oath Used by the Star Chamber and other prerogative courts, this oath required a prisoner to 'convict himself' by confessing to an unspecified crime levelled by an undisclosed informer. It was abolished by the Long Parliament in 1640.

Eyre Until the early fourteenth century judges visited the counties every seven years to hold a General Eyre and make searching inquiries about local government and the administration of justice. This generated fear with some people fleeing rather than face the judges.

Felony At common law every serious crime was a felony if conviction allowed forfeiture of the lands or goods of the offender and the penalty was capital punishment. Now redundant.

Fox's Libel Act Statute of 1792 which established the right of juries to decide as a matter of law whether or not a writing was libel and not merely that it had been published. (*Chapter 6*)

Glorious Revolution To avoid Catholic succession to the throne as plotted by James II, the Whigs and the Tories invited William, Prince of Orange, to replace James and enforce the Protestant religion. He landed in Devon in 1688 enabling a non-violent revolution. (*Chapter 5*)

Grand jury The grand jury (also known as the 'accusing' or 'presenting' jury) was established by the Assize of Clarendon in 1166 to present alleged offenders from the neighbourhood for trial for the most serious crimes. It came to consist of 12 to 23 people. Abolished in 1948.

Great Reform Act 1832 The statute which started the progression towards Parliamentary democracy in Britain by giving the vote to larger numbers of people. The franchise was enlarged (although still denied to women until 1919) and a fervour of electoral reform swept the country. (*Chapter 7*)

Hundred Historic sub-division of a county where a local court would be held every month.

Hung jury A jury which is divided and thus unable to reach a unanimous decision. Normally a new trial is ordered (subject to modern provisions enabling certain majority verdicts).

Ignoramus When an indictment was before a grand jury (above) it could find that it showed a *prima facie* case (i.e. that there was a case for the accused to answer) and should thus go for trial. It would then mark it as 'a true bill'. If, however, it found there was not a case to answer it would mark the indictment *'ignoramus'* ('we ignore') and the accused would be set free.

Indictment Written document accusing one or more people of a crime and reciting the charges in technical language - for use in the Crown Court (earlier Assizes/Quarter Sessions).

Interregnum The period of the Commonwealth (above) and Protectorate (below) combined, i.e. the total period of the interruption of monarchy in the mid-17th century. (*Chapter 4*)

Jury de mediate linguae (literally 'jury of the half tongue'). Where a foreign national was being tried in England he or she could claim that six members of the jury be of the same nationality as himself or herself. Abolished in 1870.

Jury discretion See 'nullification' below.

Jury packing In the days when jurors were chosen from lists of freeholders by sheriffs these officials sometimes packed a jury with people whom they had been bribed to select. It was an abuse sometimes denounced in statutes and strongly attacked by Jeremy Bentham.

Larceny (grand and petty) Theft of money or goods to the value of 12 pence or more, for which the penalty was death (grand larceny); or goods to the value of less than 12 pence (petty larceny: which was not a capital crime).

Lay justice An unpaid, volunteer, non-professionally qualified magistrate.

Marian trial and committal statutes In the 1550s magistrates temporarily ceased to be judicial officers and, by taking depositions and binding over witnesses to appear at a trial, became agents of the monarch to ensure efficient prosecutions of accused felons. (*Chapter 3*)

Medial verdict When an accusing jury (above) presented somebody for trial by ordeal they were not acting judicially but simply making an intermediate - or 'medial' proposal.

Mens rea The mental aspects within the definition of a criminal offence.

Misdemeanour Any indictable offence less serious than a felony which did not attract the death penalty. All distinctions between felonies and misdemeanours were abolished in 1967.

Nullification The jury's power to acquit a defendant on the basis of conscience even when, on the evidence and law, the defendant would be technically guilty.

Ordeal Ancient mode of trial in which an accused underwent a form of torture - usually involving fire or water - to ascertain guilt or innocence 'at the hand of the Almighty'.

Oyez and terminer 'Hear and determine' - hence the commission of oyer and terminer empowering a judge to try allegations of offences in a given area of the country.

Partial verdict See 'pious perjury' below.

Peine forte et jure (Hard and strong punishment) Pressing to death with weights when a defendant refused to plead. He might do so to ensure that land and goods would not be forfeited (which they would if guilty) and that his family would inherit. Abolished in 1772.

Perverse verdict A jury verdict contrary to the evidence or directions of the judge.

Peremptory challenge An unfettered objection to all or any members of a jury by the defence, i.e. without giving any reason. After 1977, this was limited to three challenges for defendants although for the prosecution there was no upper limit. Contrast 'challenge for cause'.

Petition of Right Sanctioned by Parliament in 1628, the petition proclaimed the 'rights and liberties' of Englishmen, including not to be imprisoned or detained without trial and no billeting of soldiers upon private individuals against their will. (See *Chapter 4*)

Petty jury The ordinary criminal trial jury, as distinct from the grand jury (above).

Pious perjury When capital punishment existed for many property crimes juries would frequently reduce the charge and thus lessen the sentence, often from death to transportation or whipping. An example would be reducing the value of goods to below 12 pence (see under 'larceny' above). The term was coined by Sir William Blackstone.

Pipe roll Part of a regular series of royal records begun in 1156 and in which details of some early jury trials can be found.

Popish Plot A fake plot instigated by Titus Oates alleging a Jesuit plan to murder Charles II, put the Roman Catholic Duke of York on the throne and bring a French army into Britain. The 'plot' raged from 1678 to 1681 and produced a public outcry that fostered the judicial murder of many Whig leaders after biased trials. (See *Chapter 5*)

Prerogative courts Courts controlled under the prerogative of the monarch and the Crown of which the Star Chamber was the most notorious.

Presenting jury See 'accusing jury' and 'grand jury' above.

Protectorate Period from 1653 when Oliver Cromwell assumed more dictatorial powers than he had done hitherto and became virtually a monarch (though he refused the Crown) and ending with the restoration to the throne of Charles II in 1660. (*Chapter 4*)

Royal pardon After someone was convicted of a capital offence, if the judge (or sometimes the jury) considered that for sound reasons he or she should be shown clemency they could petition the monarch for a royal pardon. This was often done to avoid capital punishment.

Quarter Sessions Area 'intermediate' level court held before two or more justices of the peace and a jury to try offenders charged with offences less serious than those tried at Assizes but beyond the province of a magistrates' court. Replaced by the Crown Court in 1972.

Sacerdotal ordeal Ordeal controlled by priests.

Scintilla juris A fragment of a right.

Seditious libel The publication of matter intended to excite disaffection, hatred or contempt against authority. The jury was permitted to decide only if publication had taken place. As it was a misdemeanour (above), counsel could appear for the defence and after a number of trials in which Thomas Erskine acted for the defence, Fox's Libel Act (above) was passed..

Seven Bishops Case In 1688 seven bishops declared that James II's Declaration of Indulgence for Roman Catholics was illegal. Charged with seditious libel, the jury found them not guilty. The case was one trigger for the Glorious Revolution. (See *Chapter 5*)

Special jury A jury drawn from a panel of those with a higher property qualification than common jurors. Abolished in 1971.

Star Chamber Set up by Henry VII, the Court of Star Chamber could not impose the death penalty for felonies but it established a wide and efficient jurisdiction, particularly over offences affecting public order and the security of the state. Gradually it became infamous for its arbitrary procedures and use of torture. Abolished in 1640. (See *Chapter 3*)

Substantive law The law setting out the ingredients of criminal offences as opposed, e.g. to procedure or rules of evidence.

Summary trial Trial by magistrates (i.e. summarily, without a jury, in a magistrates' court).

Talesmen Bystanders at court who at one time could be asked to 'make up' jury numbers.

Tourn The hundred court with the sheriff presiding over allegations by the presenting jury.

Trailbaston Commissions Special commissions with extensive powers to deal with widespread violence in the early fourteenth century. They were eventually replaced with the introduction of justices of the peace and mainly from the 1360s onwards. The word was originally used to describe a criminal carrying a stave as a weapon. (*Chapter 2*)

Unanimity From 1367 until quite modern times every criminal jury had to reach its verdict unanimously. Failure to do so meant that a retrial had to be held. Today, juries must still attempt unanimity. But if they cannot agree after two hours they may return a verdict by a majority of at least ten to two, or at least nine when the jury has been reduced to ten or eleven.

Waltham Black Act Statute of 1723 that added some 50 new capital offences to the existing total of over 200 in the 'England's bloody code'. (*Chapter 6*)

Wergild Financial compensation for injury in Anglo-Saxon times.

1794 Treason Trials Three trials - the first of an intended 800 - that were an attempt by the Pitt administration, which was alarmed at seeing the French Revolution, to introduce a reign of terror in England. The defendants were represented by Thomas Erskine, found not guilty and the remaining cases were dropped thereby making them landmark cases in English criminal and constitutional law. (*Chapter 6*)

1965 Morris Report Underlying basis for the Juries Act 1974 which democratised the jury by abolishing property qualifications for jurors and extending eligibility to everyone on the electoral roll. (*Chapter 8*)

CHAPTER 1

Introduction

A DEMOCRATIC INSTITUTION

We all know what a jury is in a criminal trial. Some people appear before juries and their freedom or livelihood may depend upon their verdicts. Others may experience them as some of the quarter of a million people who are called for jury service each year. What is significant is that the criminal trial jury gives expression to the constitutional principle that no man or woman should be imprisoned or suffer a penalty for a crime unless he or she has been found guilty by his or her peers. And underlining the importance of the jury is the point that it reaches a verdict only on the facts of the case before it, whether or not its decision is a correct one. As was said by Sir William Holdsworth, juries create no precedent and they can decide hard cases equitably without making bad law. The jury system also indiscriminately draws members of the public into the administration of justice and an understanding of legal and human rights. As Thomas Jefferson declared, the jury is the anchor which holds a government to its constitution.

The jury has always been drawn from sections of society but has been made democratic only in the last half century. In particular, since the Criminal Justice Act 2003 was passed almost all citizens of the United Kingdom are now eligible to serve on a jury. But across the years that democratisation has been partially undermined by a significant shift from the higher courts where juries sit or have sat—the Crown Court and before that Assizes and Quarter Sessions—to the magistrates' courts, where they do not in the type and seriousness level of cases tried. This process first began in 1855. Why this has been the policy of successive governments is of tremendous importance and can be better understood with a knowledge of the history of trial by jury and the inherent power of the jury.

I have endeavoured, therefore, to deal with the great political, social and legal landmarks with which that history is embroiled and to show how the criminal jury evolved and survived attacks, pressure, interference and controls to become the key democratic institution that it is. Unfortunately, such attacks and pressures still continue as society and the jury evolve further and this is examined in *Chapter 8*.

CHANGING MEANING

Trial by jury is at the heart of the English criminal trial system, having had a striking history stretching over nine centuries. Its influence on criminal law and procedure has been profound. Yet, many modern textbooks on criminal law and the jury tend to deal only with present structures and to exhibit an anti-historical bias. This is regrettable, particularly as with the criminal jury the past sheds a good deal of light on aspects of current controversies about its place and role in modern society.

Of course, the word 'jury' has changed its meaning over the centuries and what it meant to people in the thirteenth century was very different from what it means today. Accordingly, as a starting point in this book, due attention will be paid to the results of a great deal of recent research in regard to juries in ancient court pipe rolls, and other records of the king's courts, assizes and quarter sessions (see the *Glossary*). It has to be taken into account, however, that primary sources themselves can be subjective and incorporate a bias either deliberately or unconsciously. Preambles to statutes complaining about increases in crime, for example, might be simply 'rhetorical flourishes advanced by members of the royal bureaucracy to justify the expansion of its influences and an increase in its sources of revenue.'[1] It must also be noted that most of such research is confined to the midland and southern counties of England and so far evidence of jury composition and other aspects of criminal jury trial in the north of England in the early days is sparse.

Clearly, there is still a great deal of work to be done in examining the forensic records of the past, and present conclusions are often tentative and subject to ongoing revision. The contemporaneous data about early juries was written by those who could write and it may have had a purpose of which we are unaware, as we are of the views of the uneducated mass of the people living at the time. Indeed, generally speaking, jurors themselves have left virtually no record of their opinions.[2] Further, as one legal historian has pointed out:

> the varied composition and variable motives of juries prevent us from deducing the features that consigned a defendant to the verdict of his country. We can only be sure that the court records of the time [the fourteenth century] support no single or simple hypothesis about the functions of a criminal trial jury.[3]

In fact, the clerks in the early fourteenth century provided only the bare minimum of information required to keep a record of criminal trials. This included 'the mode of prosecution, the accused, the type of offence, the victim, the stolen goods (if any) and their supposed value, sometimes the hundred, town or neighbourhood providing the jury, and the result.'[4] Lists of jury members were extremely rare. Moreover, since before the eighteenth century lawyers were little involved in felony trials, law reports (apart from those of state trials which, in any event, are not always accurate) were largely barren of criminal cases. It means that 'the behaviour of juries can thus appear unpredictable and unfathomable'[5] and no work on the subject can yet, or probably will ever, be considered conclusive.

Nevertheless, valuable information can be gleaned from the evidence which is available and research in recent years has uncovered a considerable amount of material that is of inestimable value for any endeavour to understand the history of criminal trial by jury in England and Wales from its origins to the present day. To attempt to record that history is a task which it appears has not previously been undertaken.

GENESIS OF THE CRIMINAL TRIAL JURY

Inquests, some of which were no doubt brought to these islands by invaders, by appointed people have a lineage that goes back a long way in ancient English history. Similarly, the whole idea of representation has a long pedigree. In Anglo-Saxon England members of local communities took part in the administration of the criminal law in the hundred courts,[6] in effect local popular assemblies, and representation was reinforced under the Normans and Angevins. At one time or another the councils of the church were attended by representatives from each diocese; spokesmen for the *vills* (townships or parishes) gave evidence before the Domesday commissioners; representatives of the hundreds and *vills* sat in the shire courts and, later, on early presenting juries; representatives of each *vill* attended the justices in eyre;[7] and subsequently other itinerant judges were assisted by knights elected by the counties under clause 18 of *Magna Carta*.[8]

In addition, it is sometimes suggested that the 12 oath-helpers described in the laws of King Alfred constituted the first criminal jury in England. However, they testified to the truth of the evidence of one party to a case and did not pass judgment on that case. They did not fulfil the essential function of the criminal trial jury that they return a verdict of guilty or not guilty. In a sense they were witnesses to the probity of the man they supported. Indeed, each party might have his or her own oath-helpers and they are no proof of an Anglo-Saxon jury as a precursor of the modern jury.[9] Equally, although Ethelred's code, issued at Wantage in the year 997, described a group of 12 men who took an oath to judge cases fairly that was probably an institution for the Danelaw only[10] and quite distinct from Anglo-Saxon practice and procedure.

Furthermore, despite its long history the alleged direct connection of criminal jury trial with *Magna Carta* is false. As W. R. Cornish has said, 'It has always been bad history to trace the system back to *Magna Carta*, and even the juries which were being introduced in the thirteenth century were only an early species in the chain of evolution.'[11] The *judicium parium* of clause 39 of the Great Charter, of the time when trial by ordeal was still in operation, was not judgment of a defendant's peers or jurors but for the barons who wrested the Charter from King John, judges of no lesser rank than themselves.[12]

Nonetheless, the petty jury has often restrained the powers of government, as will be seen in later chapters. Although the idea that juries have a right to decide questions of law has often been pressed and rejected, they undoubtedly have the democratic if not the strict legal right to do so. One commentator has written, 'Juries may and do infuse "non-legal" values into the trial process. They are the conscience of the community: they represent current ethical conventions. They are a constraint on legalism, arbitrariness and bureaucracy.'[13] How far this has been, and still is, true will be considered at each stage in the vicissitudes of criminal jury trial in what follows.

Fortunately, the origin of the *criminal* jury trial system in England, as distinct from the jury in civil, often real property, cases, is shown clearly by the instructions the king's council gave to the judges in 1219.[14] Except for a brief incursion into what preceded trial by jury, and what the jury sprang and grew from, that is where this study will commence.

HISTORICAL CONTEXT

This will involve investigating how far early jurors were witnesses, how they reached their verdicts, and how their role changed and they came to hear evidence. Also, as part of the theme running through this book consideration will be given to the extent to which nullification[15] (the power to acquit a defendant when he or she is technically guilty) was practised by early juries and why they so acted; how they fared under stricter control by the early Tudors and Stuarts; and how far the issue of the right of a jury to decide questions of law was raised in the Interregnum. Equally, it will be examined to what extent juries, and in particular grand juries, were influenced by political interference in the reigns of the later Stuarts (*Chapter 5*); to what degree juries used discretion in cases of seditious libel and treason in the eighteenth century (*Chapter 6*); what changes in criminal trial by jury occurred in the nineteenth and twentieth centuries with the transfer of trials from the jury to magistrates(*Chapters 7 and 8*); and why, and to what extent, jury trial is under attack today (*Chapter 8*).

The main purpose of this book is to explore the exercise of jury power over the whole nine centuries of jury existence. This means asking by what process an elite body of witnesses became identified as a popular tribunal. And, to what extent the jury participated in the legal process and influenced the legitimacy of the criminal justice system, *inter alia*, through the use of discretion, including jury nullification and the avoidance of the death penalty by what is known as 'pious perjury'. As a secondary, and connected, theme it will be necessary to consider the social composition of juries at various times and how far this affected jury nullification.

As background material consideration will be given to whether the existence of the jury over the centuries suited the interests of judges, monarchs and governments in endeavouring to legitimise their own power by seeking controlled involvement of people of property in the criminal justice system.[16] In other words, must law enforcement be placed within a historically specific social and political context?[17] And, as part of the overall picture consideration will be given to whether Blackstone's eighteenth century view that the jury was 'the sacred bulwark of the nation, upholding the liberties of England'[18] was really true in his day and is true today. These are essential elements in what is in effect the story of the evolution of the English criminal trial by jury.

RECENT TRENDS

The present system of criminal trial by jury often provokes passionate attitudes of support on the one hand and strong opposition on the other. According to two writers, juries provoke comments which are little short of hysterical.[19] After all, they say,

> twelve individuals are chosen at random, often with no prior contact with the courts, to listen to evidence (sometimes of a highly technical nature) and to decide upon matters affecting the reputation and liberty of those charged with criminal offences. They are given no training for this task, they deliberate in secret, they return a verdict without giving reasons, and they are responsible to their own conscience but to no one else. After the trial they melt away into the community from which they are drawn.[20]

This seems to suggest that juries are anomalous. Nonetheless, they can be considered either to represent an ancient right and to be a 'bastion of liberty' or, not exactly as unnatural, but as an anachronism that is both too expensive and too favourable to criminals who often exploit it.[21] One academic writer also calls the jury 'an anti-democratic, irrational and haphazard legislator, whose erratic and secret decisions run counter to the rule of law.'[22] Further, Professor Glanville Williams, a respected authority on criminal law, spoke of the jury having a 'tyrannous origin' and he quoted with approval Lord Goddard as saying that 'no one has yet been able to find a way of depriving a British jury of its privilege of returning a perverse verdict.'[23]

Such views are reflected in the 2001 report of Lord Justice Auld[24] and this book will endeavour to establish how far jury intuition, in different forms, has extended throughout the history of the criminal trial jury and how deep is the threat to the existence of jury trial at the beginning of the twenty-first century. Certainly, two academic lawyers have claimed that during the twentieth century in England the scope and powers of the jury markedly declined, and criminal jury trial is increasingly seen as excessively expensive and time-consuming.[25] However, they add, 'the impetus for reform has come from immediate political concerns, high-profile cases, and anecdote as much as from systematic information or reliable research.'[26] Views of those opposed to nullification and those in favour of it are indicated and contrasted at various points in the chapters that follow, particularly *Chapter 9*.

As would be expected, over nine centuries criminal trial by jury in England has undergone considerable changes and adaptation. Perhaps most important is that whereas during most of its existence almost all serious charges were heard before a jury, today some 97 per cent of criminal cases are dealt with by magistrates.[27] Indeed, if the situation were otherwise the criminal justice system would choke on the volume of work. The remaining three per cent of cases are committed to the Crown Court for trial where most defendants plead guilty and do not face a jury at all.[28] However, these are percentage figures and a good many accused persons, charged with serious offences and facing severe penalties, are tried by juries.

Although Alexis de Toqueville considered the jury system to be 'as direct and extreme a consequence of the sovereignty of the people as universal suffrage',[29] for some years now critics of the jury have included policemen, judges and academics who often point to the fact that juries are not always logical or sometimes do not follow the law strictly. This reflects, in some cases, the logical minds of the detractors themselves, or perhaps their own interests in the criminal justice system. Metropolitan police chief commissioner Sir Robert Mark, Sir Robin Auld and Professor Glanville Williams have all been outspoken in their respective roles as police officer, appeal judge and academic.

Despite the earlier rarity of criticism of the jury system, this began to change after 1972 when, to make juries more representative of the nation, the Criminal Justice Act of that year brought the qualification for jury service largely into line with the franchise. Significantly, since that time, and the democratisation of jury service, not only has criticism of the system grown from those with an interest such as the police who often feel frustrated by jury verdicts,[30] but respective governments have sought, with varying degrees of success, to diminish the role of the jury in our society. This culminated in the Auld Report of 2001 and the subsequent Criminal Justice Act of 2003,[31] both of which will be examined in *Chapter 8*. The question is whether, in effect, the 2003 Act marks a destruction of the right to trial by a cross-section of the community for very many people, alongside breaches of fundamental rules of evidence which helped establish and maintain the presumption of innocence. It will be considered how far the history of criminal jury trial informs this current agenda.[32]

JURY 'PERVERSITY' AND THE STATE

In some cases the results of detailed research by scholars into juries in certain localities during specific periods[33] will be considered and experiences and judgments from the United States will not be ignored. In fact, academics based in the United States and Canada have made an important contribution to opening up what is known about medieval (and later) juries, a subject which until recently was largely unexplored.

The truth is, said Thomas Jefferson, that the jury is as important as democracy itself. He wrote that he considered the jury 'as the only anchor, ever yet imagined by man, by which a government can be held to the principles of its constitution.'[34] Indeed, it needs to be emphasised that the jury is a unique institution that has had a huge global impact on over 50 countries and many would argue that it represents the most important English contribution to world jurisprudence.[35]

But what is its essence? The unifying theme of this book is the friction between the idea of justice based on common sense, legal nihilism, and innate feelings of what is right and wrong on the one hand and the concept of justice represented by the state and the law on the other. There is a very basic ideological conflict here, represented in the confrontation of lay person and state servant or lawyer. The jury represents a unique dialogue between formal legality and its own intuitive power or common cultural understandings which evolve from period to period. The interpretation of how this dialogue commenced in the thirteenth century and developed to the present day is an endeavour to provide an original contribution to the knowledge of the subject of jury power.

ENDNOTES for *Chapter 1*

[1] Bernard William McLane. (1988) 'Juror Attitudes towards Local Disorder: The Evidence of the 1328 Lincolnshire Trailbaston Proceedings.' In Cockburn and Green (eds.) *Twelve Good Men and True: The Criminal Trial Jury in England, 1200-1800*. New Jersey, Princeton University Press. p. 38. He uses the words quoted, although to urge a different point.

[2] For the conclusion that this is so of eighteenth-century jurors see P.J.R. King. (1988) '"Illiterate Plebeians, Easily Misled": Jury Composition, Experience and Behaviour in Essex, 1735-1815.' In Cockburn and Green. Ibid. p. 289.

[3] J.B. Post. (1988) 'Jury Lists and Juries in the Late Fourteenth Century.' In Cockburn and Green. Ibid. p. 77.

[4] Anthony Musson. (1997). 'Twelve Good Men and True? The Character of Early Fourteenth-century Juries.' 15 *Law and History Review*. University of Illinois Press. p. 116.

[5] Musson. 'Twelve Good Men and True? *Op. cit.* p. 117.

[6] The hundred was an administrative district within a county, its size varying in different parts of the country but sometimes equivalent to 100 hides, a normal peasant landholding.

[7] Eyres were itinerant royal courts held by the king's justices in counties at intervals of several years. They took presentments by juries and all Crown pleas that had arisen since the last eyre.

[8] For much of this see Sir Frank Stenton. (1971) *Anglo-Saxon England*. Oxford, The Clarendon Press. For *Magna Carta* see Henry Marsh. (1971) *Documents of Liberty from Earliest Times to Universal Suffrage*. Newton Abbot, David and Charles Ltd. p. 43.

[9] Eric Gerald Stanley. (2000) *Imagining the Anglo-Saxon Past. The Search for Anglo-Saxon Paganism and Anglo-Saxon Trial by Jury*. Woodbridge, Boydell and Brewer Ltd. p. 118.

[10] Ibid. p. 142. This view is contrary to that of Naomi D. Hurnard. (1941) 'The Jury of Presentment and the Assize of Clarendon.' 56 *The English Historical Review*. London, Longmans, Green and Co. pp. 374-410. See *post* p. 17. Hurnard's view is strongly contested in turn by R.C. Van Caenegem

(1991) in 'Public Prosecution of Crime in Twelfth-Century England.' In *Legal History: A European Perspective.* London, Hambledon Press. Chapter 1.

[11] W.R. Cornish. (1968) *The Jury.* London, Allen Lane. p. 12.

[12] Penny Darbyshire. (1991) 'The Lamp that Shows that Freedom Lives – Is it Worth the Candle?' *The Criminal Law Review.* London, Sweet and Maxwell. p. 743.

[13] M.D.A. Freeman. (1981b) 'The Jury on Trial.' 34 *Current Legal Problems.* London, Stevens & Sons. p. 90.

[14] See *post* p. 21–2.

[15] For a formal explanation of jury nullification see *post* p. 30.

[16] Douglas Hay has argued that by the eighteenth century, if not earlier, legitimisation was directed by a ruling-class conspiracy of king, judges, magistrates and gentry aimed at the common people, with the law superseding religion in that role. Cf. Hay. (1975) 'Property, Authority and the Criminal Law.' In *Albion's Fatal Tree, Crime and Society in Eighteenth-Century England.* London, Allen Lane. p. 52. Hay's views have been sharply contested by John H. Langbein. (1983) in 'Albion's Fatal Flaws.' *Past and Present.* Oxford, The Past and Present Society. p. 96.

[17] Cynthia B. Herrup. (1985) 'Law and Morality in Seventeenth-century England.' 106 *Past and Present.* Oxford, The Past and Present Society. p. 104.

[18] Sir William Blackstone. (1830) *Commentaries on the Law of England.* London, Thomas Tegg. vol. iv. p. 344.

[19] John Baldwin and Michael McConville. (1979) *Jury Trials.* Oxford, Clarendon Press. p. 1.

[20] Ibid.

[21] *Cf.* Sally Lloyd-Bostock and Cheryl Thomas. (1999) 'Decline of the "Little Parliament": Juries and Jury Reform in England and Wales.' 62 *Law and Contemporary Problems.* Durham, North Carolina, Duke University School of Law. p. 7.

[22] Darbyshire. Op. cit. p. 750.

[23] Glanville Williams. (1963) *The Proof of Guilt: A Study of the English Criminal Trial.* London, Stevens & Sons. pp. 257 and 261. Goddard. House of Lords. [191] 85.

[24] The Auld Report. (2001) *Review of the Criminal Courts of England and Wales.* HMSO. Cm. 5563. ·

[25] Lloyd-Bostock and Thomas. (2000b) 'The Continuing Decline of the English Jury.' In Neil Vidmar (ed.) (2000) *World Jury Systems.* Oxford, Oxford University Press. p. 53.

[26] Ibid. p. 54.

[27] Sean Enright and James Morton. (1990) *Taking Liberties. The Criminal Jury in the 1990s.* London, Weidenfeld and Nicolson. p. 2.

[28] Ibid.

[29] Alexis de Tocqueville. (1840) *Democracy in America.* (1990 edn.) New York, Vintage Books, Random House Inc. p. 283.

[30] For example, Sir Robert Mark's Dimbleby lecture on BBC television in 1973.

[31] Eliz. II. c. 44.

[32] Regrettably, juries did not include women until 1919 (see *Chapter 8*), and before that people were brought before all-male juries. Certain punishments were also only inflicted on men, such as forfeiture of land and estates , since women could not own property. In the text, certain historical references are to 'he' only for this reason, rather than the more modern 'he or she'.

[33] See, for example, essays in J.S. Cockburn and Thomas Andrew Green (eds) (1988) *Twelve Good Men and True.* Op. cit.

[34] *Thomas Jefferson Papers.* (1789) Julian P. Boyd (ed) (1958) Princeton, Princeton University Press. vol. xv. p. 269.

[35] Cf. Neil Vidmar (ed) (2000) *World Jury Systems.* Oxford, Oxford University Press.

CHAPTER 2

Origin and Early Growth of Jury Trial

INTRODUCTION

Under William the Conqueror and his successors, England became essentially a colony of a foreign dynastic empire in which some one-and-a-half million people were held in subjection by a few thousand alien warlords comprising knights and men at arms.[1] Yet, despite this, the Norman/Angevin period was crucial to the creation of the concept of the criminal jury trial and of jury nullification which began at this early stage of the criminal law as a by-product of the Anglo-Saxon emphasis on clemency. It followed from the Conqueror wanting to confirm the legitimacy of his rule and largely accepting Anglo-Saxon laws and courts when he declared he would have and hold the law of King Edward the Confessor.[2]

This chapter will deal with the rise of the accusing jury and how trial by sacerdotal ordeal functioned and expressed community values. It will consider why England adopted the criminal trial jury system following the abandonment of the ordeal and not the inquisitorial method favoured on the continent. It will look at the growth of the petty jury from the earlier presenting, self-informing juries to the jury that accused and decided. This involves examining how far jurors continued to give expression to the community thinking that lay behind the ordeal. Why, for example, did they exercise clemency for all but the most serious offenders, following the Anglo-Saxon concept of *wergild* (compensatory payment based upon a man's worth) rather than the capital punishment desired by the Crown? To what extent was there opposition to trial by jury in the early days and why did a defendant have to accept a jury or face *peine et forte dure* (pressing to death)?

The chapter will also observe the responses of juries to serious local disorder. It will outline the crucial change in the role of the jury when its members ceased to be accusers and acted in a more judicial capacity, and consider how this came to be accepted by both the judiciary and the public.

THE LAWYER KING

Alongside the blood-feud, lay justice existed in Anglo-Saxon times in the hundred and shire courts[3]. On the other hand, as intimated in *Chapter 1* the jury in England began as an administrative institution dealing with a number of different matters and only later did it become confined to courts of law. We cannot do better than follow the legal historians Pollock and Maitland in defining a jury as a body of neighbours summoned by a public officer to answer questions upon oath.[4] William the Conqueror's Domesday Book, for example, was based upon enquiries and conclusions of jurors from the localities, but crucially the *criminal jury* had its direct origin in the discretion exercised by the king's judges when trial by ordeal was abolished in 1219.

When Henry II ascended the throne in 1154, following the anarchy of the 'nineteen long winters' in the reign of King Stephen, crime, often instigated by powerful barons, was widespread[5] and Henry was determined to tackle it and, above all, establish royal control over the land.[6] At the time minor crimes could still be dealt with in the hundred courts and more serious crimes in the shire courts but pleas of the Crown, committed 'against the peace of our Lord the King, his crown and dignity', were dealt with only by the king's judges on circuit or at Westminster.[7]

In a significant transformation, Henry, the 'lawyer king', unified English customary law and royal codes into the common law[8] by establishing a permanent body of professional judges, by increasing the number of circuits of itinerant judges and, with the Assize of Clarendon (1166)[9], introducing the seeds of the new mode of trial by jury. There was a shift from Anglo-Saxon feuds and *wergild* to Angevin public prosecution, and from 'predominantly private resolution through monetary compensation to predominantly capital punishment at the hands of the Crown.'[10] From this time onwards a crime was seen as a wrong not merely against the victim but also against the Crown, with the king as the symbolic victim who had to be revenged.

Apart from increasing Crown revenues, the reason for this appears to have been that if the government wanted criminals to be prosecuted it had to do so itself. According to Theodore Plucknett:

> it was useless to depend upon injured parties or their kin to maintain the difficult procedure of bringing a criminal to justice. The chances were at least even that such proceedings would be used as a means of oppression by the powerful instead of a means of prosecution and redress by the victims of crime. As for the expectation that injured parties would bring 'appeals' and engage in judicial combat with murderers, thieves, highwaymen and such like, all experience showed that there was nothing to be expected from that quarter.[11]

Nevertheless, the Angevin monarchy would not have been exempt from the dubious motives attributed here to the 'powerful'.

THE ACCUSING JURY

The first reference to the jury in criminal cases is in the Constitutions of Clarendon in 1164 where, in the case of a layman so rich and powerful that no individual dared appear against him, it was provided that 'the sheriff shall cause 12 loyal men of the neighbourhood, or of the *vill*, to take an oath in the presence of the bishop that they will declare the truth about it.'[12]

This was followed two years later by the Assize of Clarendon as part of a royal campaign against crime. The assize provided that from each hundred, 12 men of good repute and without criminal records and four lawful men of every *vill* were to report persons in the locality accused or notoriously suspected of serious crimes. If there were any, they were to be arrested and charged before the sheriff in the shire court or held until they could be brought before visiting royal justices. In either case they faced being sent to proof by ordeal.[13]

Naomi Hurnard has argued that the assize did not introduce the first presenting jury as this was done by Ethelred's law of the year 997 mentioned earlier.[14] There is, however, little evidence of the use of presenting juries before the assize and Pollock and Maitland believed that Ethelred's jury was found only in areas subject to Danelaw[15]—a view shared more recently by Eric Gerald Stanley.[16] In 1176 the Assize of Northampton[17] increased the range of felonies set out in the Assize of Clarendon so that serious crimes were now defined as treason, murder, robbery, larceny, forgery, arson and harbouring criminals.

The presenting jury exercised significant discretion in determining who would undergo the ordeal and, in doing so, broadly reflected 'communal attitudes about the sorts of persons who ought to suffer capital punishment or the sorts of offences for which persons ought to suffer such punishment.'[18] After 1220 the trial jury exercised a similar power with the judges dependent upon it for information about both the accused and the offence.[19]

Such presenters as the Clarendon assize required might act of their own knowledge but in the main they formed an investigating body which relied upon what was reputed in the neighbourhood and consequently they spoke to the prior perceptions *and judgment* of the locality.[20] Nevertheless, there is evidence that individual jurors had no hesitation in putting forward offences of which they themselves or their relatives had been victims.[21]

These juries were known as presenting juries, later grand juries, and, by chapters 2 and 12 of the Assize of Clarendon, the majority of suspects they presented were sent to the ordeal of cold water.[22] They therefore gave medial verdicts. At no time did they act in the judicial capacity of a trial jury but even at this early stage they exercised some discretionary or screening role in that they could decide not to proceed if an offence was insufficiently serious or the accused was of good fame. Even when they presented an accused, if they subsequently stated that he was 'not suspected', he would not be sent to the ordeal. In other words, they reported all those alleged to be criminals and then designated which of them they themselves suspected.[23] But, to be suspected by hundred jurors alone, i.e. without the four *vills*, there had to be supporting evidence of some kind beyond the mere suspicion of the presenters. For instance:

> Andrew of Burwarton is suspected by the jurors of the death of a certain Hervey because he concealed himself on account of that death, and therefore let him purge himself by the judgment of water.[24]

In other words, by the 1190s a simple assertion of guilt by a presenting jury, even if based on local reputation, had become insufficient and an accused could be sent to the ordeal only if the hundred jury produced inculpatory evidence and confirmed that the accused was truly suspected, or if it and the townships joined in an assertion of suspicion based upon reputation.[25] This involvement of the local community thus pre-dated the trial jury, 'the adoption of which ought to be understood as a continuation and enhancement of traditional practices, not as a revolutionary step.'[26] Indeed, Susan Reynolds has shown that community decision-making had a long history in England.[27]

By 1215 presenting juries, including representatives from the *vills*, were more than simply accusing juries. After making their accusations, they proceeded to decide which defendants should make proof by ordeal and which should not.'[28] Roger Groot says they exercised an adjudicatory power in selecting the guilty from the accused, controlling which accused persons were sent to the ordeal and 'the ultimate disposition of persons who successfully completed the ordeal'.[29] This greatly facilitated the development from the ordeal to the trial jury who reached a final verdict. And, any possible abuse was to a large extent limited by the Crown imposing fines or imprisonment upon presenting juries who were found guilty of perjury.[30] In general, however, in the early days the power of jurors to decide a prisoner's fate was almost absolute and they were not subject to punishment for a verdict if it had been come by honestly, only if they were guilty of corruption.[31]

TRIAL BY ORDEAL

In trials for felony in England prior to 1219 proof of guilt or innocence was largely determined by the ordeal. Once an accused was before the court there could be no trial on questions of fact—such a concept was unknown. A defendant was there on suspicion of criminal activity and had to seek a verdict from the Almighty by means of an appeal, oath-helpers or trial by ordeal.

An appeal of felony was a private prosecution against a perpetrator of a crime to obtain retribution with proof by battle,[32] although this was not available to women or the disabled and in any event was disliked as a Norman innovation. Similarly, since it required an individual accuser it could not arise when there was presentment by a jury. When battle was chosen the loser was deemed guilty and hanged. If an appellee wished to avoid battle he could plead that the appeal had been made from hate and spite (*de odio et atia*) and buy a writ to have a jury decide the issue. Hence, prior to 1215 there were two major forms of jury; the presenting jury and the *de odio* jury, and 'every presented person, and every appellee who sought a jury, was spared physical proof until a jury had viewed the case and found against him,'[33] i.e. that he should go to the ordeal.

If, however, an accused could produce sufficient oath-helpers (known as compurgators) to vouch for his character this was deemed conclusive evidence from the Almighty of his innocence. They did not swear to the facts but to their belief in the truthfulness of another person's oath,[34] or, to put it another way, their judgment that the accused was an honest man. On the other hand, if the accused were unable to find enough oath-helpers and refused to admit the crime he had to undergo the ordeal which was also a judgment of God.[35] The Assize of Clarendon ended compurgation in criminal cases and relied instead upon the ordeal.[36] However, Glanville explained that the court listened to argument before deciding to send a man to the ordeal.[37]

Like so much else in Christian countries the ordeal was of heathen origin but had been adapted to the use of the Church. It was inscrutable and could take various forms but was always a religious ceremony.[38] One ritual was known as the ordeal by hot water.[39] For this an iron cauldron was placed over a fire in a church. When the water boiled, the accused had to reach down into the vessel and snatch up a stone from the bottom. The hand and arm were then swathed in cloth or linen for three days, after which it would be exposed and if the flesh was uninjured God had pronounced the accused not guilty. If the flesh was scalded he was guilty and was sentenced by the court, usually to death.

ORDEAL BY HOT WATER.

In the ordeal by hot iron, the suspect had to lift a piece of red-hot metal and carry it barehanded over a distance of nine paces. The hand would then be bound and the accused found guilty or innocent according to its condition after three days.[40]

Another ritual involved the suspect walking barefoot and blindfold over nine red-hot ploughshares. If he completed the walk unharmed the verdict was not guilty. Emma, the mother of Edward the Confessor, is said to have undergone this ordeal when he accused her of adultery with the Bishop of Winchester. She appears to have emerged from it successfully.[41]

The ordeal of cold water, which was normally reserved for persons without rank, involved casting the body of the accused held by a rope into a pond near the church, after he had been given holy water to drink. Priests were paid five shillings for preparing the pool and 20 shillings for blessing it. If the accused floated, he was guilty as it was believed that consecrated water would not receive a wicked body. If he sank he was innocent, which would not help him unless he was hauled out in time.[42]

For a cleric the ordeal meant swallowing an ounce of consecrated barley bread, or an ounce of cheese, impregnated with a feather. If the suspect choked that was held to be proof from God of guilt. Sometimes this ordeal was prescribed for non-clerics. Godwin, the Earl of Kent and father of King Harold, was subjected to it when accused of murdering his brother. 'May this bread choke me if I am guilty!' he cried, and promptly fell down dead.[43]

Anyone caught red-handed in possession of stolen goods or who confessed or was of very low reputation was not sent to the ordeal but was dealt with summarily. Those who took and failed the ordeal were mutilated or executed, their goods forfeited to the king and their land to the lord from whom they held it. If they came through the ordeal successfully, and many did, by chapter 14 of the Assize of Clarendon they had to leave the country as outlaws if they were believed to be bad characters, which suggests that the ordeals were not entirely trusted by the king.[44] Indeed, in the reign of Rufus, of 50 men sent to the ordeal of iron all escaped, to the annoyance of the king who railed at God's judgment which he complained could be swayed by men's prayers. According to Pollock and Maitland, 'this certainly looks as if some bishop or clerk had preferred his own judgment to the judgment of God, and the king did well to be angry.'[45] As a pipe roll reveals that an officiant might allow the iron to cool[46] it seems quite possible that the priest arranged the acquittals.[47]

On the other hand, an over-zealous official might make the ordeal more than usually difficult. In an ordeal of the hot iron one Eadric, reeve of Calne in Wiltshire and all-powerful president of the hundred court, had the fire banked up unusually high and used a heavier than normal iron to be lifted. It is reported that he was seriously humiliated when, after three days, the defendant's hand was held to be clean and he was found not guilty. Although it was later shown that the hand was in fact damaged, once judgment had been declared it could not be changed.[48]

What needs to be remembered is that all these ordeals were inflicted not as punishments—no final verdict had yet been reached when the accused was sent to the ordeal—but as proofs. Moreover, the clergy had entire control over their conduct. This included deciding on the quality of the bandage in the ordeals of hot water and iron, the timing of the attempt to rescue the innocent in the ordeal by cold water and the size of the feather inside the bread or cheese. It is a matter of conjecture whether they endeavoured to mitigate the terrors of the various ordeals in order to conduce to 'group harmony'.[49] It has been suggested that the ordeal gave a defendant considered guilty by a jury a last opportunity of escaping punishment.[50]

That they 'were engineered to ensure a high rate of success' certainly appears likely.[51] Indeed, whilst men were generally subjected to the ordeal of cold water, women were usually sent to the ordeal of hot iron since, because of higher body fat, 'a woman was much less likely than a man to pass the ordeal of cold water'.[52]

Although to modern eyes such modes of proof were savage, most of those who suffered them probably experienced only a less severe form and appear to have survived. A body thrown into a pond with a rope attached might well start to sink initially but be quickly pulled out. Maitland found between 1201 and 1219 only one case in which the ordeal did not acquit the accused[53] and it has been said that the ordeal was not merely an appeal to the Deity as a 'supra-fact finder' but '[i]n practice, if not in theory, the ordeal provided a guilty man with a way to purge his wrong and therefore to be adjudged innocent.'[54]

Fisher, in similar vein, claims that 'the institutional brilliance of the ordeal was that it so neatly merged the appearance of divine judgment with the reality of a great measure of human control', and he extends this to the petty jury by adding that, 'in the trial jury, the English justice system managed to reproduce this very useful combination of traits.'[55] He concludes that 'it may be impossible to understand even the later history of the criminal trial jury without a theory about why the ordeal worked so well and about what its demise left lacking.'[56] It worked by relying upon the divine sanction when judgment would take the defendant's life or limb and ensuring 'discreet human control under the cover of divine judgment.'[57] This was followed with the jury having unbounded discretion to acquit.[58] As Paul R. Hyams has also written, the functioning and demise of the old proofs actually shaped the classical common law in multifarious ways.[59] Moreover, in people's minds crime continued, as time passed, to be linked with sin, evil and moral weakness.[60]

THE EARLY TRIAL JURY

In 1215, after serious theological questioning, the Church at the fourth Lateran Council held in Rome forbade the clergy from participating in what it rather belatedly discovered was a barbaric practice. This spelt the end of ordeals[61] and they were abandoned in England by 1219.[62] This has been described as, 'the most important event in the history of the criminal jury' by necessitating a search for a successor to the most common method of proof in the English criminal process.[63] However, no obvious and suitable replacement was seen immediately. Henry III was still a boy and left to themselves the judges were unclear about what to do.

After some hesitation by the judges at a time when there was serious civil commotion, in January 1219 the king's council addressed a writ to the justices in eyre which told them that nothing had as yet been decided about replacing the ordeal.[64] In the interim, it continued, those suspected of great crimes should be imprisoned without trial, though not to incur danger of life or limb; those whose crimes were less heinous should be made to abjure the realm; and those accused of small offences should be released if they found securities to keep the peace. 'We have left', the writ concluded, 'to your discretion the observance of this aforesaid order … according to your own discretion and conscience.'[65]

In regard to minor offences it meant that the council assumed that there were accused persons who were not suspected and 'thus recognised and assumed the continuation of the older medial jury verdict, which had been the mechanism that distinguished the merely accused from the truly suspected.[66] In general, however, many prisoners were either freed or temporarily imprisoned without any trial at all.

Such a situation could not last since the judges were faced with crowds of prisoners whom they were unable to try.[67] No further writ from the council followed however, and, in the event, England turned to trial by jury at the same time as many European countries, where the rules of law and procedure were more precise, adopted Roman forms of proof 'which exalted the probative power of sworn eyewitness testimony and of the accused's confession, often coerced by torture.'[68] In this way 'the law encouraged and, indeed, often required, the torture of the accused in order to produce a confession, which was considered of particularly high evidentiary value.'[69] According to Olson, the

> system of roman-canonical proof constituted an evidentiary revolution, shifting the focus of evidencing to accurate fact finding. The same, however, cannot be said of the jury trial. Unlike the roman-canonical proofs, the jury trial, like the ordeal, aimed primarily at resolve. Moreover, it was a resolve that carried a sacerdotal meaning.[70]

The important point is that although the *Inquisitio* (Roman law), based on the work of the Bologna School and the Glossators, was available from this time it was not adopted by English judges[71] who followed Bracton's dictum that the law should go 'from precedent to precedent.'[72] In contrast, western Europe, long closer than England to Rome and its influences, developed the principles of the civil law (sometimes called 'canon law') by 'means of glosses and commentaries and treatises upon the text of Justinian's books.'[73]

Since the judges in England would not follow this example and take upon themselves to decide on the facts as well as law in a judicial inquisitorial manner they began to offer the accused the opportunity of having 12 laymen from the presenting jury determine his guilt or innocence.[74] This startling and momentous innovation meant that by their verdict these 12 men would have to decide the case, as to some extent they had already done when sending an accused to the ordeal.[75] The need for torture was by-passed and the decision turned from the judgment of God to the conclusions of mortals, although they were not required to give reasons for their decisions, their oath being sacrosanct like the ordeal and possibly, in practice, because there might be as many reasons as there were jurors. Equally, their verdict could not be challenged, not simply because they were men of substance but because initially they were largely self-informing. Their decisions were regarded as 'proofs' like the ordeal with no detailed inquiry into evidence.[76] As with the ordeal, their verdict was inscrutable and remains so today.

Using community-established jurors was a means of legitimising the Angevin kings. As one writer has put it:

> At a time when the Continental sovereigns were looking to the theory of Roman law to strengthen their own pretensions to power, the English rulers had already achieved a high degree of centralisation of power in the hands of the royal government. As a result, English royal judges were able to administer justice all over the country and they soon superseded the local courts. Wherever the royal justice went, they used the jury … as a means of determining facts. The jury system was therefore an instrument of royal power, and spread as rapidly and widely as the royal courts.[77]

Nevertheless, the use of a jury meant that a defendant would be putting himself into the hands of his community. For example, in the year 1220 two men were accused of felony by one Alice, a confessed and condemned murderer, but as a female accuser she could not personally offer combat (although she could have appointed a champion to fight on her behalf). Accordingly, the men 'put themselves for good and ill (*de bono et malo*) upon a verdict, and the *vills* said that they were thieves' and they were hanged.[78] In the next case three of her suspects who 'put themselves for good and ill upon a verdict of the countryside', were also found by the *vills* to be thieves and were hanged.[79] Not before 1220 did a jury sit in judgment of an accused person with the discretion either to acquit or to condemn and, according to Groot, these defendants were the first persons properly convicted by an English jury. Yet, by 1229 criminal trial by jury was the normal mode of proof in all criminal proceedings.[80]

At the time juries exercised a significant degree of discretion based upon morals, justice and mercy. In a sense there was a continuation of community involvement in which, in the king's courts and at local and county level, lay judging was seen as an integral element of justice. It should be remembered, however, that not all members of the community could have been involved, and certainly were not after the Statute of Westminster II of 1285[81] introduced a property qualification by providing that jurors should own freeholds to an annual value of 20 shillings within a particular county or 40 shillings outside it. These sums were raised to 40 shillings and 100 shillings respectively in 1293.[82]

Standing before the court in the thirteenth century, the accused would be asked in what manner he would be tried. If, fearing the alternative of indefinite imprisonment, he answered, 'by my country' the jury would be assembled and would reach a verdict on the basis of their own knowledge of the circumstances of the case and that of their neighbours. They might act as witnesses providing information but they also had a duty to make enquiries of their neighbours, which as men of good standing they were well placed to do.[83] In what had become a quasi-judicial capacity they were to collect testimony, weigh it and state the net result in a verdict.[84] Clearly, in involving others in their assessments they were more than witnesses. As Sir William Holdsworth has written, they represented the sense of the community from which they were drawn.[85] And the finality of the jury's verdict may have arisen in part because the defendant had chosen to put himself in their hands. The consequence that the verdict was not open to challenge meant that jury discretion was an integral element of criminal justice from the beginning.[86]

However, trial by the local community could be 'trial by local prejudice' and it is significant that as early as the middle of the thirteenth century Bracton had said that a defendant might object to the inclusion of false and malicious accusers on the trial jury.[87] Thus began jury challenges. The defendant might also object to jury trial altogether, but that involved certain disadvantages, as will be seen.

OPPOSITION TO TRIAL BY JURY

In its early days trial by jury met with some opposition in criminal cases long after it was well established and popular in civil cases.[88] The primary reason for this was that there was no presumption of innocence, which was a concept as yet still unknown.[89] The defendant had to *prove* his innocence, unlike compurgation and the ordeals where he had a chance to clear himself without evidence and was frequently successful. In a trial by jury he was in the hands of people in whose choice he had no voice and who were usually the very men who had presented the charge against him. And, although in the absence of lawyers he could not normally have had the assistance of counsel before the reign of Edward I from then on he was formally denied it after the rule was announced in a case of rape.[90]

There seems to be no doubt that Charles Wells overstates his case when he concludes that, '(w)ith a jury prejudiced by its own indictment, relying on rumours and hearsay evidence, often stupid and ignorant, liable to irrational, undue, and underhanded influences and intimidation, and without individual responsibility, a conviction was almost, if not quite, a foregone conclusion.'[91] Against that judgment, Fortescue was to describe the jury as coming into court with an open mind instead of finding the verdict from their own knowledge.[92] They were, he said, 'neighbours, able to live of their own, sound in repute and fair-minded, not brought into court by either party, but chosen by a respectable and impartial officer, and compelled to come before the judge.'[93] However, it would be sensible to accept with Post that the situation varied in different courts with some juries self-informing as to the evidence and others not.[94]

Edward Powell may, however, be going too far when he puts forward the hypothesis that criminal trial juries were never entirely self-informing in the strict sense and that even in the earliest days of jury trial accusers and witnesses had the chance to inform the jury in court. He himself calls this a 'suspicion' and produces no evidence to back the idea.[95] Fisher also doubts that the early jury was entirely self-informing. If it were, he says, the defendant's right to challenge jurors for cause, as confirmed by Bracton, would have given the defendant the 'power to scuttle trial altogether unless other informed jurors waited nearby.'[96] This view is supported by Macnair in his study of the origins of the jury.[97] Furthermore, according to Cockburn, 'the central dynamics of "modern" criminal trial were in place at least as early as the beginning of the fifteenth century.'[98]

Whatever the truth, there were many acquittals. Although not necessarily a reliable source since its draftsmen may have had a purpose in mind, as early as 1275 the Statute of Westminster 1[99] complained that 'the peace is less kept, and the laws less used, and offenders less punished than they ought to be.' Ten years later the Statute of Winchester (1285),[100] which was principally concerned with urban crime, reiterated in its preface that crime was occurring more frequently than in the past and that jurors were failing to indict felons who even when brought to trial were rarely convicted. Clearly, Wells' main conclusion is refuted by the high level of acquittals, assessed by Green as often 50 per cent or more, in the majority of early homicide trials.[101]

REFUSAL OF JURY TRIAL

Groot claims to have found 'few cases in the printed post 1221 rolls in Warwick in which defendants steadfastly refused jury trial. Some mechanism, perhaps simple incarceration as in 1220, continually generated pleas *de bono et malo*' (for good and ill).[102] Further, when a defendant refused to be tried by a jury of the hundred, the judge would add 24 knights to the jury and, with fewer hopes of mercy from knights drawn from the county at large, defendants proved less likely to refuse to be tried by a hundred jury at the outset.[103] On the other hand, if the jurors from the hundred did not suspect the accused persons, participation by the townships or knights was unnecessary and the defendants could be placed under pledges of good behaviour. Equally, if the hundred jury did suspect and a case was referred to the townships the absence of suspicion by the townships terminated the prosecution.[104] In both these sets of circumstances the judge was dependent upon the jury in regard to both the accused and the offence. And the jury was exercising discretionary and screening functions, including the power to acquit regardless, which it has exercised in different contexts throughout its history.

Nonetheless, in those early days jury trial was not always popular. After all, if the presenters believed a man was guilty he would have little chance of being found innocent upon his trial compared with the ordeal. Consequently, a certain number of people accused of crime declined to put themselves on their country (i.e. before a jury). Sollom Emlyn, in his notes to Sir Matthew Hale's *History of the Pleas of the Crown* which he edited, spoke of people arraigned of felony in the reign of Edward III standing mute who were not pressed 'but had judgment to be hanged'. It seemed at that time, he said, to have been the usual practice that if the prisoner stood willfully mute 'a jury of twelve were impanelled *ex officio*, and if they found him guilty another jury of twenty-four were chosen to examine the verdict of the former; and if they were of the same opinion the prisoner was sentenced to be hanged.'[105] So, at first an accused who refused to plead might be tried anyway.

PRESSING TO DEATH

It has been said that 'the clearest evidence of the system's sense of illegitimacy in the early years after the ordeal's death was its failure to force trial by jury upon those accused of crime.'[106] This may be because the authorities recognised that in the ordeal a man had the opportunity of clearing himself by his own act whereas with trial by jury he was in the hands of others, the very men who had accused him in the first place. At any event, the number of refusals to accept jury trial continued to increase and legislative action was called for. Accordingly, in an effort to overcome refusals, the first Statute of Westminster (1275)[107] made jury trial compulsory by providing that if an accused refused to agree to trial by jury and stood mute when charged he was to be kept in a hard and strong prison, *prison forte et dure*, until he changed his mind. This could result in long delays, however, and the courts decided to attempt to compel prisoners to accept jury trial and changed 'hard prison' into 'hard pain', *peine forte et dure*.[108] In his *Second Institute*, Sir Edward Coke described the meaning of this judgment of penance as it was called as follows:

The man or woman shall be remanded to the prison and laid there in some low and dark house where they shall lie naked on their backs on the bare earth. One arm shall be drawn to one part of the house with a cord and the other to another part. The same shall be done with their legs and there shall be laid upon their bodies iron and stone—as much as they shall bear and more . . . The following day they shall have three morsels of barley bread without any drink. The second day they shall drink thrice of the water that is next to the prison (except running water), without any bread, and this shall be their diet until they be dead. So they shall die by weight, famine and cold. [109]

Since someone who would not plead could not be tried, those who submitted to this torture[110] and accepted such a frightful death did so to ensure that their lands and goods would not be forfeit but would pass to their families. It is not possible to know how many prisoners did submit to it but later records show that 48 persons were put to *peine forte et dure* at the Old Bailey sessions between 1558 and 1625.[111] In cases of treason however, pressing could not arise since the accused who refused to plead was condemned as if convicted.[112]

As late as 1658 a prisoner was pressed to death but in 1772 *peine forte et dure* was abolished by statute and replaced by a plea of guilty.[113] In 1827 this in turn was replaced by a provision that a plea of not guilty should be entered when an accused remained mute.[114]

CHALLENGING JURORS

Although it may not have been perceived by defendants, it is interesting that Musson shows quite clearly that in rolls for sessions held in Oxfordshire, Berkshire and Buckinghamshire in 1326 'there was no noticeable bias toward conviction when the majority of the trial jurors had also brought the accusation.[115] For instance, John Rolond was acquitted of theft when there were present ten of the jury that had indicted him and John Kempe and Richard Warcheyn were acquitted by a jury made up of 11 of those who had presented their offences of assault.[116] It is impossible to know, but these may have been examples of jury nullification to preserve the defendants from capital punishment.

In spite of what Musson's research has revealed, in 1352 a landmark statute[117] was passed enabling the accused to challenge a trial juror on the ground that he had been a member of the presenting jury. From this time the trial jury began to be quite distinct from the grand jury (which was so named because it had up to 23 members) in that the grand jury still decided whether to present a person, after sifting substantial complaints from casual accusations,[118] whereas the trial jury acted judicially and decided if someone were guilty or innocent. By statute, as late as 1368 however, petty jurors were still required to 'have best Knowledge of the Truth, and be nearest'[119] (i.e. to be from the vicinity of the crime).

According to Lord Chief Justice Fortescue, the accused was permitted to challenge peremptorily (i.e. without the need to give any reason) as many as 35 jurors[120] and evidence from the Norfolk rolls indicates that challenges were not infrequent.[121] At a Norwich session in 1351 John Munch challenged 29 jurors and in sessions at Northampton, John Dounedale of Geytington so challenged the jury that he exhausted three dozen of them. Deciding that he would not place himself upon a jury at all he was sent to *peine forte et dure* where he died.[122] And Sayles records a case in Dublin where a defendant successfully challenged 60 jurors.[123] However, a prisoner in a state trial could not find out from the court how many challenges he had or the grounds for challenging a juror. If he asked he could be told by the judges that they were not there to provide him with legal counsel.[124]

The right to challenge trial jurors was an essential consequence of their gradual change from witnesses to men who had no previous knowledge of the cases they tried but who nevertheless might be biased against a defendant. Musson has shown that jury challenges were common until the disappearance of a substantial overlap between presenting and trial juries.[125] That may explain why Post found no trace of jury challenges in the public record office documents of the late fourteenth century. He claims that if they were common in criminal trials, some trace would have been left in the documents and suggests that it seems very likely that the typical defendant was not allowed to challenge the jury and thus delay his trial. A better method of affecting the composition or character of the jury, he says, was the 'simple expedient of bribery which was far from unknown.'[126]

Presumably, however, to secure delay would not normally be the reason for challenges and not only was the challenge a right given by statute but it is unlikely that many defendants would have been able to afford to bribe the jury. In any event, it seems more than likely that in small communities there would be a strong dislike of some jurors who would be known to those who were accused and were thought to be acting with malice. Most importantly, jurors were ceasing to be the very people who had accused the defendant in the first place.

VERDICTS

Initially if a jury split, the majority would prevail. As laid down by Britton, in a trial of felony, 'If they cannot agree let them be separated and examined why. If the majority know the facts and the minority know nothing, judgment shall be given in accordance with the voice of the majority.'[127] And Hale was to say that in case of jury disagreement the lesser number would be dispensed with and an equal number added until the 12 were unanimous.[128] Not that it was always so simple. Charles Wells found instances in early assize rolls where, in one case in Lancashire in the reign of Edward I, a juror was placed in custody for 'contradicting the verdict of his associates without reasonable cause' and, in another case in Gloucestershire, in the reign of Henry III, a juror was fined for his disagreement.[129]

In the early days, as today, unanimity was generally considered desirable and Hale mentioned an important case of a juror, who held out against the majority, being imprisoned by the judge. However, meeting together, all the judges subsequently set him free on the ground that 'men are not to be forced to give their verdict against their judgment.'[130] It was in this leading case in 1367 that the courts rejected earlier precedents and held that a majority verdict was void.[131] The jury were now required to provide the same unambiguous judgment as the ordeal had done.

Moreover, by statute[132] the jurors were to be kept together without meat, drink, fire or candle, until they were unanimously agreed upon their verdict. Although this rule was meant to prevent delay and intimidation, and force them to agree on a verdict,[133] it was an onerous requirement and may well have led to hasty verdicts of acquittal, particularly if a case lasted longer than a day, although most lasted a lot less. Had they not arrived at a decision by the time the itinerant judges were due to leave the town (or city) the jurors were subject to a rule that they might be carried round the circuit from town to town in a cart.[134] Surprisingly, the statutory requirement was not abolished until the Juries Act 1870.[135]

The most common observable fault of medieval jurors in the fourteenth century was their persistent failure to appear, particularly at Westminster which for many involved considerable travelling and expense. As G. Sayles wrote, 'the declaration that no jury came is one of the most monotonous commonplaces of the records' of the Westminster courts.[136] Securing a jury of 12 was an haphazard and rushed procedure and reliance upon talesmen (bystanders in or about the court) was common, with an arbitrary sample indicating that half the juries were supplemented in this way in the fourteenth century.[137]

TRAILBASTON COMMISSIONS

In the fourteenth century the preambles of some statutes and the large number of *trailbaston*[138] commissions (special commissions with extraordinary powers) indicated that crime was endemic.[139] The main reason appears to have been that peasant land-hunger and seigniorial oppression led to a widespread breakdown of manorial discipline at all levels and a serious collapse of public order.[140] Armed bands, often led by noblemen, infested the countryside committing homicides, robberies and other serious crimes and could not be dealt with effectively by the infrequent eyres. They caused considerable concern to the central authorities who in 1304, assigned justices to investigate the activities of 'malefactors and peacebreakers who are moving about the woods and parks and committing murders, depredations, burnings and other misdeeds to the peril of travellers and dwellers' in Lincolnshire and the rest of England.[141] Even in urban London, the parliament of 1305 promulgated an Ordinance of Trailbaston for the capital and the commission sat in that year and 1306.[142]

These special commissions were also to deal with those who threatened jurors so that they would not tell the truth and those who, 'by reason of their power and state', protected criminals in return for fees.[143] Such commissions did not survive the fourteenth century but the evidence of the Lincolnshire trailbaston proceedings in 1328 has been studied by Bernard McLane and is useful in revealing juror attitudes toward local disorder at that time.[144]

The Lincolnshire commission was composed of a judge of the Court of Common Pleas, a sergeant at law and two local magnates. They commenced their sittings at Lincoln on 6 June when juries began to make their presentments.[145] A total of 248 men have been identified as jurors sitting in court during the sessions of June and July 1328. Eighteen served both on presentment and trial juries (an interestingly low number for the time), another 148 only on presentment juries and 82 others only on trial juries.[146] Local notables were far more likely to serve as presentment jurors than just as trial jurors which may be because bringing these serious criminals to trial was considered even more important than dealing with them when charged. Fifty-three per cent of the offences dealt with were felonies, 27 per cent were trespasses committed by non-officials and 20 per cent trespasses by local and royal officials.[147] The last indicates considerable corruption by those holding power of one kind or another over others.

It is interesting that similar offences committed by different persons (or groups) were sometimes treated as felonies and in other cases as trespasses which McLane considers depended on the presenting jurors taking into account the reputations of the parties;[148] an attitude to defendants that was to be followed by trial juries for centuries to come.

Apprehending offenders was a serious problem and in Lincolnshire at this time only one-third of the accused were brought before royal justices to answer the charges against them. When they were tried, convicted trespassers were usually imprisoned for a brief period and then released after being fined, the fine being levied according to the ability of the accused to pay rather than the seriousness of the offence. For instance,

> Ralph Payknave was accused in six presentments of assault, false imprisonment, and extortion, as well as being a 'common malefactor,' while Hugh Tyler was presented only once on a charge of conspiracy. Yet Tyler was fined £10 and Payknave only 40 pence. The reason, no doubt, was that Payknave was of moderate means in the city of Lincoln and Tyler was one of the city's wealthiest citizens.[149]

Felony convictions, on the other hand, were punishable by execution, although only 18 per cent of the alleged felons who were tried were found guilty and few of those were hanged. The remainder were acquitted and released.[150] As an extraordinary 72 per cent of those accused of felony did not appear and were outlawed, it is possible that those who did appear were innocent or the jury could not decide if they were guilty[151] which would confirm that trial jurors, at least in trailbaston, were largely no longer self-informing by this time, many of them coming ten or more miles away from the scene of the crime.[152] Or perhaps they thought the penalty of death was too high for the crime, such as, for example, homicide without malice aforethought.

Trial jurors' leniency towards accused felons, especially alleged killers, is seen by McLane as a consequence of the inflexibility of the common law regarding felonies and the death penalty. In many cases, he says, trial jurors may have acquitted the defendants because they believed that they did not deserve to be hanged, even though they may actually have committed the crime for which they were being tried. Alternatively, they would declare that an alleged killer had killed in self-defence, thereby making him eligible for a royal pardon.[153] If so, these were other examples of the use by juries of their power to exercise nullification, particularly as pardons were very common at the time.

Green also suggests that 'from the community's point of view' it was legitimate for a violent attack to be met with a violent response. 'A man whose life was threatened did not have to seek some means of escape; indeed, he need not do so though he was not in danger of losing his life.'[154]

It is also possible that jurors had been threatened and in some cases were too frightened to find some accused persons guilty, even though they considered that they were. The original trailbaston commission in 1304 spoke of 'those who have disturbed jurors on assizes, that they dare not speak the truth, for if they do so they cause them to be so beaten and ill-treated that many lose their lives, or are maimed for ever more, so that for fear of them the truth cannot be known before the king's justices.'[155] This was repeated in summarised form by the 1328 commission and McLane gives examples of corrupt practices and coercion including cases where the jurors simply did not appear or actually fled.[156] Musson also found that in gaol deliveries in Norfolk at this time jury default occurred frequently with, for example, juries defaulting in Norwich on six out of the 14 sessions held from 1324 to 1328.[157] After 1361, when justices of the peace were first appointed,[158] their sittings in quarter sessions and assizes made trailbastons unnecessary and they were not repeated.

At the same time as justices of the peace were introduced in 1361 the eyre declined, but the system of jury presentment remained, with the juries generally bringing accusations of criminal offences before the sheriff at his tourn, the coroner, the justices of the peace, stewards of liberties, bailiffs of towns and itinerant judicial commissioners such as justices of *oyer and terminer*.[159] Yet, by this time the division between presentments and indictments was being eroded to the extent that the words 'indict' and 'present' appear to have become interchangeable.[160]

EARLY JURY NULLIFICATION

Green concludes that the great majority of defendants in felony trials in the thirteenth and fourteenth centuries were acquitted by conscious jury nullification of the law[161] which has been defined as the power 'to acquit the defendant on the basis of conscience even when the defendant is technically guilty in light of the judge's instructions defining the law and the jury's finding of the facts'.[162] Further, as Green adds, historically some cases of nullification 'reflect the jury's view that the act in question is not unlawful, while in other cases the jury does not quarrel with the law but believes that the prescribed sanction is too severe.'[163] This is not to be confused with the jury not believing a witness or failing to understand the directions of the judge. Nullification in order to convict seems to be remote in practice except possibly in modern times as an expression of prejudice based on race.[164]

It has been said that 'from the outset of the common law period, trial juries were prepared to voice a sense of justice fundamentally at odds with the letter of the law'.[165] As a consequence 'the tension between jury law finding and limitations on jury discretion emerges as a critical shaping force in the development of substantive legal principles ... [including] the growth of concepts like criminal intent and justification as discrete arenas that grew by shielding and fostering jury discretionary judging.'[166]

In homicide cases, for example, Green says that juries systematically imposed upon the courts a distinction that the formal legal rules did not draw. With murder, they established a difference between actual murder and what today is seen as manslaughter long before the distinction was legally recognised in the late sixteenth century. As a consequence, trial rolls of the thirteenth to fifteenth centuries and earlier reveal juries acquitting the great majority of those charged with simple homicide and sending murderers to the gallows about 50 per cent of the time.[167] Equally, although theft of goods to a value of 12 pence and over was a felony it was often treated as a trespass with only about one third of those tried being convicted.[168]

Groot has examined what occurred in regard to larceny in some detail.[169] It has been thought, he says, that the Statute of Westminster I in 1275[170], by providing that one indicted for 'Petty Larceny that amounteth not [above the Value] of twelve-pence' should be bailable, created the distinction between grand and petty larceny—the former a felony and the latter a misdemeanour. On the contrary, he argues from cases he cites, the statute simply recognised an existing practice from the 1220s of juries declaring that stolen goods were of little value to ensure the judges could not impose the capital penalty.[171] Thus, in effect, the juries were deciding who should live and return to the community and who should die.[172] Hence, the statute did not create petty larceny but, as a consequence of a rule determined by juries, clarified that the dividing line between petty larceny and grand larceny was 12 pence and dealt with precisely what it purported to deal with—pre-trial disposition of those accused of the minor form of larceny.[173]

Green himself argues that jury behaviour to some extent slowed the development of a policy aimed at reducing serious crime, but sees this as 'an ironic result of the dialectical process created by the combined adoptions of a general capital sanction for felony and a lay criminal trial jury.'[174] One writer, among others, has claimed that trial by ordeal was used to determine someone's standing in the community rather than guilt or innocence and that the trial jury carried this forward, giving nullification a long pedigree.[175]

CONCLUSION

It seems clear that even in the early days the criminal trial jury was exercising its power of nullification to a considerable extent. Anglo-Saxon justice had given prominence to a compensatory payment (*wergild*) as the penalty for many crimes including murder if not premeditated and carried out by stealth. Such a concept remained in people's minds in Norman and Angevin times and gave rise to jury nullification which Green says the judges might have countenanced in cases of simple homicide, self-defence and theft.[176] At the same time, jury discretion may possibly have been fuelled by Anglo-Saxon feelings of resentment against the harsh treatment meted out by William I and his successors.

On the other hand, as Olson has indicated, 'From the beginning of the jury trial, the acquittal rate was overwhelmingly high, the justices accepted these verdicts, and their accuracy was often doubtful.' Yet, 'often the jury acted not to express disapproval of a law or of a sanction but to bestow mercy … upon a defendant. It is within the details of this act that one may find the jury's affinity with the ordeal as a penitential act of purgation.'[177]

Trial by ordeal, according to Fisher, bespoke 'an unwillingness to take life or limb without divine sanction'[178] and later, by 'forbidding conflicts of oaths in capital cases' (secured by not allowing one side, i.e. defendants, to give evidence or call witnesses under oath), 'the system assured that a jury's verdict of guilt would seem to bear a divine imprimatur.'[179]

One commentator, dealing with the fourteenth and fifteenth centuries in England, has said:

> Jurors are the unsung heroes of the common law. Jurors gave the verdicts that made the whole system possible. Without the enforced co-operation of jurors, the tiny number of royal justices—usually 12 or 13 at any one time—could not possibly have resolved the thousands of disputes that came to judgment every year in the expanding jurisdiction of the common law.[180]

From its inception, and perhaps until Tudor times, the jury was the source of practically all of the evidence put before the court.[181] Because the presenting jurors were notables from the local hundred and largely self-informing, the judges and the kings did little to interfere with or control juries at this time beyond endeavouring to ensure by statute that they continued to be composed of men of property.

But changes occurred nonetheless and for a variety of reasons. The close of the period from 1219 to Tudor times saw the end of a tightly-knit feudal society in England[182] and, with economic developments and the growth in size and importance of the towns, the social and community significance of the jury was changed. As life improved for some people they were more inclined to move and take up work elsewhere than the place in which they were born and this was encouraged by the Black Death and other plagues.[183] At the same time, although there was no system of precedent in the law as we know it today the recording of trials had commenced, often by students, and a legal profession formed which was growing and, as prosecutors, would use witnesses and evidence to enhance their cases.[184] All this meant that involvement in jury composition from the hundreds was on the wane, with jurors often drawn from as far as ten miles away from the scene of the crime.[185] The jury did, however, remain a county and community institution and clearly continued to exercise to a high degree its significant power of nullification in cases of felony and larceny.

ENDNOTES for *Chapter 2*

[1]   See Arthur Bryant. (1984) *Set in a Silver Sea*. London, Collins. vol. i. p. 66.
[2]   F.W. Maitland. (1908) *The Constitutional History of England*. Cambridge, Cambridge University Press. p. 7.
[3]   Sir Frank Stenton. (1985) *Anglo-Saxon England*. Oxford, The Clarendon Press. p. 298-301.
[4]   Pollock and Maitland. (1895) *The History of English Law Before the Time of Edward I*. Cambridge, Cambridge University Press, vol. i. p. 138.
[5]   See G.N. Garmonsway. (1977) *The Anglo-Saxon Chronicle*. London, J.M. Dent & Sons. p. 264.
[6]   W.L Warren. (1973). *Henry II*. London, Eyre Methuen. p. 354.
[7]   A.K.R. Kiralfy. (1958) *Potter's Historical Introduction to English Law and its Institutions*. London, Sweet & Maxwell. chaps 2 and 3.
[8]   Warren. Op. cit. pp. 360-1.
[9]   12 Hen.2, c.1.
[10] Thomas Andrew Green. (1988) 'A Retrospective on the Criminal Trial Jury, 1200-1800'. In J.S. Cockburn. and T.A. Green (eds.) *Twelve Good Men and True: The Criminal Trial Jury in England, 1200-1800*. New Jersey, Princeton University Press, p. 359.
[11] T.F.T. Plucknett. (1960) *Edward I and Criminal Law*. Cambridge. Cambridge, University Press. p. 66.
[12] William Forsyth. (1852) *History of Trial by Jury*. London, John Parker, p. 195.
[13] 12 Hen. 2. c. 1.
[14] Naomi D. Hurnard. (1941) 'The Jury of Presentment and the Assize of Clarendon.' 56 *The English Historical Review*. London, Longmans, Green & Co. pp. 374-410. See *ante*. p. 14.
[15] Pollock & Maitland. Op. cit. p. 142.
[16] See *ante*. p. 11. note 9.
[17] 22 Hen. 2 c. 7.
[18] Green. 'Retrospective'. Op. cit. p. 359.
[19] Ibid.
[20] See Mike Macnair. (1999) 'The Origins of the Jury: Vicinage and the Antecedents of the Jury'. 17 *Law and History Review*. University of Illinois. p. 590-1.
[21] Anthony Musson. (1997) 'Twelve Good Men and True? The Character of Early Fourteenth-Century Juries.' 15 *Law and History Review*. University of Illinois Press. p. 120.
[22] See *post*. p. 20.
[23] Roger D. Groot. (1988) 'The Early-Thirteenth-Century Criminal Jury.' In Cockburn and Green. *Twelve Good Men and True*. Op. cit. pp. 5-6.
[24] G. Wrottesley, (ed.) (1882) *Staffordshire Suits: Collections for a History of Staffordshire*. 3: 94. Quoted by Groot, Ibid. p. 6.
[25] Groot. 'The Early-Thirteenth-Century Criminal Jury.' Op. cit. pp. 16-17.
[26] Green. 'Retrospective'. Op. cit. p. 363.
[27] See Susan Reynolds. (1997) *Kingdoms and Communities in Western Europe, 900-1300*. Oxford, Clarendon Press.
[28] Groot. 'The Early-Thirteenth-Century Criminal Jury.' Op. cit. p. 7.
[29] Groot. (1982) 'The Jury of Presentment Before 1215.' 26 *The American Journal of Legal History*. Carolina, North Carolina University Press. p. 1.

[30] Thomas Andrew Green. (1985) *Verdict According to Conscience. Perspectives on the English Criminal Trial Jury 1200-1800.* Chicago. University of Chicago Press. p. 19.

[31] Ibid.

[32] J.B. Thayer. ((1969) *A Preliminary Treatise on Evidence at the Common Law.* New York, Augustus M. Kelly. p. 65.

[33] Groot. 'The Early-Thirteenth-Century Criminal Jury.' Op. cit. pp. 8-9.

[34] Ibid. p. 25.

[35] George Fisher. (1997). 'The Jury's Rise as Lie Detector.' New Haven, 107 *Yale Law Journal.* p. 587.

[36] Thayer. Op. cit. pp. 36-7.

[37] Paul R. Hyams. (1981) 'Trial by Ordeal: The Key to Proof in the Early Common Law.' In Morris S. Arnold and others (eds.) *On the Laws and Customs of England. Essays in Honour of Samuel E. Thorne.* Chapel Hill, The University of North Carolina Press. p. 112. note 182.

[38] Pollock & Maitland. Op. cit. vol. ii. p. 598.

[39] Dick Hamilton. (1979) *Foul Bills and Dagger Money: 800 Years of Lawyers and Lawbreakers.* London, Book Club Associates. p. 4.

[40] Robert Bartlett. (1986) *Trial by Fire and Water: The Medieval Judicial Ordeal.* Oxford, Clarendon Press. p. 23.

[41] Hamilton. Op. cit. pp. 3-4. However, Bartlett claims the account is fictional. Bartlett. Ibid. p.17.

[42] Fisher. Op. cit. p. 585.

[43] Forsyth. Op. cit. p. 81.

[44] Plucknett. Op. cit. p. 70.

[45] Pollock and Maitland. Op. cit. vol. ii. p. 599.

[46] Pipe Roll. 21 Henry II. Pipe Roll Society, vol. 22, London, 1897. p. 131. Quoted by Hyams, p. 116.

[47] Hyams. Op. cit. p. 116.

[48] Ibid. pp. 93-4.

[49] Trisha Olson. (2000) 'Of Enchantment: The Passing of the Ordeals and the Rise of the Jury Trial.' New York, *Syracuse Law Review.* p. 132.

[50] Thayer. Op. cit. p. 39.

[51] Margaret Kerr *et al.* (1992) *Cold Water and Hot Iron: Trial by Ordeal in England.* 22 J. Interdisc. Hist. p. 582.

[52] Ibid.

[53] F.W. Maitland. (1888) *Select Pleas of the Crown.* London, Selden Society. p. 75.

[54] Olson. Op. cit. p. 113.

[55] Fisher. Op. cit. p. 601.

[56] Ibid. p. 587.

[57] Ibid.

[58] Ibid. p. 601.

[59] Hyams. Op. cit. p. 91.

[60] Cynthia B. Herrup. (1987) *The Common Peace: Participation and the Criminal Law in Seventeenth-century England.* Cambridge, Cambridge University Press. p. 3.

[61] Hyams, Op. cit. pp. 90, 101 argues that the ordeal was brought to a slow end by social developments but Bartlett shows that it was flourishing in the eleventh and twelfth centuries. Bartlett. Op. cit. pp. 42-3.

[62] Thayer. Op. cit. p. 37.

[63] Groot. 'The Early-Thirteenth-Century Criminal Jury.' Op. cit. p. 3.

[64] Patent Rolls. 1216-25. p. 186.

[65] Ibid.

[66] Groot. 'The Early-Thirteenth-Century Criminal Jury.' Op. cit. p. 11.

[67] Plucknett. Op. cit. p. 74.

[68] Fisher. Op. cit. p. 587.

[69] Barbara J. Shapiro. (1983) *Probability and Certainty in Seventeenth-Century England. A Study of the Relationships between Natural Science, Religion, History, Law and Literature.* New Jersey, Princeton University Press. p. 174.

[70] Olson. Op. cit. p. 112.

[71] See Sir William Holdsworth. (1966) *A History of English Law.* London, Methuen & Co. vol. iv. pp. 221-243.

[72] Ibid. vol. ii. p. 243.

[73] Ibid. vol. iv. p.220.

[74] Thayer. Op. cit. p. 82.

[75] Groot. (1983) 'The Jury in Private Criminal Prosecutions Before 1215.' 27 *The American Journal of Legal History*. North Carolina University Press. p. 113.

[76] Cf. Macnair. Op. cit. p. 545.

[77] Morris Ploscowe. (1935) 'The Development of Present-Day Criminal Procedures in Europe and America.' 48 *Harvard Law Review*. Cambridge, Mass. Review Association. p. 455.

[78] *Curia Regis Rolls*. 8:274. Cited by Groot. 'The Early-Thirteenth-Century Criminal Jury.' Op. cit. pp. 17-18.

[79] Groot. Ibid.

[80] Ibid. pp. 18 and 35.

[81] 13 Edw. 1.

[82] Musson. Op. cit. p. 130.

[83] Holdsworth. Op. cit. vol. i. p. 317.

[84] Pollock and Maitland. Op. cit. vol. ii. pp. 624-5.

[85] Holdsworth. Op. cit. vol. i. p. 317.

[86] Green. *Verdict*. Op. cit. pp. 19-20.

[87] Leonard W. Levy. (1999) *The Palladium of Justice: Origins of Trial by Jury*. Chicago, Ivan R. Dee. pp. 22, 63.

[88] Charles L. Wells (1914) 'Early Opposition to the Petty Jury in Criminal Cases'. 117 *The Law Quarterly Review*. London, Stevens & Son. pp. 97-110.

[89] Ibid. p. 97.

[90] Year Books. 30 and 31, Edw. I. 529-30.

[91] Wells. 'Early Opposition.' Op. cit. p. 103.

[92] Sir John Fortescue. [1468] (1997) *On the Laws and Governance of England*. Shelley Lockwood (ed). Cambridge, Cambridge University Press. pp. 36-7.

[93] Ibid. p. 40.

[94] J.B. Post. (1988) 'Jury Lists and Juries in the Late Fourteenth Century.' In Cockburn and Green, Op. cit. p. 73.

[95] Edward Powell. (1988) 'Jury Trial at Gaol Delivery in the Late Middle Ages: The Midland Circuit, 1400-1429.' In Cockburn and Green. Op. cit. p. 116.

[96] Fisher. 'The Jury's Rise as Lie Detector.' Op. cit. pp. 592-3 and note 47.

[97] Mike Macnair. (1999) 'The Origins of the Jury: Vicinage and the Antecedents of the Jury.' 17 *Law and History Review*. Illinois, University of Illinois. pp. 537-554.

[98] J.S. Cockburn. (1991). Review of Cynthia B. Herrup's *The Common Peace*. 9 (2) *Law and History Review*. University of Illinois Press. p. 179.

[99] 3 Edw. c. 12.

[100] 13 Edw. c. 1.

[101] Green. *Verdict*. Op. cit. p. 34.

[102] Ibid. p. 35.

[103] Groot. 'The Early-Thirteenth-Century Criminal Jury.' Op. cit. pp. 30-31.

[104] Ibid. p. 32.

[105] Sir Matthew Hale. (1736) *The History of the Pleas of the Crown*. London, E. & R. Nutt and Others. vol. ii. p. 322.

[106] Fisher. 1The Jury's Rise as Lie Detector.' Op. cit.p. 589.

[107] 3 Edw, 1. c.12.

[108] Kiralfy. *Potter's Historical Introduction*. Op. cit. p. 247.

[109] Coke. (1797b) *Second Institute*. London. E & R Brooke, p. 179.

[110] John H. Langbein argues that it was not torture because it was not directed to extracting evidence or information by confession. (1977) *Torture and the Law of Proof: Europe and England in the Ancien Regime*. Chicago, University of Chicago Press. pp. 76-7.

[111] Cockburn. (1985) *Introduction to Calendar of Assize Records. Home Circuit Indictments: Elizabeth I and James I*. London, HMSO. p. 72.

[112] Coke. (1797) *Third Institute*. London, E & R Brooke p. 217.

[113] 12 Geo. III. c. 20.

[114] 7 & 8 Geo. IV. c. 28.

[115] Musson. Op. cit. p. 137.

[116] Ibid. pp. 137-8.

[117] 25 Edw. III. 5. c. 3.

[118] Herrup. *The Common Peace*. Op. cit. p. 93.

[119] 42 Edw. 3, c. 11.

[120] Fortescue. *On the Laws.* Op. cit. p. 40.

[121] Musson. 'Twelve Good Men.' Op. cit. p. 133.

[122] H.R.T. Summerson. (1983) 'The Early Development of *Peine Forte et Dure.*' In E.W. Ives and A.H. Manchester (eds). *Law, Litigants and the Legal Profession.* London, Royal Historical Society. pp. 118-20.

[123] G.O. Sayles (ed.) (1938) *Select Cases in the Court of King's Bench under Edward I.* (Selden Society), London, Bernard Quaritch. p. 127.

[124] 1 Howell's *State Trials.* col. 1318.

[125] Musson. Op. cit. pp. 117, 133.

[126] *Post.* 'Jury Lists.' Op. cit. p. 71-2.

[127] F. M. Nichols. (1865) *Britton.* Oxford, Oxford University Press. vol. i. 31.

[128] Hale. (1971) *The History of the Common Law of England.* Chicago, University of Chicago Press. p. 78.

[129] Charles L. Wells. (1911) 'The Origin of the Petty Jury.' *The Law Quarterly Review.* London, Stevens and Sons. p. 351.

[130] Hale. *History of the Pleas of the Crown.* Op. cit. ii. p. 297.

[131] Year Book. Mich 41. Edw. 3. 31 pl. 36.

[132] 24 Edw. 3. c. 75.

[133] David J. Seipp. (2002) 'Jurors, Evidences, and the Tempest of 1499'. In *The Dearest Birthright of the People of England: The Jury in the History of the Common Law.* Cairns and McLeod (eds.) Oxford, Hart Publishing. pp. 75, 88.

[134] A. H. Manchester. *A Modern Legal History of England and Wales 1750-1950.* London, Butterworth & Co. Ltd. p. 92.

[135] 33 & 34 Vict. c. 77.

[136] Sayles. Op. cit. p. 103.

[137] *Post.* Op. cit. p. 68.

[138] So-called after the staves carried by criminals as weapons.

[139] Bernard William McLane. 'Juror Attitudes to Local Disorder: The Evidence of the 1328 Lincolnshire Trailbaston Proceedings.' In Cockburn and Green. Op. cit. pp. 36-7.

[140] Colin Platt. (1978) *Medieval England.* London, Routledge & Kegan Paul Ltd. p. 108.

[141] McLane.'Juror Attitudes to Local Disorder'. Op. cit. p. 37.

[142] Ralph B. Pugh. (1975) *Calendar of London Trailbaston Trials under Commissions of 1305 and 1306.* London, HMSO. Introduction.

[143] McLane.'Jurors' Attitudes to Local Disorder'. Op. cit. p. 40.

[144] Ibid.

[145] *Cf.* The Public Record Office, file JUST 1/516.

[146] McLane. 'Jury Attitudes.' Op. cit. p. 41.

[147] Ibid. p. 43.

[148] Ibid. p. 52.

[149] Ibid. p. 54.

[150] Ibid.

[151] Ibid. p. 56.

[152] Ibid.

[153] Ibid. p. 58.

[154] Green. *Verdict.* Op. cit. p. 38.

[155] McLane. Op. cit. p. 62.

[156] Ibid.

[157] Musson. Op. cit. p. 130.

[158] C. 34 Edw. III.

[159] Musson. Op. cit. p. 118.

[160] Ibid. p. 119.

[161] Green. *Verdict.* Op. cit. p. 34.

[162] Alan Scheflin and Jon Van Dyke. (1980) 'Jury Nullification: The Contours of the Controversy'. 43 *J.L. and Contemporary Problems.* Durham, North Carolina, Duke University. p. 56.

[163] Green. *Verdict.* Op. cit. p. xiii.

[164] Jack B. Weinstein. (1993) 'Considering Jury "Nullification": When May and Should a Jury Reject the Law to do Justice?' 30 *American Criminal Law Review.* University of Illinois Press. p. 239.

[165] Green. *Verdict.* Op. cit. p. 52.

[166]   Michael H. Hoffheimer. (1987) Review of Green's *Verdict According to Conscience*. 56 *University of Cincinnati Law Review*. p. 563.

[167]   Green. *Verdict*. Op. cit. pp. 22, 34 and 52.

[168]   Ibid. p. 61.

[169]   Groot. (2002) 'Petit Larceny, Jury Lenity and Parliament.' In Cairns and McLeod. (2002) *"The Dearest Birthright of the People of England"*: Op. cit. Oxford, Hart Publishing. pp. 47-61.

[170]   3 Edw. I. c. 15.

[171]   Groot. 'Petit Larceny,' Op. cit. p. 47.

[172]   Ibid. pp. 58-60.

[173]   Ibid. p. 61.

[174]   Green. *Verdict*. Op. cit. p. 76.

[175]   Robert C. Palmer. (1986) 'Conscience and the Law: The English Criminal Jury.' 84 *Michigan Law Review*. pp. 792-94.

[176]   Green. *Verdict*. Op. cit. pp. 35, 61.

[177]   Olson. Op. cit. pp. 173-5.

[178]   Fisher. Op. cit. p. 588.

[179]   Ibid. p. 602.

[180]   David J. Seipp. (2002) 'Jurors, Evidences and the Tempest of 1499'. Op. cit. p. 75.

[181]   Green. *Verdict*. Op. cit. pp. 26-7.

[182]   Kiralfy. *Potter's Historical Introduction to English Law*. Op. cit. p. 37.

[183]   E.F. Jacob. (1997) *The Fifteenth Century: 1399-1485*. Oxford. Clarendon Press. p. 370.

[184]   According to Fortescue, English lawyers were the wealthiest advocates in the world. *On the Laws and Governance of England*. Op. cit. p. 72.

[185]   McLane. Op. cit. p. 56.

CHAPTER 3

Tudor and Stuart Political Control

INTRODUCTION

According to Green in 1985 'Very little is yet known about the institution of the trial jury in Tudor and Stuart England, about governmental policy towards juries or about the vicissitudes of jury power.'[1] This is no longer entirely true today. Since his work was written the results of the researches by Lawson into the composition and behaviour of juries in Hertfordshire from 1574 to 1624[2] and of Cockburn on the trial jury at assizes from 1560 to 1670[3] have cast fresh light on juries at the time. The Crown's policy towards juries, and the vicissitudes of jury power are also clearer nowadays.

After the divisions in the country during the Wars of the Roses, the Tudors and early Stuarts set about establishing a strong central government and a nation state.[4] 'The royal power created a machinery to make its power effective throughout the land' and 'writ all over the period is the compelling force of the royal sovereignty.'[5] It has become apparent that this included exercising more control over the justice system, including juries, than monarchs had in earlier times. The result was a growing ascendancy of bench over jury power. Nevertheless, after subsiding for a time, jury nullification (as discussed in *Chapter 2*) gradually re-asserted itself.

As part of its search for strong government, the Crown was well disposed towards the continental civil law, with the central role of the judge and the exercise of torture, and it will be shown that this not only reduced the availability of benefit of clergy (by statute) but also led to torture under cover of the royal prerogative.

This chapter looks at the importance of the introduction of evidence in changing the character of juries from pre-Tudor self-informing to judicial bodies[6] and causing changes in trial procedures. Additionally, there was the introduction on a regular basis of public prosecutions once jurors ceased to be self-informing and started evaluating evidence.[7] Under the Tudors, the Marian bail and committal statutes of the 1550s established that magistrates were not judicial officers but agents of the king who should ensure effective prosecution of accused felons.[8] Witnesses for the prosecution were bound over to appear at trial whilst the accused could not compel the attendance of witnesses and could not know the exact nature of the indictment or have access to the depositions of prosecution witnesses.[9]

Henry VIII, in particular, greatly extended the statutory scope of the law of treason including the uttering of mere words.[10] And when the judges began to 'cow' jurors[11] and fine and imprison them for 'perverse' verdicts, it is pertinent to ask to what extent this was done in order to undermine jury discretion. If it was significantly so, did this result in the number of executions increasing and in general in this period was the jury less independent than before and seen as part of the wealth and power structure? Certainly, there was a constant and pervasive interference by judges, who wasted little time in addressing juries who were faced with a pace of proceeding that could be described as 'rushing through the [assize] calendar like a wild elephant through a sugar plantation.'[12] During this period the property qualification was raised to secure wealthier jurors more amenable to the government and attempts to interfere with the selection of juries also grew.

Paradoxically, the jury may also have 'helped the royal administration of criminal law to function, perhaps even alleviated tensions that might have brought it to a halt, by exercising its mediatory powers ...'[13] Cockburn believes that in the period he deals with (1558-1714) there were few discretionary verdicts before about 1590, and that they reflected judicial rather than jury initiatives. After that date, however, there were signs of a change in the courtroom balance of power with discretionary verdicts becoming more common as the expression, according to Lambarde, of a novel, and unwelcome, assertiveness by both grand and trial jurors.[14] There is, indeed, evidence of jurors acting 'lawlessly' and once again nullification and jury independence, resulting in more acquittals, were becoming significant features.

MODIFYING BENEFIT OF CLERGY

With the strong central government of the Tudors came an increase in the severity of the penal law and an attempt to modify the palliative effects of the benefit of clergy. The origin of 'benefit' lay in the murder of Thomas à Becket in Canterbury Cathedral in 1170. This led Henry II to accept the bizarre situation whereby a cleric could not be punished in a secular court.[15] The definition of a cleric was already wide when in 1352 it was enacted that 'all manner of clerks, as well secular as religious ... shall freely have and enjoy the privileges of the Holy Church.'[16] The judges then extended the 'benefit' to all who could read and made the only test of literacy an ability to read the first verse of the 51st psalm—appropriately known as the 'neck verse' because it might save a person from hanging by the neck– even if recited from memory by an illiterate person.[17] The verse reads: 'Have mercy on me, O God, according to thy loving kindness; according to the multitude of thy tender mercies, blot out my transgressions.' It was even known for judges to send a prisoner who had been found guilty back to the cells to learn the verse before being returned to court to be set free.[18] Serjeant Daniel apparently saved a convict's life by lending him his spectacles so that he might read the 'neck verse'.[19] And on one occasion, a Kent justice of the peace called out, as a prisoner claimed benefit of clergy, 'He will read as well as my horse!'[20] Because it was used as a measure of mercy, benefit of clergy was to bedevil attempts to reform the penal law for hundreds of years to come. Sir James Fitzjames Stephen claimed that for centuries 'benefit' must have 'reduced the administration of justice to a sort of farce.'[21]

Treason and witchcraft were never clergyable, but in the preamble to a statute of 1489, it was deplored that many people who could read had come to rely on the privilege of clergy 'to be bold in committing murder, rape, robbery and theft.'[22] In response the Act provided that those not actually in holy orders who had once benefited from their 'clergy' should not be able to do so again. Accordingly, murderers obtaining immunity from execution were to have branded on their left thumb with a hot iron the letter 'M' and thieves a 'T'. Accessories before the fact however were by statute to be hanged for their principal's first offence,[23] which seems somewhat illogical. In regard to property crimes this strengthening of the law brought about more undervaluing of goods by juries.[24]

Until a statute of 1624[25] the benefit was not available to women and even after that date no woman accused of the theft of goods valued at more than ten shillings could ask for benefit so that for many alleged crimes or allegations of violence juries still had no easy way to punish a woman without placing her life at risk.[26] The 1624 Act recited that 'many women do suffer death for small causes' but full rights to clerical privilege (a nice irony) were not granted to women until 1691.[27]

Despite benefit of clergy, the number of persons sent to the gallows in the sixteenth century was extremely high. Stephen claimed that there were some 800 executions in the year 1598 alone.[28] And Coke wrote,

> What a lamentable case it is to see so many Christian men and women strangled on that cursed tree of the gallows, insomuch as if in a large field a man might see together all the Christians that but in one year, throughout England come to that untimely and ignominious death, if there were any spark of grace, or charity in him, it would make his heart bleed for pity and compassion.[29]

This is in contrast to earlier, and later, times when the death penalty was far less widely executed, largely due to jury discretion and nullification.[30]

TORTURE

Another expression of Tudor and early Stuart authoritarianism was the use of torture. Confessions under torture left no room for a judicial finding by a jury, a situation well established in continental practice.[31] Although Fortescue emphasised that torture was hardly ever used in medieval England, he wrote nevertheless, 'O Judge, in what school of humanity did you learn this custom of being present while the accused suffers agonies?' By way of contrast, he pointed to France where, 'criminals and suspected criminals are afflicted with so many kinds of tortures ... that the pen scorns to put them into writing.'[32]

Later, on the trial of John Felton, who had assassinated the Duke of Buckingham at Portsmouth in 1628, all the 12 judges declared unanimously that he should not be tortured on the rack, 'for no such punishment is known or allowed by our law.' This clearly indicates, however, that the judges knew of the existence and use of the rack and they avoided the question 'whether the law recognised its own subjection to absolute prerogative.'[33] Notwithstanding this unambiguous statement of the position at common law, partly from the influence of continental jurisprudence,[34] torture was used extensively by the Star Chamber to secure confessions and persuade prisoners to implicate others. Indeed, under Elizabeth I alone a long list of priests are said to have been put to death after suffering torture.[35] And, although the majority of cases involving torture between 1540 and 1640 involved crimes of state, more than a quarter of torture warrants were issued in cases involving murder, robbery, burglary and horse stealing.[36]

During all the Tudor reigns, the rack was in constant use in the Tower of London but specific instructions from either the monarch or the council, using the royal prerogative, were always required before the torturer could act. However, a confession under torture denied a jury the opportunity of reaching a verdict on the facts of the case.

That torture was not only used, but covered-up, by the Tudors and early Stuarts was revealed by David Jardine, a nineteenth-century barrister and writer on historical and legal matters.[37] His researches into the registers of the proceedings of the council and original torture warrants in the state papers office revealed the extensive use of the rack for dislocating limbs in order to persuade victims to 'confess' to treason, murder or robbery. Letters from successive monarchs, including Elizabeth, and the council were discovered which instructed the lieutenant of the tower to use torture, and not with the rack alone. Guy Fawkes was not the only prisoner to be very badly tortured by other means before his trial.[38] For instance, in December 1577, Thomas Sherwood, a Roman Catholic accused of attending mass, was placed in a dungeon in the Tower below the high-water mark. Water flowed in and out with the tides bringing with it rats which tore the flesh from his arms and legs. He was subsequently put to the rack. Despite such cruelty he admitted nothing and was executed for high treason.[39]

Such blatant torture was brought to an end along with the Star Chamber by the Long Parliament in 1641. But, in any event, despite the prerogative, the use of torture had not been regularised in English criminal procedure.[40] Although the Tudor and Stuart monarchs admired continental practices, they were unable to bring together their new activist judges and the practice of torture to avoid the need for a jury entirely. This was because of the outspoken opposition of Fortescue and Coke and the widespread public acceptance of jury trial together with the fact that torture could be used anyway under the prerogative. As a consequence, the jury standard of proof, instead of adjudication by professional judges, gave England no cause to institutionalise torture.[41]

EVIDENCE OF WITNESSES

By the fourteenth century witnesses from outside the ranks of the jury began to make their appearance in criminal cases although it was not until 1468 that Fortescue was the first judge and jurist to refer to witnesses giving evidence.[42] Edward Powell has examined the circuit gaol delivery records of Derbyshire, Leicestershire and Warwickshire between 1400 and 1429[43] and his conclusions are both instructive and contrary to what has been widely believed before. The trial jury in these years, he says, was not usually self-informing or drawn from the neighbourhood where the offence occurred. It often relied for its information upon the hearing of evidence in court and by 1400 the active medieval jury had begun to give way to the passive triers of the modern courtroom.[44]

This was a transformation in jury trial that accelerated under the Tudors and it was the very existence of flexible decision-making, unlike the Roman canon method, that made it possible. The Tudors were undoubtedly moving towards Roman law but 'once again the common law stood impregnable upon the foundations laid by Henry II.'[45] According to Plucknett, the reason was that,

> The close organization of the profession and the numerous vested interests which it contained, the strong tradition of its educational system centring in the Inns of Court, and the practical impossibility of superseding the courts by a newer system, had the result of entrenching the common lawyers within the tangles of their feudal learning, which moreover, had become the basis of every family fortune in the land.[46]

It should be remembered, however, that it was not until 1504, towards the end of the reign of Henry VII, that statutes for the first time referred unequivocally to the giving of evidence—a new word in the official vocabulary of the English criminal law.[47] According to Barbara Shapiro, several developments 'subtly altered English trials and created the need for some kind of law of evidence.'[48] By the sixteenth century these were:

> Juries were no longer so likely to be familiar with the facts of a case. As society became more complex and as mobility increased, juries increasingly came to rely on the testimony of witnesses for information …Without giving up their right to consider their own personal knowledge in reaching a verdict, juries increasingly relied on witnesses and documents which they now had somehow to evaluate for truthfulness and accuracy.[49]

So rapidly was change occurring that in 1563 legislation[50] created a legal process for compelling the attendance of witnesses in civil cases and made perjury a crime.[51] Moreover, in criminal trials the Crown alone could call witnesses and it could already compel them to attend court to testify against the prisoner by a statute of Philip and Mary.[52] This statute helped perpetuate private prosecutions and 'channelled the English pretrial procedure away from Continental-style public prosecution.'[53] By ensuring preliminary evidence from justices of the peace it also encouraged judicial control over trials.

As Green has argued, in Tudor and Stuart England juries exercised a mediatory power in two distinct but related ways. In individual cases they prevented the imposition of sanctions they deemed too harsh in the light of the defendant's behaviour, reputation, or the hardship he or she had already suffered. And, more generally, they reflected the interests of the local community as opposed to those of central authorities. However, by the middle of the fifteenth century, as the jury became less self-informing and the judges less dependent on their knowledge, the bench began to reduce jury power.[54] As judges began to put pressure on jurors who acquitted against the wishes of the bench, by fining or imprisoning them or sending them to the Star Chamber, the number of convictions at assizes grew strikingly higher than in the late Middle Ages when it was generally less than 25 per cent.[55]

But although witnesses were now appearing in court for the prosecution it is widely considered that a defendant was not permitted to call witnesses.[56] And, although practices and procedures in felony trials did not always follow the same rules as in treason trials, they appeared to do so in the denial of hearing defence witnesses.[57] The general position was shown clearly in the trial of Sir Nicholas Throckmorton in 1554 when a witness for the defendant, John Fitzwilliams, was summarily dismissed from the courtroom and was not allowed to speak. Throckmorton asked the court why they were not as prepared to hear the truth from him as untruth against him? He reminded the judges that Queen Mary herself had told the court that defence witnesses should be heard, but it was to no avail.[58]

Again, in the trial of Puritan minister John Udall for seditious libel at Croydon assizes in 1590 the defendant offered some witnesses and it was declared that because the evidence was against the Queen's majesty they could not be heard. To which he sensibly replied, 'which seemeth strange to me, for methinks it should be for the Queen to hear all things on both sides, especially when the life of any of her subjects is in question.'[59] Since prosecutions were taken in the name of the monarch it was logical that a similar rule applied to felonies as well as in state trials and in a felony case in the reign of Edward I the court had told the prisoner, in terms similar to those used to Udall about his witnesses, that he could not have counsel 'against the King.'[60]

Nevertheless, Langbein argues that there was no rule excluding defence witnesses, at least in felony trials, and that 'we have no reported instance of defence witnesses being refused audience after the supposed events in Udall's trial in 1598.'[61]

In treason trials a point of law included an error in procedure such as an omission to mention an overt act when the indictment concerned compassing the King's death, or a lack of two witnesses, or a jury drawn from the wrong place.[62] Not that this always assisted prisoners, some of whom complained bitterly but unsuccessfully when only one witness against them was produced. In felony trials it became openly possible for the defence to produce witnesses following *Tyndal's Case* in 1632,[63] although they were not permitted to take the oath.[64]

Yet Coke in his *Third Institute* had mentioned a statute[65] which allowed witnesses on oath to the accused in certain trials for felony, 'for the better information of the consciences of the jury and justices.' To which he added, 'To say the truth, we never read in any act of parliament, ancient author, book case, or record, that in criminal cases the party accused should not have witnesses sworn for him, and therefore there is not so much as *scintilla juris* against it.'[66] Notwithstanding that, as Sir Matthew Hale wrote after *Tyndal's Case*, 'Regularly the evidence for the prisoner in cases capital is given without oath, though the reason thereof is not manifest … neither is counsel allowed him to give evidence to the fact, nor in any case, unless matter of law doth arise.'[67] These eminent jurists could not explain this restriction on defence witnesses but it has recently been argued that, after the end of trial by ordeal, when there was a legal presumption that all sworn evidence was truthful because of divine vengeance for lies, the system could not cope with sworn conflicts of testimony.[68]

COUNSEL

In felony trials in Tudor times defendants were still not permitted to have counsel except to deal with points of law and most cases were dealt with without them. It was Coke who first put forward reasons for the denial in all capital cases that were much quoted in later years, including 1836 when Parliament debated the Prisoners' Counsel Bill that finally allowed defendants to have counsel represent them on all aspects of their cases.[69] 'The true reasons of the law', he said, 'are, first, that the testimony and the proofs of the offence ought to be so clear and manifest, as there can be no defence to it; secondly, the court' (i.e. the judge) 'ought to be instead of counsel for the prisoner.'[70]

He was followed by the eminent jurist Serjeant Hawkins who argued that the denial of a full defence by counsel was an advantage to an innocent person. Although admitting that many had complained that the rule was very unreasonable, Hawkins thought that everyone could speak to a matter of fact as if he were the best lawyer. 'The simplicity, the innocence, the artless and the ingenious behaviour of one acquitted by his conscience,' he wrote, 'has something in it more moving and convincing than the highest eloquence of persons speaking in a cause not their own.'[71] Ideals of perfection indeed.

In cases of treason, the right to counsel was granted to defendants and witnesses were allowed to take the oath by the Treason Trials Act of 1696,[72] in the main because of the lack of credibility of the witnesses brought by the later Stuarts against unsworn but truthful witnesses for the defence.[73] As will be seen, '[t]his flowed from the Revolution of 1689 as a means of redressing a wrong the now-dominant Whig political class had suffered in the previous decade—the use of charges of treason to destroy political opponents.'[74] For felony, witnesses could be sworn only from 1702.[75] As for defence counsel in felony trials, they were increasingly allowed by judges from the early 1700s for reasons which will be discussed in *Chapter 6*.

JURY MEMBERSHIP

By the sixteenth century, residence within the county rather than the neighbourhood of the crime was an adequate qualification for jury service[76] and probably the majority of jurors were yeomen or craftsmen.[77] Jury service could, however, be oppressive and was accordingly unpopular.[78] It took the jurors away from their occupations, disrupted their daily lives and cost them time and money to appear at court, often travelling from one end of the county to another, or sometimes several counties.[79] Although it is difficult to say how widespread the practice was, Cockburn gives numerous examples of malpractices by sheriffs allowing jurors to avoid service and of their absences causing serious problems.[80]

This tended to weaken the jury system and led to fears that the less substantial men on the jury were more susceptible to threats and bribes. In fact, embracery (trying to influence a juror to favour one side or the other by means of threats or bribes) was a crime but it was nevertheless common, as numerous complaints in Parliament and elsewhere testified.[81] Even Shakespeare added his voice in *Measure for Measure* when Angelo argues:

> The jury passing on the prisoner's life
> May in the sworn twelve have a thief or two
> Guiltier than him they try. What's open made to justice,
> That justice seizes. What knows the laws
> That thieves do pass on thieves?[82]

It had led in the fifteenth century to a property qualification of 100 shillings annual value of land or rents, although Parliament reduced this to 40 shillings annual value for jurors in cases of homicide,[83] with a smaller income probably accepted for lesser felonies. This property qualification was the general rule for over three centuries and when eroded by inflation was believed to have again caused a lowering of the social class of jurors.[84] To obtain a more wealthy type of juror, in the mid-1580s the 40-shilling qualification for jury service was raised by statute to four pounds[85] at which it remained until 1664 when it was increased by a Juries Act to £20[86] for

reformation of abuses in Sheriffes and other Ministers, who for reward doe oftentimes spare the ablest and sufficientist, and returne the poorer and simpler Freeholders lesse able to discerne the Causes in question, and to beare the charges of appearance and attendance thereon.[87]

Powell found that in the early fifteenth century in Derbyshire in the Midland circuit, nearly 60 per cent of jurors who served twice or more, and nearly 30 per cent of those who served once only, were gentry, or 35 per cent of jurors overall. There was a striking incidence of coroners and bailiffs among trial jurors in Derbyshire and Warwickshire, which appeared to cause no concern even though some of the prisoners were likely to have been indicted before the coroners.[88] The remainder, he presumes on some but not very conclusive evidence, were yeomen and prosperous husbandmen.[89]

Powell also found that juries generally tried several cases at a time and on one occasion 39 prisoners were arraigned before a single jury at Nottingham in 1420.[90] In all three counties that he studied the vast majority of trial juries included at least one or two jurors from each hundred where the offences had been committed. But within the hundreds there was no consistent geographical correlation between the location of offences and the domicile of jurors, and where three or more prisoners were tried at one time, even that tenuous correlation tended to break down.[91] For example, a trial jury sitting at Hertford assizes in 1615 heard five different cases which originated in four different parishes that were located in three different hundreds. Not a single juror came from a parish in which one of the offences had occurred and six of the 10 jurors whose residences are given did not even come from one of the three relevant hundreds. Clearly, jurors were no longer self-informing witnesses.[92]

In Hertfordshire in Elizabethan and Jacobean times, it was men of property, yeomen, lesser gentry and wealthy husbandmen and craftsmen who formed the social backbone of the county's jury system. This meant that they were recruited from a relatively small section of the population.[93] In other words, 'the social context of the jury system was in a very precise sense a class institution.'[94] Jurors were drawn, Lawson says, from lists of propertied men who exercised a tangible power over the lives of members of their own communities and the jury must have been seen from the perspective of most village men and women as a ruling-class institution.[95] This was true, however, of most trial juries until the abolition of the property qualification in modern times.

SELECTION OF JURORS

Despite the property qualification there were constant criticisms by the government that the sheriffs were nominating men for jury service who were unqualified, with a heavy reliance on talesmen.[96] Certainly, the trial juror of substance was less likely to serve than in earlier times. Many trial jurors, it appears, were unqualified men serving for payment in one form or another, or men who had been dragooned into the post by sheriffs and their officers.[97] And, by the 1620s,

Seventeenth-century under-sheriffs commonly oscillated between two equally unacceptable courses: they either warned indiscriminately all the county's freeholders to attend for jury service, or failed to summon any at all. In consequence bailiffs customarily took up 'men of all sorts' at assize time to form the *tales de circumstantibus* [jury members made up from bystanders] by which deficient juries might be made up … By the 1620s, 'contrary to the ancient writs and forms of law', more Western Circuit causes were tried by tales-men than by jurymen proper.[98]

According to G. R. Elton, '[j]uries at this time were certainly open to corruption by interested parties.' For instance, to support a man to be indicted at Guildford Assizes Sir Matthew Browne, a justice of the peace, 'asked the sheriff to impanel a favourable jury, offered its members bribes and favours and appeared at the trial to speak for the accused and impress the jury by his presence.' Evidence shows that he was successful.[99] This and other examples, taken mainly from Star Chamber records, are given by Elton although he accepts that the position was complex and that, outside state trials, juries were 'thinking men and could take a line of their own.'[100]

Robert Persons wrote of the accused's life depending on 'the verdict, malice, ignorance or little Conscience or care of twelve silly little men', who had to decide 'without time or means to inform themselves further, than that which they have heard there at the Bar.'[101] Yet this has always been a common complaint and cases such as Throckmorton's (see below) show that some jurors, even if chosen with care by the Crown, had minds of their own which made them face the prospect of a large fine or imprisonment for dissent with some steadfastness.

JUDICIAL ATTACKS ON THE JURY

On 11 April 1554 Sir Thomas Wyat was executed for leading a rebellion against the Catholic Queen Mary who was planning to marry Philip of Spain. Six days later Sir Nicholas Throckmorton was charged with high treason in adhering to the queen's enemies as Wyat's accomplice.[102] Endeavouring to secure a jury that was unbiased he reminded the court of a case where one judge said to another, 'I like not this jury for our purpose, they seem to be too pitiable and charitable to condemn the prisoner' but the second replied there was no cause for apprehension: the prisoner would 'drink the same cup his fellows have done' since the jurors were 'picked fellows for the nonce' (the occasion).[103] Throckmorton's judges were unimpressed.

After a spirited defence Throckmorton was found not guilty by the jury, a rare acquittal in a state trial under a special commission. The judges—Sir Thomas Bromley, the lord chief justice; Sir Thomas White, the lord mayor of London; and an assortment of earls and knights—were aghast and asked for the verdict not only from the foreman but from the other jurors individually as well. An incensed Lord Bromley told the jury, 'Remember yourselves better, have you considered substantially the whole evidence as it was declared and recited? The matter does touch the Queen's highness, and yourselves also. Take good heed what you do.'[104]

The foreman of the jury asked that they be not molested for discharging their consciences truly.[105] This had no effect however and they were committed to prison for arriving at a 'perverse' verdict. Four of them accepted that they had offended and were freed. Regardless of the effect on themselves and their families, the remaining eight held firm and their homes were sealed up and they themselves were imprisoned for six months. At the end of that time they were taken before the Star Chamber. There, the foreman and two others were ordered to pay the astronomical sum of £2,000 each within a fortnight and the other five 1,000 marks each. An English mark was worth 13/4d (66.8p). All were then sent back to prison.

In the event, six weeks later five jurors were discharged on paying £220 each and nine days later the rest followed on paying £60 each—still huge sums at the time. The effect on potential jurors of other jurors facing death for honouring their oath may be left to the imagination.

Even earlier, those who had found the Bishop of Rochester guilty of treason in 1535 said afterwards that their verdict was 'full sore against their conscience'. But they feared 'for the safety of their goods and lives which they were all well assured to lose, in case they acquitted him.'[106] It is little wonder that Throckmorton was one of only two Tudor subjects acquitted on charges of treason. Moreover, as a direct result of the example presented by the imprisonment and impoverishment of the jurors, Throckmorton's brother John was quickly found guilty of high treason on the same evidence on which his brother had been acquitted.[107] He was then executed. Sir Nicholas himself was unlawfully kept a prisoner in the Tower for a year after his acquittal but later became a favourite of Queen Elizabeth who sent him to be her ambassador, first to Paris and afterwards to Scotland.[108]

According to Cockburn, many juries at the time were partisan and understood little of the principles of evidence. As a consequence judges often attempted to cow them and by the 1570s the right to threaten them to secure the reversal of unacceptable verdicts was an accepted convention, with the powers of the Star Chamber in the background.[109] Furthermore, in state trials, which were really show trials, juries were handpicked for the particular case[110] from knights, esquires or gentlemen,[111] and in Tudor and early Stuart reigns were sometimes rehearsed by the Star Chamber in the case of the prosecution before the hearing.[112]

It is interesting that in the reign of Henry VIII the fining and imprisonment of jurors were authorised by a statute for Wales and the Marches (i.e. the border regions) in cases when they gave 'an untrue verdict against the king, contrary to good and pregnant evidence ministered to them by persons sworn before the justices …'[113] C.J. Vaughan, in *Bushell's Case* in 1670, drew the inference from this statute that such treatment was not legal without it, or at all outside Wales.[114]

Equally interesting is that in Tudor times most criticism of treason trials was around the trial jury who would have been specially selected for such cases. On trial for treason, both Edmund Campion and Richard White asked to be tried by a jury with more learning. And, John Udall, in his trial for seditious libel at Croydon assizes in 1590 said, 'I do desire to be tried by an inquest of learned men; but seeing I shall not, I am contented to be tried by the ordinary course, as these men before me are, that is, as you used to say, by God and the country.'[115] Clearly, these defendants did not consider that they were being tried by their peers.

CONVICTIONS

Under the Tudors, although jury nullification continued,[116] there was a considerable rise in the number of felony convictions.[117] One of the reasons for this was the fact that victims of crime were more likely to attend the court now that they could bring witnesses with them whose evidence would influence juries. Further, a statute[118] in 1529 offered restitution in cases of carrying away of property if the victim gave evidence that secured the conviction of the suspect. Another statute[119] in 1555, gave justices of the peace power to bind over witnesses to a felony to appear at the trial and this also would have strengthened the case of the prosecution. Monitoring of juries by the prerogative courts was also likely to be a factor. There is evidence however that by the end of the sixteenth century the trend of increasing rates of conviction had begun to reverse.[120]

With a rather complicated example Herrup also shows that juries often knew exactly what they were doing.[121] Briefly, four separate charges of theft were made over a period of six months against Francis Pankhurst of Heathfield in Sussex. At the quarter sessions held in October 1637, Pankhurst was accused by John Ellis for, first, the theft of several bushels of wheat and, secondly, the taking of a goose from Ellis's father, Thomas. Three months later Pankhurst was back at the quarter sessions, this time at the demand of Anne Williams, who claimed that he had stolen an iron pot and, on another occasion, feathers worth four shillings. A grand jury rejected the charge for the larceny of the goose; the trial for the theft of the pot ended in an acquittal. The other two cases brought convictions; one was eased by the trial jurors revaluing the stolen property to ten pence instead of three shillings, and the other was softened by the justices of the peace who accepted Pankhurst's plea for benefit of clergy. Details of the evidence in the first three cases show that they were decided in accordance with the facts, although two of the verdicts reveal the exercise of jury discretion.

JURY AUTONOMY

The Tudor and early Stuart reigns saw the final decline of the role of jurors as witnesses since, as Edward Powell has shown, jurors were often no longer necessarily part of a small local community and the rules of procedure were undergoing change. Now jurors were often yeomen and frequently heard evidence from independent witnesses. According to Hale they could be of the county with only two from the hundred and *inter alia* they were to take evidence from witnesses.[122] Furthermore, although in 1554 the common law judges ruled that they could not fine or imprison jurors the period saw the Star Chamber judges continuing to do so as a means to coerce them and bring them more under the control of the bench.[123] The number of acquittals and verdicts of self-defence fell but was complemented by an increase in the number of convictions on charges that left the defendant eligible for benefit of clergy (by now branding and after 1576 the possibility of one year's imprisonment).[124] According to Green this made juries feel more merciful with the less serious felonies.[125]

Lawson found in Hertfordshire between 1573 and 1624, that jurors 'occupied a position of importance within the early-modern structure of wealth and power.'[126] This meant that they were educated and skilled enough to exercise a practical degree of independence. He confirms that in many cases they were not drawn from either parishes or hundreds where the offences had occurred and in Hertfordshire, as in other counties, they were the yeomen, lesser gentry, wealthy husbandmen and craftsmen.[127]

Of the known verdicts of the assize trial jury in Hertfordshire between those years, 41.3 per cent were acquittals, 48.3 per cent were absolute convictions and 10.4 per cent were partial verdicts.[128] On a lesser scale, Cockburn found that on the home circuit from 1560 to 1680 an average of approximately 25 per cent of all those indicted were reprieved by jury mitigation. Trial juries, he says, 'saved an indeterminate number from the gallows by undervaluing stolen goods in order to reduce the offence from grand larceny, punishable in the last resort by death, to petty larceny, commonly punishable by a public whipping.'[129] Hence, nullification was still practised even in this period of growing attempts to control juries.

As part of nullification with regard to homicide, Green holds that there was a passing over of the Anglo-Saxon notion that only those who committed homicide through secrecy or stealth were guilty of murder and had to pay with their life. This caused popular resistance to the extension of capital punishment to those guilty of killing who would have paid compensation under Anglo-Saxon law, with juries, by means of acquittals and verdicts of self-defence, imposing upon the courts their long-held notions of justice.[130] This links with the continuing influence of the ordeal. Did the early jury act, asks Olson, 'not to express disapproval of a law or of a sanction but to bestow mercy ... exhibiting an affinity with the ordeal as a penitential act of purgation?'[131]

By the 1590s 'assize judges on the home circuit were attempting in vain to discourage the unauthorised exercise of discretionary powers by both trial and grand jurors.'[132] However, this was replaced in part by an informal system of judicially controlled plea bargaining. By this means the judges were able to 'exclude the jury from between 10 and 30 per cent of the criminal cases heard on each circuit in the 30 years after 1590.'[133]

Some latitude was permitted to jurors by judges and James I in his Proclamation for Jurors in 1607 made clear their autonomy, saying:

> [of jurors] also the Law of this our Realm does ascribe such trust and confidence, as it does not so absolutely tie them to the evidences and proofs produced, but that it leaves both supply and testimony, and the discerning and credit of testimony to the juries consciences and understanding.[134]

Accordingly, the stealing of horses to sell for profit was treated seriously by juries but although there was a small percentage of thefts of food among serious crimes, juries mitigated 31 per cent of those tried as felonies.[135] Herrup has shown that in parts of East Sussex between 1592 and 1640 the crime of horse theft resulted in an order to hang for 95 per cent of those convicted. This reflected the morality of the time since whereas horse thieves were vilified because they were notoriously successful at selling their booty well and quickly, excusing those who stole from hunger dated from at least the canonists of the twelfth century and had deep roots in the commonsense notion of justice.[136]

LAWLESS JURIES?

Dealing with the composition and behaviour of juries in Hertfordshire, Lawson discusses whether trial juries in particular were 'lawless' in the sense of exercising powers of nullification.[137] He says that by implication they emerge 'as articulators of a widely shared body of norms that might limit, even contradict, the formal criminal law.'[138] He also cites Herrup as suggesting that in addition to the formal legal definitions of culpability, there existed in the seventeenth century 'an informal, religiously inspired, community-based set of definitions.'[139]

Alternatively, as Cockburn suggests, did trial procedure undercut the independence of juries and strengthen the position of the judge, thereby ensuring that the behaviour of juries was in large part determined by the bench?[140] From his research, Lawson considers that, at the time, 'symptoms of jury lawlessness are clearly apparent.' Partial verdicts point in that direction as do contemporary complaints that juries were willing to acquit against the evidence. But, he says, this does not mean that in doing so juries were representative members of their communities since 'they occupied ... a position much closer to those who made the laws than those who bore the brunt of their enforcement.'[141] Nonetheless, he concludes that, to the extent that they adopted a flexible approach to their task, Elizabethan and Jacobean juries can be described as lawless. But, while they violated the letter of the law they did not violate its spirit. He says:

> Early modern criminal justice was founded on the logic of exemplary punishment, and this logic demanded that the law be enforced selectively rather than absolutely ... it was this demand that ensured that the jurors were likely to convict men more than women, 'old offenders' more than inexperienced offenders, and serious offenders more than those who committed less serious crimes ... Far from attempting to moderate the law, the jurors emerge as willing and largely obedient participants in the early-modern system of law enforcement.[142]

Jurors, he adds, were men of property whose natural social alignment was with the larger landowners immediately above them in the social structure rather than the landless and near-landless people below them who supplied the bulk of the prisoners who stood before them in court.[143]

CONCLUSION

Green sees the first great watershed in the history of trial practice being the development in Tudor times of a formal prosecution.[144] But this could occur only because juries had ceased to be self-informing and because witnesses and evidence had come to the fore. The period from the ascension to the throne of Henry VII in 1485 to the execution of Charles I in 1649 reveals juries being drawn less and less often from a small community and having direct knowledge of the accused and their cases. Instead, they were increasingly drawn from the counties and judged both the witnesses themselves and their evidence. Significantly, Hale wrote that the credit of the testimony of a witness 'is left to the jury, who are judges of the fact, and likewise of the probability or improbability, credibility or incredibility of the witness and his testimony.'[145] Nevertheless, although judges allowed juries some discretion, with a growth in the number of witnesses and the amount of evidence before the court it became possible for the bench to take on a more powerful role alongside the growing power of the Crown with its use of torture and the weakening of benefit of clergy. Furthermore,

> Crown officials then took increasing responsibility for the initiation and prosecution of criminal cases and for the management of the trial itself. The effects of these changes upon the jury were substantial. For one thing, the government sometimes used great art in persuading juries of the defendant's guilt; perhaps more significantly, the jury lacked the means to manipulate the evidence, to suppress whatever might give the lie to the way it chose to view the facts. Moreover, perhaps as a result of these changes, the bench brought pressure to bear upon some juries that

acquitted in the face of inculpatory evidence, binding them to appear before Star Chamber or even fining and imprisoning them directly.[146]

Nonetheless, such measures clearly indicate sufficient discretion to disturb the authorities. And, as Lawson contends, although to an extent juries adopted a flexible stance and sometimes violated the letter of the law they did not violate its spirit since logically it had to be enforced selectively.[147]

This period saw for the first time the fining and imprisonment of jurors, and sending them to the Star Chamber for punishment for 'perverse' verdicts. It is interesting that at the assizes in one county, Kent, partial verdicts were unknown in the 1560s, very uncommon before 1590 and increased thereafter until by the 1660s more than 31 per cent of all convictions were the product of partial verdicts.[148]

In a detailed study of the courts of assizes at the beginning of the seventeenth century, Cockburn concludes that in the criminal trial 'the role of the jury was subordinate to and determined by the bench.'[149] He also endorses the view of Beattie that when, for example, a jury reduced a charge of grand larceny to petty larceny, in many instances the jury's intention may have been to strengthen judicial sanctions by substituting a more painful, and public, whipping for the formal branding that followed a successful plea of benefit of clergy.[150] But whilst whipping could be more painful than branding, the latter was hardly less public in the long term.

The Tudor and Stuart state saw the empowerment of the judges with a growing mastery of written materials and domination of the procedure following the Marian reforms. For felonies, the Marian statutes[151] directed justices of the peace to certify their preliminary examinations of suspects and witnesses to the next gaol delivery. The law of criminal evidence presented by witnesses began to form with the justices replacing the old accusing jury and providing the judges with written prosecution evidence.[152] This meant that the judge was now possessed of evidence that enabled him to be more directly involved in the decision making. Nevertheless, at the same time, the Marian scheme enhanced the position of the trial jury. Alongside the jury's growing inability to inform itself, the statutes instituted a procedure to assure it a regular flow of information from justices of the peace, who investigated crime and organized the prosecution, thereby reinforcing its role as a trier of fact and easing its transition from a medieval to a modern body.[153]

Nevertheless, juries were relatively more subordinate during the Tudor and early Stuart reigns than before. This was because Crown officials were more likely to manage trials than they had been earlier and the bench brought pressure to bear by binding juries over to appear before the Star Chamber, or fining and imprisoning jurors themselves. In addition, there was interference with the selection of jurors. Despite all this, however, and the fact that for a time the number of acquittals reduced, they increased again in the latter part of the period with juries increasing their autonomy and power and the impact of nullification.

ENDNOTES for *Chapter 3*

[1] Thomas Andrew Green. (1985) *Verdict According to Conscience. Perspectives on the English Criminal Trial Jury 1200-1800. Chicago, Chicago University Press.* p. 105.

[2] P.G. Lawson. (1988) 'Lawless Juries? The Composition and Behaviour of Hertfordshire Juries, 1573 –1624.' In Cockburn and Green (eds) . *Twelve Good Men and True. The Criminal Trial Jury in England 1200-1800.* New Jersey. Princeton University Press. pp. 117-157.

[3] J.S. Cockburn. (1988) 'Twelve Silly Men? The Trial Jury at Assizes, 1560-1670.' In Cockburn and Green. Ibid. pp. 158-181.

[4] J.D. Mackie. (1992) *The Earlier Tudors 1485-1558.* Oxford, Clarendon Press. p. 562.

[5] Ibid. pp. 562-3.

[6] J.B. Post. (1988) 'Jury Lists and Juries in the Late Fourteenth Century.' In Cockburn and Green (eds.) *Twelve Good Men and True: The Criminal Trial Jury in England.* New Jersey, Princeton University Press. pp. 29-32

[7] John H. Langbein. (1973) 'The Origins of Public Prosecution at Common Law.' 17 *The American Journal of Legal History.* North Carolina, University Press. pp. 313-14. And (1974) his *Presenting Crime in the Renaissance; England, Germany, France.* Cambridge, Mass. Harvard University Press.

[8] 2 & 3 P. & M. c. 10. (1555).

[9] J.M. Beattie. (1991) 'Scales of Justice: Defense Counsel and the English Criminal Trial in the Eighteenth and Nineteenth Centuries.' 9 (2) *Law and History Review.* University of Illinois Press. pp. 222-3.

[10] 26 Hen. 8. c. 14. (1539).

[11] J.S. Cockburn. (1972) *A History of English Assizes from 1558 -1714.* Cambridge, Cambridge University Press. p. 123.

[12] Cited in ibid at p. 122 from the condemnation by the Cairns Commissioners of 1869.

[13] Green. *Verdict.* Op. cit. p. 105.

[14] Cockburn. 'Twelve Silly Men?' Op. cit. pp. 179-80.

[15] Theodore F.T. Plucknett. (1956) *A Concise History of the Common Law.* 5th edn. London, Butterworths. p. 439.

[16] 25 Edw. 3. st. 3, c.4.

[17] A.K.R. Kiralfy. (1958) *Potter's Historical Introduction to English Law and its Institutions.* 4th edn. London, Sweet & Maxwell. p. 362.

[18] Sir Matthew Hale. (1736) *The History of the Pleas of the Crown.* London, E. and R. Nutt and Others. vol. ii. p. 379.

[19] Cockburn. *A History of English Assizes 1558-1714.* Op. cit. p. 126.

[20] J.A. Sharpe. (1985) '"Last Dying Speeches": Religion, Ideology, and Public Execution in Seventeenth-Century England.' 107 *Past and Present.* London, Past and Present Publishers. p. 167.

[21] James Fitzjames Stephen. (1883) *A History of the Criminal Law of England.* London, Routledge/Thoemmes Press. vol. i. p. 463.

[22] 4 Hen. VII, c. 13.

[23] Hale. Op. cit. p. 374. 4 & 5. P & M c.4.

[24] Green. *Verdict.* Op. cit. p. 280.

[25] 21 Jas I, c. 6.

[26] Cynthia B. Herrup. (1987) *The Common Peace. Participation and the Criminal Law in Seventeenth-century England..* Cambridge, Cambridge University Press. p. 143.

[27] 3 W. & M. c. 9. (1691). Herrup. Ibid. p. 143.

[28] Stephen. Op. cit. vol. i. p. 468.

[29] Sir Edward Coke. (1797b) *Third Institute.* London, E & R Brooke. Epilogue.

[30] Green. *Verdict.* Op. cit. p. 34.

[31] *Cf.* John H. Langbein. (1977) *Torture and the Law of Proof: Europe and England in the Ancien Regime.* Chicago. University of Chicago Press. p. 4.

[32] Sir John Fortescue. [1468] (1997) *On the Laws and Governance of England.* Shelly Lockwood (ed.) Cambridge, Cambridge University Press. p. 60.

[33] James Heath. (1982) *Torture and English Law: An Administrative and Legal History from the Plantagenets to the Stuarts.* Westport, Connecticut. p. 162.

[34] Edward Peters. (1986) *Torture.* Oxford, Basil Blackwell Ltd. p. 80.

[35] Antonia Fraser. (1996) *The Gunpowder Plot. Terror and Faith in 1605.* London, Weidenfeld & Nicolson. p. 177.

[36] Langbein. *Torture.* Op. cit. pp. 73-4.

[37] D. Jardine. (1836).'A Reading on the Use of Torture in the Criminal Law of England prior to the Commonwealth'. Delivered at New Inn Hall, Michaelmas Term. Published in 67 *Edinburgh Review*. (1838).

[38] Fraser. Op. cit. p. 179.

[39] Jardine. Op. cit. p. 26.

[40] Langbein. *Torture*. Op. cit. pp. 73, 77-8.

[41] Ibid.

[42] Fortescue. Op. cit. pp. 38-9.

[43] Edward Powell. (1988) 'Jury Trial at Gaol Delivery in the Late Middle Ages: The Midland Circuit, 1400-1429.' In Cockburn and Green. Op. cit.

[44] Ibid. p. 115.

[45] Plucknett. *A Concise History of the Common Law*. Op. cit. p. 44.

[46] Ibid.

[47] J.G. Bellamy. (1984) *Criminal Law and Society in Late Medieval and Tudor England* Gloucester, Alan Sutton. p. 35.

[48] Barbara J. Shapiro. (1983) *Probability and Certainty in Seventeenth-Century England. A Study of the Relationships Between Natural Science, Religion, History, Law, and Literature*. New Jersey, Princeton University Press. p. 176.

[49] Ibid.

[50] 5 Eliz. c. 9.

[51] Plucknett. *A Concise History*. Op. cit. p. 436.

[52] Ibid. 2 & 3 P. & M. c. 10. (1555).

[53] John H. Langbein. (2003) *The Origins of Adversary Criminal Trial*. Oxford, Oxford University Press. pp. 42-43.

[54] Green. *Verdict*. Op. cit. pp. 105-6.

[55] J.G. Bellamy. (1998) *The Criminal Trial in Later Medieval England*. Stroud, Sutton Publishing. p. 97.

[56] George Fisher. (1997) '*The Jury's Rise as Lie Detector*'. New Haven. 107 *Yale Law Journal*. p. 603.

[57] Ibid. p. 604, and see next page.

[58] 1 *State Trials*. cols. 809-902. The first full report of a criminal trial.

[59] Ibid. *cols*. 1271-1281.

[60] Year Books. 30 & 31 Edward 1 (Rolls Series) pp. 529-32. Quoted by David J.A. Cairns. (1998) *Advocacy and the Making of the Adversarial Criminal Trial 1800-1865*. Oxford Clarendon Press. p. 26.

[61] Langbein. *The Origins of Adversary Criminal Trial*. Op. cit. p. 55.

[62] John Bellamy. (1973) *An Introduction to the Tudor Law of Treason*. London, Routledge and Kegan Paul. p. 143.

[63] Cro. Car. 291.

[64] J.B. Thayer. (1898) *A Preliminary Treatise on Evidence at the Common Law*. Boston, Little Brown & Co. p. 160.

[65] 4 James I. c.1, s.6 (1606).

[66] Coke. *Third Institute*. Op. cit. p. 39.

[67] Hale. *History of the Pleas of the Crown*. Op. cit. ii. p. 283.

[68] Fisher. Op. cit. p. 584.

[69] *Hansard*. 3rd series. vol. 34. cols. 763-4.

[70] Coke. *Third Institute*. Op. cit. p. 29.

[71] William Hawkins. (1716) *Treatise of the Pleas of the Crown*. London. J. Walthoe. vol. ii. p. 400.

[72] 7 & 8 Wm. III. c.3, s.1.

[73] Fisher. Op. cit. p. 618. 7 & 8 Will. III c. 3.

[74] Beattie. 'Scales of Justice'. Op. cit. p. 224.

[75] 1 Anne. c.9, s.3.

[76] J.S. Cockburn. (1985) *Calendar of Assize Records, Home Circuit Indictments Elizabeith I and James I. Introduction*. London, HMSO. p. 57.

[77] Cockburn. 'Twelve Silly Men?' Op. cit. p. 161.

[78] Ibid. p. 160.

[79] Plucknett. *A Concise History of the Common Law*. Op. cit. p. 131.

[80] Cockburn. *Calendar Introduction*. Op. cit. pp. 57-60.

[81] J.G. Bellamy. (1973) *Crime and Public Order in England in the Later Middle Ages*. London, Routledge & Kegan Paul, p. 149.

[82] W. Shakespeare. (1991 edn) *Measure for Measure*. Oxford, The Clarendon Press. p. 111.

[83] 2 Henry V, st, 2, c. 3 (1414).

[84] See, however, Douglas Hay, *post.* p. 84.

[85] 27 Eliz. 1. c. 6.

[86] 16 Car. c. 3.

[87] 16 &17 Car. 2, c.3.

[88] Powell. Op. cit. pp. 90-1.

[89] Ibid. p. 95.

[90] Ibid. p. 84. In Hertfordshire by the late sixteenth century, however, Lawson found that the typical number of prisoners dealt with at one time by trial juries was seven.

[91] Ibid. p. 88.

[92] Lawson. 'Lawless Juries?' Op. cit. p. 123.

[93] Ibid. p. 133.

[94] Ibid. p. 137.

[95] Ibid.

[96] Lawson. 'Lawless Juries? Op. cit. p. 124.

[97] Cockburn. *Introduction to the Calendar of Assize Records.* Op. cit. pp. 60-1.

[98] Cockburn. *A History of English Assizes:* Op. cit. p. 118.

[99] Star Chamber. 2/22/50. Cited by G.R. Elton. (1972) *Policy and Police.* Cambridge, Cambridge University Press. pp. 310-26.

[100] Elton. Ibid.

[101] Bellamy. *The Tudor Law of Treason.* Op. cit. p. 177.

[102] 1 *State Tryals* (1719) London, Timothy Goodwin and others. pp. 47-60.

[103] Ibid. p. 48.

[104] Ibid. p. 61.

[105] Ibid.

[106] 1 Howell. (1818) *State Trials* col. 395.

[107] Ibid.

[108] J.B. Black. (1959) *The Reign of Elizabeth 1558-1603.* Oxford. The Clarendon Press. pp. 46, 68.

[109] Cockburn. *A History of English Assizes.* Op. cit. p. 123.

[110] John H. Langbein. (1978) 'The Criminal Trial before the Lawyers'. Chicago. 45 *The University of Chicago Law Review.* p. 266.

[111] James C. Oldham. (1983) *The Origins of the Special Jury.* Chicago. 50 *The University of Chicago Law Review.* p. 154.

[112] Bellamy. *The Tudor Law of Treason.* Op. cit. pp. 167-8.

[113] 26 Hen. VIII. c. 4.

[114] Thayer. *A Preliminary Treatise on Evidence.* Op. cit. p. 162.

[115] 1 *State Trials.* col. 1277.

[116] Green. *Verdict.* Op. cit. pp. 106-7.

[117] Cockburn. *Introduction to Calendar of Assize Records.* Op. cit. pp. 175-81.

[118] 21 Hen. VIII, c. 11.

[119] 2 and 3 P. & M. c. 10.

[120] Cockburn. *Introduction to Calendar of Assize Records.* Op. cit. pp. 175-81.

[121] Herrup. *The Common Peace.* Op. cit. pp. 146-7.

[122] Sir Matthew Hale. (1971) *The History of the Common Law of England.* Chicago, Chicago University Press. pp. 160-67.

[123] Green. *Verdict.* Op. cit. p. 141.

[124] Green. 'A Retrospective on the Criminal Trial Jury 1200-1800.' In Cockburn and Green. *Twelve Good Men and True.* Op. cit. pp. 360-61.

[125] Ibid.

[126] Lawson. Op. cit. pp. 119-20.

[127] Ibid. p. 133.

[128] Lawson. Op. cit. p. 150.

[129] Cockburn. *A History of English Assizes 1558-1714.* Op. cit. p. 128.

[130] Green. *Verdict.* Op. cit. p. 31.

[131] See Trisha Olson. (2000) 'Of Enchantment: The Passing of the Ordeals and the Rise of the Jury Trial.' New York, 50 *Syracuse Law Review.* p. 174.

[132] Cockburn. *Assize Introduction.* Op. cit. p. 70.

[133] Ibid.

[134] Herrup. *The Common Peace:* Op. cit. p. 148. For a highly critical review of Herrup's methodology see Cockburn (1991) in 9 (2) *Law and History Review.* University of Illinois Press.

[135] Ibid. p. 158.

[136] Herrup. (1985) 'Law and Morality in Seventeenth-Century England.' 106 *Past & Present*. Oxford, The Past and Present Society. pp. 114-5.

[137] Lawson. Op. cit. pp. 117-157.

[138] Lawson. Ibid. pp. 117-8.

[139] Ibid. p. 117. Herrup. 'Law and Morality in Seventeenth-Century England.' pp. 102-23.

[140] Cockburn. *Introduction to Assize Records*. Op. cit. pp. 131-3.

[141] Lawson. 'Lawless Juries'. Op. cit. pp. 119-20.

[142] Ibid. p. 157.

[143] Ibid.

[144] Green. *Verdict*. Op. cit. p. 267.

[145] Hale. *The History of the Pleas of the Crown*. Op. cit. vol. ii. pp. 276-7.

[146] Green. *Verdict*. Op. cit. p. 106.

[147] Lawson. Op. cit. p. 157.

[148] Ibid.

[149] Cockburn. *Introduction to Assize Records*. Op. cit. pp.131-33.

[150] Cockburn. 'Twelve Silly Men?' Op. cit. p. 172.

[151] 1 & 2 P & M c. 13. and 2 & 3 P & M c. 10 (1554-5).

[152] John H. Langbein. (1974) *Prosecuting Crime in the Renaissance: England, Germany, France*. Cambridge, Mass. Harvard University Press. pp. 1-2.

[153] Ibid. pp. 22-3 and 119.

CHAPTER 4

The Jury in the Interregnum

INTRODUCTION

The Anglo-Saxon legal and cultural background to the English trial jury system and the form that system took from its inception[1] enabled jury nullification to play a significant role through the thirteenth to the fifteenth centuries. This was partially modified later by the control exercised by the strong central government of the Tudors and early Stuarts. Theirs was a time when the nation state was established and the prerogative courts were approaching the height of their powers.

In response, and with the aid of the rapid expansion of the printing industry, a propaganda war exploded in the early seventeenth century around the growth of Puritanism. This included the demand, by Levellers, Diggers and other radical sects, for the reinstatement of what they perceived to have been an earlier non-centralised legal system with the jury dominant over the judge on questions of both fact and law.

At this time, the selection of jurors sometimes suffered from interference but in the second half of the century jury foremen, sitting and re-elected frequently, could bring a high degree of stability to jury trial.

This chapter considers, among other things, the demand of the Levellers, and in particular their leader, lieutenant-colonel John Lilburne, for 'jury right' to decide the law: for the first time as a clear-cut constitutional issue.[2] It will also show the response of jurors themselves in the trials of Lilburne when they were interrogated by the council about their 'perverse verdicts', and the role the judges could play in regard to the composition of the jury and their potential for influence upon it.

The country was riven by the civil war and its aftermath but at a deeper level:

> The definition of the common law as common justice and the identification of both with ideals of virtue infused the legal and social structures of early modern England. The intimate interweaving of criminal law and morality found expression not only in the courts but also in contemporary sermons, literature and legal dicta.[3]

It will be considered whether or not this mixture of morality and law prompted juries to a greater exercise of their power of discretion.

LAW REFORM

Parliament's disputes with King Charles I were intended to destroy the arbitrary rule of the monarch together with the prerogative courts like the Star Chamber that sat without a jury. However, it is significant that Parliament itself dispensed with the jury when appointing a new High Court of justice during the commonwealth which was given the power to sentence to death for treason—a power the Star Chamber did not possess.[4]

After the civil war Cromwell endeavoured to go further than destroying the Star Chamber. He wanted to secure reform of the law, for which he appointed a strong commission under the chairmanship of Sir Matthew Hale who was charged with preparing Bills for that purpose.[5] However, although the commission produced 16 Bills for reform it said little about criminal jury trial apart from a regressive proposal to raise the property and educational qualifications of jurors. Even in proposing that *peine forte et dure* be abolished it desired instead that it be replaced by a refusal to plead being taken as a plea of guilty with conviction following automatically—a strange means of mitigating an inhuman law, unless the purpose was to ensure the forfeiture of the estates of those remaining mute.

Opposition to the political aims of Cromwell came from the Leveller movement which advocated political and judicial reform, near-universal male suffrage and local justice.[6] The Levellers also held the belief that all trials should be before juries who, they said, should be judges of law as well as fact for the first time in England's history. This demand was to persist among dissenters and radicals during the eighteenth and nineteenth centuries with far-reaching consequences. The Levellers were well supported in the army but once Cromwell had obtained power he became less well disposed towards them than formerly. They turned against him when he stood by the men of property and when he had three soldiers shot after a short-lived mutiny by regiments proclaiming 'England's freedom, soldiers' rights.'[7]

THE LEVELLERS AND THE JURY

During the Interregnum the authorities endeavoured to crush radical opposition by use of the courts, and the Treasons Act of 1649[8] extended treason to cover verbal expressions of opinion, in addition to the government appointing the High Court of justice for criminal trials which, as we have seen, sat without a jury. All this led to the jury's role in the criminal process being re-examined. In particular, 'responding to the government's increased use of criminal prosecutions as a means of silencing its opponents, political and religious dissenters began asserting the jury's right to judge the "legality" and fairness of the law.'[9] It also led to Lilburne claiming that the government was infringing the right of trial by 12 sworn men of the neighbourhood[10] who should decide law as well as fact.

As early as 1646 Lilburne had called for all trials to be held monthly in the local courts and judged by 'twelve men of free and honest condition.'[11] Two years later, he claimed, in a pamphlet addressed to the House of Commons that 'all tryalls should be only of twelve sworn men, and no conviction but upon two or more sufficient known witnesses.'[12] The first, and still operative, Statute of Treasons of 1352[13] stipulated that no person should be indicted, arraigned or convicted unless accused by two sufficient, lawful and willing witnesses, but it was confined to high treason and was often ignored.

Lilburne characterised the jury as 'that great and strong hold of our preservation.'[14] Cromwell, for his part, was critical of the method of selection of juries, considering that the jury system encouraged 'the ensnaring of the weak and the tempting of the avarice of the more subtle, wholly in wait for their own advantage.'[15] In a letter to Major-General Desborough on 29 January 1656 he said, 'The law and justice hath been much liable to be perverted by the way that is generally held by deputy sheriffs in the choice of juries.'[16] Instead, he suggested that justices of the peace put forward to the sheriffs the names of freeholders of 'clearest integrity and prudence, of honest and blameless conversation.'[17] In other words, he was advocating more control over the selection of jurors, as he did with MPs. In Devon, the county Roberts is dealing with in the works just quoted, defendants came from all over the county, but trial jurors were almost exclusively composed of those who lived nearest to the venue of the trials.[18] What is clear is that during this period Cromwell was seeking to win over yeomen and, where they were not royalists, the gentry also in the counties as a support for his own rule. This was not confined to jurors, however, and was not unusual for any ruler or government.

INDEPENDENCE OF JURIES

In Somerset in January 1648 a book of freeholders eligible for jury service was completed. Afterwards a number of additions, sometimes in a different hand, were made to the original constables' returns. A large number of these freeholders were called upon to serve when the cases to be considered by the grand jury had political overtones, ten out of 19 at one time being from those added.[19] And, at the later trial of Lady Alice Lisle in 1685 for high treason, Lord Chief Justice Jeffreys 'ordered the sheriff to take care, that a very substantial jury should be returned, of the best quality in the county.'[20]

Dealing with juries at quarter sessions in Devon between 1649 and 1670, Roberts argues that at least in that county in the mid-seventeenth century, trial jurors, who were mainly small businessmen and farmers, were allowed little independence of judgment from their social superiors in questions of life and death but were 'stooges' of the gentry. He found that the jury was 'patrolled and policed by the class immediately above it and was forced into the Procrustean mould of deference and passivity cast for it by the gentry.'[21] This does not appear, however, to have been the case in other counties and, in any event, his research deals with juries at quarter sessions, and there was an undoubted difference between those who were called for jury service there and at the assizes.[22] Nevertheless, the justices in quarter sessions maintained a campaign to reduce the degree of uncertainty in composing a jury and officers charged with delivering the summons to individual jurors were fined and badgered into a semblance of reliability.[23]

Even at this stage juries could be more tolerant than Parliament and were known to use what later became known as 'pious perjury' to dilute the consequences of statutes they considered to be too severe. An example is a statute passed on 10 May 1650 and sent to every parish in England[24] that made adultery a felony punishable with death.[25] Unusually for the time, it provided that persons indicted might produce witnesses at the trial, and the judges might examine those witnesses on oath. But juries generally refused to convict for adultery and in a period of ten years only one person was sentenced to death at the Middlesex Quarter Sessions on this charge, namely an Ursula Powell on 30 August 1652.[26] This picture was largely repeated in other parts of the country where such sentences were also very rare.[27]

JURY FOREMEN

Prior to 1640 the foreman of the petty jury appears to have been simply the first among equals, presumably being selected from its literate members.[28] The situation then changed and Cockburn deals with the question of the foreman of the jury from about 1640, but predominantly at the Kent assizes so his examples and his conclusions may not reflect what was happening in the rest of the country. They are, however, of considerable and surprising interest. One assize juror, Robert Day, served over 13 years, during which he participated in at least 118 trials, 111 of them as foreman. Another man, Bernard Ellis, was directly involved in the trials of almost 400 prisoners and at one period was sworn to at least 50 juries, on 41 of which he was the foreman. Thomas Brewer was sworn to at least 40 juries, on 31 of which he served as foreman.[29] As a consequence, during the years 1653 and 1660 only six of the 40 juries sworn were not presided over by one of these three men.

Yet, during the same period, whilst 14 different judges rode the Home circuit, only four of them did so on more than three occasions. 'Looked at from this point of view,' Cockburn says, 'the most stable element in criminal justice administration in Kent during these years was the trial jury.'[30] And, although 'Ellis and Brewer had, as far as we know, no formal legal training, their experience of the criminal law in action compared favourably with that of any member of the Home circuit establishment.'[31]

Cockburn suggests that the members of this 'foreman elite' also exercised an extraordinary degree of control over the jury's deliberations and verdict. His general conclusion is that '[t]he introduction of a virtually institutionalised foreman and serial service for rank-and-file jurymen brought an unprecedented degree of stability to the Kent trial jury in the second half of the seventeenth century.'[32]

LILBURNE ON TRIAL

On 24 October 1649 the lord mayor of London was one of 40 dignitaries who attended the Guildhall to constitute an extraordinary commission of *oyer and terminer*. They were to try, with a jury, the Leveller leader, lieutenant-colonel John Lilburne. Held in the Tower, he was charged with high treason for publishing sundry 'scandalous, poisonous and traitorous books asserting that Cromwell's government was tyrannical, usurped and unlawful.'[33] It is worth considering the case in some detail to indicate his belief that the jury should decide issues of law as well as fact and how far this appealed to the jury. Moreover, his views represent a good deal of influential dissenting opinion of the period.

In court, Lilburne first declared that the commission of *oyez and terminer* to try him for uttering or publishing words in time of peace was illegal.[34] Then, summoned by the trier to hold up his hand, Lilburne instead addressed Mr Justice Keble who was the presiding judge. He would claim no mercy except from God, he declared. 'All the privilege that I shall crave this day at your hands,' he continued, 'is no more but that which is properly and singly the liberty of every free-born Englishman, namely the benefit of the laws and liberties thereof, which by my birth-right and inheritance is due to me and which I have fought for as well as others have done.'[35] With a supreme flight of fancy he claimed that other courts, including the Star Chamber, which had once tried him for treason had granted him this right.

Before he would plead, Lilburne asked for counsel to assist him on points of law and to see the indictment under which he was charged, but these requests were refused and after prolonged argument he pleaded not guilty. He constantly out-talked the judges and when two of them whispered together he jumped up to claim that to do so was against the liberties of Englishmen. When they replied that it was nothing to his detriment he did not hesitate to reply that there was no way he could know that.[36] Holding in his hand a book of Sir Edward Coke—'that great Oracle of the Laws of England'—he argued that his trial by the special commission of *oyer and terminer* was contrary to the *Petition of Right 1628* and to the Act of 1641which abolished all such extraordinary tribunals.[37] The power of all courts, he maintained, must be 'universal … to administer the law to all the people of England indefinitely, who are all born free alike, and not to two or three particular persons solely.'[38]

Judges mere ciphers

After denying all the charges against him, and refusing to say anything that might incriminate him, he asked if he would be allowed to speak to the jury on matters of law. They were his countrymen, he said, upon whose integrity depended the lives and liberties of all the honest men of the nation, since they were the judges not only of fact but of law.

Keble, the judge, expressed his fury at the suggestion that juries could decide on the law. Upon which Lilburne burst out, 'You that call yourselves judges of the law are no more but Norman intruders; and indeed and in truth, if the jury please, are no more but ciphers to pronounce their verdict.'[39] This was a direct appeal from the Levellers' belief that the jury was born in Anglo-Saxon times before the Normans had cast their alien yoke on the country. The concept of the Norman Yoke had a patriotic appeal and was of significance to the Puritans struggling against what they saw as an alien aristocracy.[40] The Leveller theory was that the Norman invasion broke England from its Anglo-Saxon past. Their myth of Anglo-Saxon liberties held that in that past age all men were free, held their land freely, met in free popular assemblies, declared the law, and judged one another in popular, local courts.[41] This theory drew disdain from the judges but was calculated to be popular with juries. It certainly was to the spectators who crowded the courtroom at Lilburne's trial. On hearing him say that the jurors had inherent in them alone 'the judicial power of the law as well as fact,' they cried in a loud voice, '"Amen, Amen" and gave an extraordinary great hum, which made the judges look something untowardly about them, and caused Major-General Skippon to send for three more fresh companies of foot soldiers.'[42]

Finally, Lilburne addressed the jury in a direct and personal way. He defiantly returned to his theme that the jurors were the judges of both fact and law. They, he resoundingly declared, 'by the law of *England* are the Conservators and sole Judges of my Life, having inherent in them alone the judicial Power of the Law, as well as Fact … I desire you to know your Power and do your Duty.'[43]

'Perverse' verdict

After Lilburne had addressed the jury Keble told them, 'you will clearly find that never was the like treason hatched in England.'[44] Notwithstanding this direction, the jury found the prisoner not guilty of any of the alleged treasons. Whereupon, 'immediately the whole multitude of people in the hall gave such a loud and unanimous shout as is believed was never heard in Guild Hall, which lasted for about half an hour without intermission.'[45] Amidst wild jubilation bonfires were lit and church bells rung throughout London with the army celebrating with the people in support of the supposed ancient rights of the jury.[46] The government however continued to detain Lilburne in prison until they could no longer withstand the clamour for his release.

After the trial, the jurors were themselves taken to the Old Bailey for individual examination on their 'perverse' verdict—a procedure the commonwealth had not dispensed with. Several of them said that they had only discharged their consciences and others vowed that despite what the judges had told them they took themselves to be 'Judges of Matters of Law' as well as of fact.[47] Nevertheless, subsequently they were set free, no doubt because of the feelings running high in the capital at the time.

Cromwell is reported to have looked upon the acquittal of his former friend as a greater defeat than the loss of a battle[48] and, although the press of the commonwealth avoided all mention of the trial, the Levellers had the last word. They struck a medal with a portrait of their hero on one side and the names of the jurors on the other. Its inscription read: 'John Lilburne, saved by the power of the Lord and the integrity of his jury, who are Judge of law as well as fact. October 26, 1649.'[49] It is not clear from the report of the trial, however, whether the verdict was an example of nullification or the jury believed there were procedural bars to conviction.

The Levellers were concerned about the limited nature of the franchise and, in their second *Agreement of the People* in 1648, proposed that property qualifications should be abolished and that men of 21 years and over, except beggars and those receiving alms, should be enfranchised.[50] Cromwell, however, believed that anything approaching manhood suffrage would lead to the overthrow of property and the destruction of civil society.[51] As a consequence, despite some changes, under the commonwealth and protectorate the franchise remained limited and largely unreformed and those without a vote (most men and all women) looked to the jury to protect such rights as they had from oppression.

Because of the jury, the mysteries of the law had to be rendered in lay language and Levellers and other radical sects wanted it to counterbalance the advantages of the legal establishment. They saw the jury as a representative institution whose origins were as old as the ancient law itself and whose capacities included that of finding and interpreting law. Judges had little role to play, merely explaining the law and maintaining order in the courtroom; judge-made law was condemned.[52] Under the Levellers' third *Agreement of the People* published in 1649 it was to be unconstitutional to try a man for his life, liberty or property except by 12 sworn men of the neighbourhood, to be freely chosen by the people and not 'picked and imposed' as before.[53]

Jury as judges of law

John Jones, who was not a Leveller but was sympathetic to many of their ideas,[54] published in May and August 1650 two books arguing for total jury control over the law. They were *The Judges Judged Out of Their Own Mouthes*[55] and *Jurors Judges of Law and Fact.*[56] Like the Levellers themselves, and to some extent like both Coke and Hale, Jones described a mythical Anglo-Saxon society where juries were themselves the judges; a society of popular local justice that was destroyed when the court of King's Bench was imposed upon it. And amazingly, the king's justices in eyre before whose visits the localities trembled, were translated by Jones into men who were 'chosen by the people.'[57] In the *Jurors Judges* etc. he stated that in all the courts in use before King Alfred's time, 'the jurors were the judges, and their then untraversable verdicts were the judgments in all causes.'[58] This meant not only 'jury right' but a decentralised system of justice with complete jurisdiction being granted to local courts. And Leveller Richard Overton desired that, 'according to the old law and custom of the land long before and after the Conquest, there may be courts of judicature for the speedy trial and determination of all causes, whether criminal or civil, erected and established in every hundred.'[59]

These demands were a response to the attempts of the government to silence dissent, not by new general laws, but through the Treason Act of 1649 mentioned earlier, which extended the crime from deeds to words, and the new High Court at Westminster. William Walwyn, perhaps the most attractive of the Leveller leaders, also said that the jury was the 'preserver of our fundamental, essential liberty, and acted judicially whilst the judge acted ministerially.' However, he too believed that William the Conqueror had been unable to take away an already existing criminal jury.[60]

The view of the jury taken by Lilburne and the Levellers was not, however, without its critics. In particular Henry Parker, a longstanding opponent, declared, in a tract attacking Lilburne's stand at his trial:

> The judges because they understand the law are to be degraded and made servants to the jurors; but the jurors because they understand no law are to be mounted aloft, where they are to administer justice to the whole kingdom. The judges because they are commonly gentlemen by birth and have had honourable education are to be exposed to scorn, but the jurors because they be commonly mechanics bred up illiterately to handicrafts are to be placed at the helm … cobblers must now practise physic instead of doctors; tradesmen must get into pulpits instead of divines and ploughmen must ride to the sessions instead of justices of the peace.[61]

Radical views

Lilburne continued to dissent, however, as he revealed in 1653 when he was subjected to a second prosecution by the commonwealth. This produced an argument about the jury that was to re-appear with embellishments when adopted by the Whigs during the events leading to the Glorious Revolution of 1689. In December 1651, on the grounds of an alleged slander against an MP, Parliament summarily and without hearing him, sentenced Lilburne to perpetual banishment from the country on pain of death if he returned.[62] By June 1653 Cromwell had dissolved the rump parliament and Lilburne decided he was free to return. However, Cromwell's nominated parliament, when it met on 4 July 1653, did not repeal the statute under which Lilburne was banished and he was brought to trial at the Old Bailey on 13 July for returning to England. Some three weeks earlier, however, his defence was anticipated by a tract entitled, *A Jury-man's Judgement upon the Case of Lieut. Col. John Lilburne,*[63] written anonymously but probably by Lilburne himself. The pamphlet argued strongly that the statute of banishment was unconstitutional and void and the sentence of death if he was in the country following a 'trial' without a jury or due process was an unlawful sentence for a minor crime.

In his trial at the Old Bailey,[64] he surprisingly won the rights to see the indictment before pleading not guilty and to have the assistance of counsel. But in his speech to what he called his 'honourable jury and keepers of the liberties of England' he called upon them to decide the law as well as fact and to acquit him on the ground that the Act, the judgment and the subsequent indictment were all null and void under the true fundamental law of England.[65] In claiming that the statute was null and void he was following the decision of Coke in *Bonham's Case* in 1610[66] that the common law could, where an Act was against reason, repugnant or impossible to perform, adjudge it to be void.[67] This idea of a natural law principle of judicial appeal found no fertile ground in England but had an immense influence in the United States.[68]

'Whatsoever is the issue of my trial,' Lilburne continued to the jurors, 'will hereafter be drawn into a precedent, either for the good or evil of all the people of England.' If such an Act as had banished him and could do him to death, neither they nor their wives nor children would be safe.[69] In the event, on 20 August, the jury found him 'not guilty of any crime worthy of death.' Three days later the jurors were closely examined by the council of state. Five said they had discharged their consciences and would answer no further questions. Three of them stated that they did not believe the prisoner was the same John Lilburne as the one mentioned in the Act. One juror, Gilbert Gayne a grocer, supported by two others, asserted that, notwithstanding the charge from the bench that they were judges only of fact, 'the jury were otherwise persuaded from what they heard out of the law books.'[70] Although acquitted for a second time, Lilburne was imprisoned for two years following the trial and died shortly thereafter.[71]

In this trial Lilburne had extended his claim that the jury were judges of law. He invoked it as a shield, asking them to reject void law and to act on behalf of the people, whose powers of delegation of authority to true representatives had been wrongfully usurped. He invoked the jury's duty to examine the charges against the defendant and to reject them if it found the facts did not amount to a crime under the common law and he planted the seeds of the dream of the jury's right to decide the law[72] which was later to dominate Restoration literature on the trial jury.[73]

THE DIGGERS

Of the wealth of seventeenth century sects the Diggers, or True Levellers as they were sometimes known, also clashed directly with the existing jury system. They aimed at a far more radical change in society, and agriculture in particular, than did the Levellers who were based more in the towns and the army. Community cultivation was to be carried out on a voluntary basis with the abolition of private property in land as an ultimate goal. With the Levellers they believed that a 'Norman Yoke' had been imposed on an idyllic Saxon England by William the Conqueror and his successors, and their leader, Gerard Wynstanley, claimed that 'the best laws that England hath are yoaks and manicles, tying one sort of people to be slaves to another.'[74] Unlike the Levellers the Diggers were opposed to the trial jury altogether since, as Wynstanley complained, its composition meant that it sided with the landowners, and jurors had dispossessed them from their settlement at St. George's Hill on Walton Heath in Surrey. They were composed, he said, of 'rich freeholders and such as stood strongly for the Norman power.'[75]

The Diggers challenged the rights of two lords of the manor, at St. George's Hill and at Cobham, not merely by squatting on the commons and cultivating them, but also by defiantly felling timber. In consequence, the lords of the manor had the Diggers' settlements and cottages destroyed and turned cattle into the growing corn.[76] The Diggers were also harassed with legal actions in the assize court at Kingston-upon-Thames where in one case a court official said, 'If the Digger's cause was good he would pick out such a jury as should overthrow him.'[77] It is little wonder that, unlike the Levellers, the Diggers had no faith in local justice or in the trial jury.

BENCH CONTROL OVER THE JURY

In the seventeenth century, the judge could exercise considerable power over a case and the jury. Before proceedings commenced he could alter the composition of a jury,[78] he could give specific instructions to the grand jury and during the trial he could influence the jury by interventions, comments and questions as well as in his summing up. Apart from the arbitrary fining of jurors by the bench for 'perverse' verdicts, Hale indicated the occasions on which in the seventeenth century he said that juries could be properly fined.[79] These were:

- if any of the jury ate or drank without the licence of the court before they had given their verdict.[80] In earlier times this had voided the verdict but no longer;
- if a juryman before he was sworn took information about the case, despite it having once been proper to do so. This had been stopped because it led easily to bribery and tampering with juries;
- if a juryman had evidence in his pocket and after the jury were sworn he showed it to the others. But this would not make the verdict void;
- if the jury questioned a witness while considering their verdict that made the verdict void as not having been done in open court and in the presence of the parties;
- if a juryman was one of the indictors in the case and did not discharge himself from the jury;
- if the jury said they were agreed and it then turned out that they were not. In this case each juror would be fined;
- for acquitting persons against 'pregnant' evidence of their guilt; and
- in one case where the jury acquitted a notorious robber in the King's Bench against great evidence they were bound over for the good behaviour of the prisoner.

Most of this was to be swept away by *Bushell's Case* which, as the next chapter will show, made the jury's verdict unassailable.

CONCLUSION

During the Interregnum, an obstacle to law reform was the prestige of the common law. With the abolition of the Star Chamber and the other prerogative courts the common law courts had acquired even greater power and prestige than in the time of Sir Edward Coke.[81] Furthermore, Barbara Shapiro argues that an examination of the credibility of witnesses and a concern for truth beyond a reasonable doubt had become standard.[82] According to Hale, evidence in history and law might be 'of high credibility, and such as no reasonable man can without any just reason deny.'[83] However, there can be little doubt that the republic was doomed to fail because in the temper of the times, Cromwell had to accept the common law and make his claims to legitimacy in legal terms that in the final analysis were based on a monarchial-type system of rule.[84]

Despite a deluge of pamphlets and tracts urging reform, there was little official change in the function of the jury except that it was required to be largely passive, which it was perhaps because of war weariness or the rule of the army. Those in Lilburne's trials appear to have been exceptions due to his immense popularity.

There was also coercion of the jury which the Levellers saw as ending community control of the law in favour of the Westminster bench and the lawyers. The main jury issue during the period was that of juries being judges of law. This appears to be the first time the question was raised publicly. However, this demand of the Levellers was based upon their vision of a past which never existed in the form in which they saw it. Nonetheless, Lilburne's trials gave it a platform and a resonance which enabled it to be taken up later by the Quakers, by the Whigs at the end of the century, again at the end of the eighteenth century and as will be seen it survives in a weakened form in the present day. It also spread to and germinated in the American colonies, and is still fiercely debated in the United States.[85]

ENDNOTES for *Chapter 4*

[1] See *Chapter 1*.

[2] T.A. Green. (1985) *Verdict According to Conscience. Perspectives on the English Criminal Trial Jury 1200-1800.* Chicago, University of Chicago Press. p. 153.

[3] Cynthia Herrup. (1987) *The Common Peace: Participation and the Criminal Law in Seventeenth-century England.* Cambridge, Cambridge University Press. p. 7.

[4] Sir William Holdsworth. (1966) *A History of English Law.* London, Methuen & Co. Ltd. vol. i. p. 431.

[5] The Minutes of the Hale Commission are available at the British Library in Hardwicke Papers. *Add. MSS.* 35863.

[6] Christopher Hill. (1966) *The Century of Revolution 1603-1714.* London, Thomas Nelson & Sons. pp. 129-32.

[7] H.N. Brailsford (ed. Christopher Hill). (1976) *The Levellers and the English Revolution.* Manchester, Spokerman Books. p. 519.

[8] *Laws and Statutes 1648-51.* (1651) London, J. Field.

[9] Warshawsky. (1996) 'Opposing Jury Nullification: Law, Policy, and Prosecutorial Strategy.' Washington, 85 *Georgetown Law Journal.* p. 195.

[10] John Lilburne. *England's New Chains Discovered.* In W. Haller. (1944) *The Leveller Tracts 1647-1653.* New York, Columbia University Press. p. 161.

[11] *The Just Man's Justification.* (10 June 1646). London, BL. E 340. (12).

[12] Lilburne. (1648) *The Humble Petition.* In G.E. Aylmer (ed.). (1975) *The Levellers in the English Revolution.* London, Thames and Hudson. p. 135.

[13] 25 Edw. III. c. 3.

[14] Lilburne. *England's New Chains Discovered.* Op. cit. p. 161.

[15] Stephen Roberts. (1982) 'Jury Vetting in the 17th Century.' 32 *History Today.* London, Trueword Ltd. p. 26.

[16] Stephen Roberts. (1988) 'Juries and the Middling Sort: Recruitment and Performance at Devon Quarter Sessions, 1649-1670.' In Cockburn and Green. *Twelve Good Men and True. The Criminal Trial Jury in England 1200-1800.* New Jersey, Princeton University Press. p. 195. Roberts is quoting from W.C. Abbott. (1947) *The Writings and Speeches of Oliver Cromwell.* Cambridge, Mass. iv. pp. 87-8.

[17] Ibid.

[18] Roberts. 'Jury Vetting.' Op. cit. p. 29.

[19] J.S. Cockburn. (1972) *A History of English Assizes: 1558-1714.* Cambridge, Cambridge University Press. p. 242.

[20] 11 *State Trials.* cols. 297 and 311.

[21] Roberts. 'Juries and the Middling Sort.' Op. cit. pp. 212-3.

[22] See J.S. Cockburn. (1988) 'Twelve Silly Men? The Trial Jury at Assizes, 1560-1670.' In Cockburn and Green, *Twelve Good Men and True.* Op. cit. p. 161.

[23] Roberts. 'Jury Vetting.' Op. cit. p. 27.

[24] State Papers, 16 May 1650.

[25] Statute, 1650, c.10.

[26] F.A. Inderwick. (1891) *The Interregnum 1648-1660: Studies of the Commonwealth, Legislative, Social and Legal.* London, Sampson Low, Marston, Searl & Rivington, pp. 34-35.

[27] Ibid.

[28] Cockburn. 'Twelve Silly Men?' Op. cit. p. 167.

[29] Ibid. pp. 168-9.

[30] Ibid. p. 170.

[31] Ibid.

[32] Ibid. pp. 168-9.

[33] 1 *State Tryals.* (1719) London, T. Goodwin & Others. pp. 580-640.

[34] Ibid. p. 583.

[35] Clement Walker. (1649) *The Trial of Lt. Col. John Lilburne ... Being as Exactly Penned and Taken in Shorthand, as it was Possible to be Done in such a Crowd and Noise.* London, Theodorus Verax. Cited by Brailsford. Op. cit. p. 604.

[36] *State Tryals.* Op. cit. p. 603.

[37] Ibid. p. 582. Lilburne excluded ordinary commissions of *Oyer and Terminer.* He was attacking only special commissions.

[38] Ibid.

[39] Ibid. p. 627.

[40] D. Veall. (1970) *The Popular Movement for Law Reform, 1640-1660.* Oxford, The Clarendon Press. p. 105.

[41] Green. *Verdict.* Op. cit. pp. 162-3.

[42] *State Tryals.* Op. cit. p. 633.

[43] Ibid.

[44] *State Trials.* Op. cit., col. 1402.

[45] Brailsford. Op. cit. p. 603.

[46] Ibid. p. 602.

[47] *State Tryals.* Op. cit. pp. 638-40.

[48] Brailsford. Op. cit. p. 603.

[49] Ibid.

[50] Brailsford. Op. cit. p. 528.

[51] Ibid. p. 490.

[52] James Epstein. (1996) ' "Our real constitution:" trial defence and radical memory in the Age of Revolution.' In James Vernon (ed). *Re-reading the Constitution: New Narratives in the Political History of England's Long Nineteenth Century.* Cambridge, Cambridge University Press, p. 33.

[53] Aylmer. Op. cit. p. 166.

[54] Veall. Op. cit. p. 103.

[55] John Jones. (1650) London, BL. Thomason Collection. E. 1414(1).

[56] Ibid. BL. E. 1414(2).

[57] *Judges Judged.* p. 79.

[58] *Jurors Judges.* pp. 24-5.

[59] R. Overton. (1647) *'An Appeal from the Commons to the Free People'*. In Don M. Wolfe. (1967) *Leveller Manifestoes of the Puritan Revolution*. London, Frank Cass. p. 190.

[60] Walwyn. *Juries Justified*. (1651) London, Robert Wood, BL. E618(9).

[61] Henry Parker. *A Letter of Due Censure ... to Lt. Col. John Lilburne*. 21 June 1650. Quoted by Donald Veall. Op. cit. p. 159.

[62] Pauline Gregg. (1986) *Free-Born John A Biography of John Lilburne*. London, J.M. Dent & Sons Ltd. p. 310.

[63] (London. 22 June 1653). BL. E. 702(6).

[64] 5 *State Trials*. (1886) cols. 407-460.

[65] Ibid. 444.

[66] Coke. (1827) 8 *Reports*. London, Butterworth & Son. p. 375.

[67] Ibid. 118b.

[68] *Cf.* S.E. Thorne. Lecture on Coke in the Hall of Lincoln's Inn on 17 March 1952. Published 1957 in London by the Selden Society.

[69] Gregg. Op. cit. p. 332.

[70] 5 *State Trials*. col. 450.

[71] Warshansky. Op. cit. p. 196.

[72] Andrew D. Leipold. (1996) 'Rethinking Jury Nullification.' Virginia, 82 *Virginia Law Review*. Virginia Law Review Association. p. 286.

[73] Green. *Verdict* . Op. cit. pp. 198.

[74] G.H. Sabine (ed). (1941) *The Works of Gerard Wynstanley*. Cornell University Press. p. 303.

[75] Ibid. p. 327.

[76] Brailsford. Op. cit. p. 657.

[77] Christopher Hill. (1972) *The World Turned Upside Down: Radical Ideas during the English Revolution*. London, Temple Smith. p. 91.

[78] Sir Matthew Hale. (1736) *The History of the Pleas of the Crown*. London, E. & R. Nutt and Others. vol. i. pp. 155, 296.

[79] Ibid. pp. 306-11.

[80] In 1577-8 'And for that a certain box of preserved barbaries and sugar candy and sweet roots were found with John Mucklow, one of the jurors aforesaid, after he had departed from the bar here to advice together with the other jurors ... therefore the same John Mucklow was fined 20 shillings.' *Weleden v. Elkington*. Plowd. 516, 518.

[81] Holdsworth. *A History of English Law*. Op. cit. vol. i. p. 516.

[82] Barbara J. Shapiro. (1983) *Probability and Certainty in Seventeenth-Century England: A Study of the Relationships between Natural Science, Religion, History, Law, and Literature*. New Haven, Princeton University Press. p. 168.

[83] Sir Matthew Hale. (1677) *The Primitive Origination of Mankind*. p. 128. Cited by Shapiro. Ibid. p. 180.

[84] *Cf.* Stuart E. Prall. (1966) *The Agitation for Law Reform during the Puritan Revolution, 1640-1660*. The Hague, Nijhoff. p. 1.

[85] See Warshansky. Op. cit. and Leipold. 'Rethinking Jury Nullification.' Op. cit. pp. 253-312.

CHAPTER 5

Juries after the Restoration

INTRODUCTION

Before Charles II was restored to the throne in 1660 he issued the Declaration of Breda in which he offered a general pardon, except for the regicides, and promised he would allow liberty of conscience, provided Parliament agreed.[1] He would also assent, he said, to a statute to secure these objects. Some MPs wanted to subject the king to wider conditions[2] but this did not suit General Monck who arranged for his speedy return to England. The Cavalier Parliament, however, had a majority who exhibited a zeal for King and Church that destroyed any hope of religious moderation. The Act of Uniformity of 1662[3] was followed a year later by the Conventicles Act[4] (see below) to which the Quakers in particular fell foul.

The Stuart use of the judiciary for political purposes led to conflict between the judges, whom the king had appointed, and juries who were being urged by Quakers to decide questions of law. For Green, it is clear that in this period assize criminal trial jurors were among the upper orders of English society. They were experienced in the affairs of local government and came from elements that, in many matters, 'looked for leadership from, and alliance with, England's most exalted rulers.'[5] On the other hand, these exalted rulers were split between those who were becoming known as Tories and those known as Whigs. The Whigs, led by the Earl of Shaftesbury, were concerned to prevent a Catholic succeeding to the throne whilst the Tories supported Charles and the government. And at this time, jurors, particularly grand jurors, did not always follow the requirements of the Crown.

Following earlier examples, there was coercion of juries by Kelyng and other judges and this led to the principle of non-coercion being established in *Bushell's Case*, which is examined in detail later in the chapter. And, although the view of Lilburne that it was the jury who were the true law-finders had been a dissident position, 'it gained support on the eve of the Glorious Revolution from an important segment of the political establishment.'[6] After 1689 Englishmen were left to draw different conclusions about 'the legitimacy of the tradition, about its relationship to merciful application of the law in routine cases, and about its place in the evolving English constitution.'[7]

In *Bushell's Case* Chief Justice Vaughan did not deal explicitly with nullification, and that left it open for partisans of jury law-finding to gloss his opinion in arguing for jurors to be judges of law[8] and, following widespread debate in public tracts, the case became the cornerstone of the modern doctrine. This chapter also considers the extent of jury packing in this period and the implications of the *Seven Bishops' Case*.

RETURN TO COERCION OF THE JURY

Prior to his death on 29 August 1657, John Lilburne joined the Quakers[9] some of whom, including William Penn, were also attracted by the idea of the jury deciding law as well as fact. The Quakers, who were a sizeable minority in the country and a dynamic force in English dissent,[10] were being subjected to harassment under the later Stuarts in the latter's efforts to destroy nonconformist religious meetings. Persecution of Quakers had grown after the 1662 Quaker Act[11] and the passing in 1664 of the Conventicles Act which endeavoured to increase the power of the Anglican Church by making illegal all assemblies of five or more persons over 16 years of age under pretence of religion, but not according to the forms of the Anglican church.[12]

Although the preamble to the Conventicles Act 1663 declared that Parliament sought to suppress seditious conventicles, the judges ruled that proof of seditious purpose was not required for a conviction since it was presumed by law.[13] Quakers, however, who were disqualified from sitting on juries because of the juror's oath (Quakers are opposed to oath taking), exhorted jurymen to demand proof of sedition as 'the law required.' The problem for the authorities was how to establish in court that a Quaker meeting conducted in silence had the 'character of religion', and the placing of the burden of proving otherwise on the defendants was not popular with juries. Yet, to the authorities the Quakers were threatening public order by 'making a mockery of the law and bringing courtroom proceedings to a virtual standstill.'[14] Added to which the 'perverse' verdicts of juries were frustrating the judges.

Lord Chief Justice Kelyng

The answer to the dilemma, as far as the royalists were concerned, was for the judges to use their authority in order to influence juries and Mr Justice Kelyng, a committed royalist, was the man to lead the way. In the trial of *R. v. Wagstaffe* at the Old Bailey in 1665[15] Kelyng instructed the jury that evidence of a meeting was sufficient to establish the offence charged and that the defendants had to prove the meeting did not have the character of non-Anglican worship. In fact, although evidence was given during the trial that people had assembled at conventicles and had bibles with them, the jury would not find them guilty of holding an illegal meeting and when they acquitted the Quakers, Kelyng fined Wagstaffe and the other jurors 100 marks each. The jurors appealed to the Exchequer court to have their fines remitted. Sir Matthew Hale, chief baron of the Exchequer, referred to the case in his *History of the Pleas of the Crown*. He wrote that fines upon jurors who found against the direction of the judge in a criminal case carried little weight with him and in the case of *Wagstaffe* the jury had taken out a writ of *habeas corpus* and 'by the advice of all the judges of England (only one dissenting) fining of jurors was ruled to be against law.'[16]

Kelyng continued, however, to attempt to control jury verdicts by fines and imprisonment, and not only in Quaker cases, and this led to charges of bullying and harrying juries being brought against him in Parliament. In December 1667 a House of Commons committee set forth its charges against him and resolved,

> that the proceedings of the Lord Chief Justice, in cases now reported, are innovations in the trial of men for their lives and liberties; and that he hath used an arbitrary and illegal power, which is of dangerous consequences to the lives and liberties of the people of England; and tends to the introducing of an arbitrary government.[17]

No action was taken against Kelyng, even though he declined to make an apology, but the Commons declared that the fining and imprisonment of juries for giving a verdict against the judge's summing up was illegal. A Bill to give effect to this was introduced in the House but after a great deal of debate it was abandoned in committee. It had been supported by John Vaughan who, as Chief Justice, soon afterwards was to give the decision of the court in *Bushell's Case* (below) in 1670. In the meantime jurors continued to be coerced, although their acting as a check on royal despotism increased their popularity.[18]

THE PENN AND MEAD TRIAL

With the Friends' Meeting-house in Gracechurch Street in London closed, like so many others under the Conventicles Act, Quaker William Penn addressed a congregation outside in the open air. He was arrested, with a Captain William Mead, and taken to Newgate prison. Both of them were brought to trial at the Old Bailey on 1 September 1670, charged with conspiring to assemble tumultuously a large concourse of people to the great terror and disturbance of many of the King's subjects.[19] The judges were: the lord mayor of London, Samuel Starling; the recorder of London, Thomas Howell; four aldermen and two sheriffs.

The defendants did not deny the fact of the indictment, admitting that they had assembled to preach, but pleaded not guilty on the ground that as a matter of law the indictment was not legal and, even if the evidence against them were true, they had not broken any law.[20] Two witnesses for the prosecution gave evidence that they were called to disperse the meeting of some 400–500 people to whom Penn was speaking but owing to the noise they could not hear what he was saying. At this point, Mead turned to the jury and observed that the witnesses were saying that they heard Penn *preach* despite the fact that they could not hear what was being said.[21]

Following some argument with the recorder as to what law the indictment was based on, Penn, who appealed to the jury as 'my sole judges',[22] was roughly handled out of the courtroom. Then, when Mead told the jury, whom he also called 'my judges,' that he and Penn relied upon the liberties of the common law, the mayor told him, 'You deserve to have your tongue cut out.'[23] Mead too was then taken away and the recorder virtually instructed the jury to find the defendants guilty and to ignore what had been sworn against them 'at your peril.'[24]

Jury vilified and judges disgraced
When the jury returned from their retirement the foreman told the court that, in effect deciding on the law, they found Penn guilty only of speaking in Gracechurch Street. On this refusal to find that he had conspired to cause a tumultuous assembly, without which the indictment failed, the judges abused and vilified the jurors and told them they could not be released until they had given a proper verdict.[25] After asking for pen and paper the jury then retired again only to produce the same verdict on Penn and to find Mead not guilty. So much at that stage for the charge of conspiracy between the two of them, as Penn was quick to point out!

One member of the jury, but not its foreman, was Edward Bushell. The mayor addressing the jury now said, 'What, will you be led by such a silly fellow as Bushell, an impudent canting fellow?' He was followed by the recorder who could hardly contain himself and told them that they would not be dismissed until the court had a verdict it could accept. 'You shall be locked up,' he said, 'without meat, drink, fire and tobacco ... we shall have a verdict, by the help of God, or you shall starve for it.' Their request for a chamber pot was refused.[26]

The following day the jury were called back to the court and again returned the same verdict. Addressing Bushell the mayor complained, 'That conscience of yours would cut my throat.' 'No, my Lord,' replied Bushell, 'it never shall.' Not to be placated the angry mayor retorted in ire, 'But I will cut yours as soon as I can,' and was soon to offer to cut his nose also.[27] Penn asked, 'What hope is there of ever having justice done, when juries are threatened, and their verdicts rejected?' On his claiming that justice demanded that the verdict of the jury be recorded, the mayor shouted, 'Stop his mouth, gaoler, bring fetters and stake him to the ground!' On the following day the jury, now near starvation and freezing, said that they found Penn also not guilty.[28] For not taking the advice the court had given them, said the recorder, they would be fined 40 marks each and held in Newgate prison until the fines were paid.[29]

After the trial Penn published an account of the proceedings to which Starling published a tract in reply. In it he denounced Penn's notion, '[t]hat the jury were the proper judges both of law and fact.' And, directing his remarks to the Westminster bench he said, '[n]ow Gentlemen of the long robe look to yourselves, and your Westminster Hall; If these learned reformers of religion shall likewise reform your laws ... and make twelve jurymen, eleven of which it's possible can neither write nor read to be the sole judges of both law and fact; farewell then to your great acquisitions.'[30] Penn responded from Newgate prison that jurors were indeed judges of law as well as fact, otherwise the judge might require a verdict of guilty for 'the most lawful act imaginable, it being such as he cannot deny, and is proved by evidences.'[31]

BUSHELL'S CASE

On 9 November 1670 a writ of *habeas corpus* was taken out in the Court of Common Pleas to show cause why Edward Bushell should not be released from prison. The case is a landmark in English jury history and the names of Bushell and his co-jurors are still commemorated by a plaque in the great hall of the Old Bailey for their resistance to judicial tyranny, which reads:

> Near this site William Penn and William Mead were tried in 1670 for preaching to an unlawful assembly in Gracechurch Street.
>
> This tablet commemorates the courage and endurance of the Jury, Thomas Vere, Edward Bushell and the others, who refused to give a verdict against them although they were locked up without food for two nights and were fined for their final verdict of Not Guilty.
>
> The case of these jurymen was reviewed on a writ of *Habeas Corpus* and Chief Justice Vaughan delivered the opinion of the court which establishes the Right of the Juries to give their Verdict according to their conviction.

As the plaque indicates, the writ came before Chief Justice of the Common Pleas John Vaughan.[32] He was himself no friend of dissenters but the writ may have been issued in the Common Pleas because Kelyng was still chief justice of the King's Bench.

First, Vaughan dismissed the contention that the jury acquitted the prisoners against the direction of the court on a matter of law. 'No evidence ever was, or can be given to a jury of what is law, or not; nor can such oath be given to, or taken by, a jury, to try matter in law ... We must take off this veil and colour of words', he continued, 'which make a show of being something, and in truth are nothing.'[33] The jury could not try a matter in law and any such direction was invalid. What he did not say is that nullification was almost impossible to detect and prevent. The jury, he continued, find on questions of fact and their full reasons may not be known to the judge since—in a vein contrary to modern day thinking—they might have personal knowledge beyond the evidence given in court which is all the judge could learn.[34] He could not punish the jury for going against the evidence when he could not know what evidence they had or that they were nullifying. In this sense, progressive as Vaughan's ruling was, it was not based upon a forward-looking approach to the rights of juries (it was not laid down that a jury could not give a verdict using their private knowledge[35] until 1816, by Lord Ellenborough). It was an example of the so-called 'genius' of the common law—using ancient precedent for progressive purposes.

The chief justice then proceeded to draw, more clearly than ever before, the distinction between two types of misconduct of which juries might be guilty. One was ministerial, for example refusing to give a verdict or receiving evidence privately from a party to the proceedings. For this they could be fined. However, the verdict itself was not a ministerial act but a judicial one and given according to the best of their judgment. For this, he said, they could not be fined and any other conclusion would be absurd.[36] On the desirability or otherwise of nullification he was silent. His statement that juries 'resolve both law and fact complicatedly' meant that in reaching a general verdict juries had to apply the law, as directed by the judge, to the facts as they find them.[37]

The verdict of a jury on questions of fact was, he said, unassailable—as it remains today. He asked, what was the use of the jury if a judge could order it on pain of punishment to take his view of the facts? They might as well be abolished, which, he said, would be 'a strange new-found conclusion after a [form of] trial so celebrated for many hundreds of years.'[38]

Such reasoning was conclusive. It is interesting that Vaughan was at first opposed to granting the *habeas corpus* on the technical ground that Common Pleas heard cases between subject and subject whilst in a criminal case the plea was between the King and the prisoner and the appropriate court was the King's Bench. However, Kelyng ruled there and Vaughan, outvoted by his fellow justices, gave the decision, in which they all concurred. The arguments met the mood of the proto-Whigs of the time and the reasoning was so obviously correct that it has been accepted as good law to this day, although it is ironic that a trial such as that of Penn and Mead would today be dealt with in a magistrates' court and not before a jury.

There have been exceptions to Vaughan's ruling and judicial domination of the trial process continued to be quite common. The case of the soldier who deserted in 1687 and was found guilty after a repentant Mr Justice Holloway, in his own words, had 'solicited and menaced the jury very much' to do so[39] is one example. And,

Langbein found that at the Old Bailey, after *Bushell's Case*, the judge exercised so much influence over the jury that it was difficult to characterise it as functioning autonomously. The judge, he said, dominated jury trial and had no hesitation about telling the jury how it ought to decide, in many cases to acquit.[40] However, although even in modern times judges have been known to press juries too hard, as in the case of Clive Ponting,[41] nevertheless *Bushell's Case* did establish the crucial principle of non-coercion of jurors.

Although this was very far from an assertion of the jury's right to nullify the law, Vaughan's defence of jury independence was an essential pre-condition for nullification and was translated into a considerable debate in the early 1680s around, and in defence of, the exercise of discretion by both trial and grand juries.[42] For instance, John Hawles, a lawyer who later became solicitor-general, wrote that juries must attend to 'matter of Law as it *arises* out of, or is *complicated* with, and *influences* the Fact',[43] and suggested that law-finding was routinely a duty of the jury, as held by Littleton and Coke.[44]

> For to say ... the jury are not to meddle with, or have respect to law in giving their verdicts, is not only a false position, and contradicted by every day's experience; but also a very dangerous and pernicious one, tending to defeat the principal end of the institution of juries, and so subtlely to undermine that which was too strong to be battered down.[45]

Hawles' tract enjoyed wide readership, many successive reprints and frequent quotation.[46]

It has been asserted that *Bushell's Case* 'constitutes an important milestone in the history of jury nullification in Anglo-American law.'[47] After the case, the Whigs treated the merger of law and fact as a common occurrence and argued that, 'while judges were political appointees who needed to please the Crown in order to stay in office, juries had no such political dependencies.'[48] It is interesting that in America the right of the jury to decide questions of law was widely recognised until well into the nineteenth century.[49]

JUDICIARY AND POLITICS

Resistance of juries to coercion by judges who were part of late-Stuart authoritarianism helped bring about Whig praise of the jury system and the Glorious Revolution. As one legal historian has said,

> The intellectual origins of the Whig sanctification of jury trial lie, ironically enough, in the struggles of extremist libertarian sects to defend themselves against repression during the seventeenth century. Trial rights established by Leveller and Quaker activists were, later in the century, triumphantly mobilised by the Whigs in their own power struggle with the Stuart monarchy. Within just a few decades, demands for free jury trial were to mark the significant transition from the manifestos of radical libertarian Puritanism to the mainstream ideology of the dominant political class.[50]

However, the sheriffs were responsible for the selection of jurymen and in 1682 it was possible for Charles II to persuade London grand juries to act on behalf of the Crown in political cases against the Opposition. This had been impossible in the years 1679-81—hence the dismissal of the Crown's charges against Shaftesbury. Charles had felt strong enough to arrest Shaftesbury, the leader of the newly formed Whigs, and have him indicted for high treason before a grand jury at the Old Bailey on 24 November 1681. Although a great deal of evidence was heard, the Whig grand jury brought in an *ignoramus* (we cannot approve) 'upon which', it was said, 'the people fell a-hollowing and shouting.'[51]

Fearful about the religion of the Catholic heir to the throne (James, Duke of York), in October 1680 the House of Commons introduced an Exclusion Bill that was intended not only to debar James from the throne but also provided that if he returned to England from his exile in Brussels after November 5 he would be guilty of high treason. The Bill was defeated in the House of Lords amidst scenes of violence.[52]

During Charles's reign there were 12 judges of the King's Bench, Common Pleas and Exchequer, and probably at no time had the English judiciary been more intimately associated with politics.[53] In the first 16 years of the reign the judges generally supported the Crown but thereafter where they failed to do what Charles wanted, they faced dismissal. After the retirement from the bench of Sir Matthew Hale in 1676, tenure of judicial office became insecure and confidence in the judiciary declined.[54]

THE PROTESTANT JOINER

One of many people arrested by order of the king during the Popish Plot manufactured by Titus Oates in 1678 was Stephen Colledge, known as 'the Protestant joiner.'[55] When Colledge was brought before a grand jury in London in 1681 charged with seditious words and actions, in allegedly saying that nothing could be expected of the king but popery and arming himself, the jury threw out the indictment with an *ignoramus*, after having been addressed by counsel in secret.[56] As a result, the foreman of the jury was sent to the Tower, and later was forced to flee abroad.[57] However, jury packing was common and not confined to one side alone.[58]

As a consequence, Colledge was transferred to Oxford where the secretary of state, Sir Leoline Jenkins, wrote on July 11 to the official who would select the jury, Lord Norreys, asking for 'a good, honest, substantial grand jury ... consist[ing] of men rightly principled for the Church and the King.'[59] This grand jury, after meeting in secret with the prosecution witnesses, endorsed a 'true bill' on the indictment and on August 17 Colledge stood his trial in Oxford before Lord Chief Justice North and other judges, with George Jeffreys as one of the prosecution counsel.

One interesting feature of the case is that Colledge claimed that his papers had been taken from him and although the court refused to return them, they did read them and decided that they were counsel's advice on how to conduct his defence. They then not only ignored the fact that prior to the trial the king in council had made an order that counsel and a solicitor might visit Colledge in prison but they had his solicitor, Aaron Smith, arrested for delivering the papers to him in prison.[60] The judges seized the papers and shared them with the prosecution, 'who then changed their evidence, withdrawing witnesses whom Colledge had been prepared to cross-examine or to refute.'[61] This caused Fitzjames Stephen to call their action 'one of the most wholly inexcusable transactions that ever occurred in an English court.'[62]

The jury was then sworn, with a Gabriel Merry being excused as 'being almost 100 years of age.'[63] Colledge pleaded not guilty and the same prosecution witnesses were called as had been disbelieved by the grand jury in London. Colledge maintained that the witnesses were Papists who had been paid to give evidence against him, whereas he had been brought up a Protestant and would die one. The Lord Chief Justice, in the judicial spirit of the time, responded that although Colledge professed to be a Protestant, his actions promoted Papist ends and Papists should be destroyed by a steady prosecution of the laws against them. At the end of the trial, and after Colledge had appealed to the jury as judges of law and fact,[64] once they had been allowed to refresh themselves with two bottles of sack, they found him guilty. Continuing to declare his innocence and his religion he was executed at the gate of the castle at Oxford on 31 August 1681. Colledge was adopted as the first Whig martyr and one modern authority described the trial as 'one of the most unfair in a period abounding in judicial murders.'[65] It appears that a person convicted in the King's Bench for drinking to the pious memory of Colledge was sentenced to pay a fine of £1,000, to stand in the pillory, and to find sureties for his good behaviour.[66]

Following the trial, Henry Care published a book which examined the relationship between legitimacy and jury nullification. He praised the unanimity rule and the privilege of trial by juries which, he said, is 'amongst the choicest of our Fundamental Laws, which whosoever shall goe about openly to *Suppress,* or craftily to *Undermine* … does *Ipso Facto* attacque the Government, and brings in an Arbitrary Power.'[67] He then went on to say that 'the Jury are the proper and *only* Judges' of the evidence, and that 'the Judge has nothing to do to Intermeddle, he is bound by their Verdict.' It was a matter of everyday practice for jurors to 'apply matter of Fact and Law together.'[68]

JURY PACKING

It is clear that the London grand juries were selected by Whig sheriffs and were plainly partisan.[69] It is also true that, despite being a freeman of the City of London which should have prevented him being tried elsewhere, Colledge was transferred to Oxford, precisely because the jury there would be royalist. So, at least in political trials, juries were selected on a basis of bias and according to Havighurst the important constitutional issues of 1681-2 were the relation of sheriffs to juries and the relation of juries to common law judges.[70] When Shaftesbury, leader of the Whigs, was arrested, disputes between the judges and the grand jury went against the judges with the king complaining that he had not obtained justice. Two Tory sheriffs were then installed in 1682 and the judges supported the council in sending two former Whig sheriffs, Shut and Pilkington, to the Tower. Other former Whig officials were successfully prosecuted and there was no further trouble with Middlesex and London juries[71]—who were now selected by different sheriffs with a different bias.

Grand juries at this time were clearly combining politics with their judicial duties. Attitudes to them varied and earlier in the century, in Cheshire in 1624, Sir Richard Grosvenor in a charge to the grand jury at quarter sessions described them as 'the eyes of your country to spy out and bring such [offenders] to their deserved punishment.' He went on however, to say,

I have observed in my time three main enemies which hinder the perfection of this service: the first is fear to offend great men our superiors; the second is favors and affection we bear towards our friends and neighbors; the third is foolish pity extended where not deserved.'[72]

Half a century later he might have added a fourth: political bias.

Cockburn asserts that in Crown suits with political overtones trial juries from an early period might also be ruthlessly packed.[73] But according to one historian, 'there has never been a period of English history when the art of jury-packing was practised so extensively as this one.'[74] In Devon, 'behind-the-scenes consultations between sheriffs and bailiffs would ensure that unsuitable freeholders were simply overlooked.'[75] It is of interest that in 1665 a statute had attacked the 'abuses in Sheriffes and other Ministers, who for reward doe oftentimes spare the ablest and sufficientest, and returne the poorer and simpler Freeholders lesse able to descerne the Causes in question, and to beare the charges of appearance and attendance thereon'[76] Then, in 1696 another Act spoke of the 'partiality and favour of sheriffs, the corruption of officers, and many other evil practices' that had very frequently caused unfit persons, taken as talesmen, to serve as jurors.[77]

Thirty-four years later an Act for the Better Regulation of Juries claimed that 'many evil practices' were used in 'corrupting of jurors' and 'many neglects and abuses' were found in the making up of lists of freeholders to serve on trials.[78] More importantly, jurors could not be fully representative of the people when, in addition to the property qualification that kept most people off juries, some sheriffs corrupted the selection process by which some were chosen to sit from the relatively short lists of the eligible.

Moreover, there were allegations that jurors themselves could be corrupt. Zachary Babington, an assize clerk on the Oxford circuit, complained that jurors at the assizes in the middle years of the seventeenth century 'seldom serve, but to serve a turn … to obey a superior, pleasure a friend, or to help away a quick dispatch of practice.'[79] In state trials during the Tudor and Stuart reigns juries 'were probably chosen for their presumed loyalty and were discouraged from disappointing royal expectations,'[80] not to mention expectations of their betters. Many juries were considered to be ignorant, unwilling to serve and easily swayed. And, they were not helped by inadequate accommodation frequently forcing them to consider their verdicts in private houses and, on occasion, even in alehouses or inns.[81] In fact, the 1607 Proclamation for Jurors by James I had declared that jury service:

oftentimes resteth upon such as are either simple and ignorant, and almost at a gaze in any cause of difficultie, or else upon those that are so accustomed and inured to passe and serve upon Juries, and they have almost lost that tendernesse of Conscience, which in such cases is to bee wished, and make the service, as it were an occupation and practice.[82]

And as Titus Oates said to Judge Jeffreys in 1685, 'My Lord, it goes a great way with the jury to have the judges' opinion.'[83]

At the same time jury service was unpopular and resort was frequently had to making up juries' numbers with talesmen who were picked from bystanders in and around the court who had the leisure or a reason to be there.[84] In fact, about this time according to Cockburn, 'contrary to the ancient writs and forms of law, more western circuit causes were tried by *tales*men than by jurymen proper.[85] There was apparently no property qualification for talesmen until 1692, when it was established at one-half of that for regularly impanelled jurors.[86] On the other hand at the Stafford assizes in the eighteenth century Douglas Hay found that over the century talesmen accounted for only four per cent, two per cent and less than one per cent of jurors sworn at the assizes over successive periods and some of them may have been qualified freeholders. In the quarter sessions for Stafford the position was similar.[87]

JAMES II AND *THE SEVEN BISHOPS' CASE*

Charles II died in 1685 after receiving the sacrament as a member of the Roman Catholic Church. Despite all the efforts of Parliament earlier to prevent it, he was succeeded by the Duke of York who became James II. Although Charles had finally obtained a judiciary favourable to him and his policy, James still removed 12 judges in four years and replaced them with others who would better serve his interests. In this period, politics and law were inseparable, with politics determining law.[88]

George Jeffreys had already been elevated to the King's Bench on 28 September 1683. There had been some delay since Charles doubted his abilities, but because he was insatiably ambitious and totally unprincipled he was soon to be one of the king's most trusted judges after no fewer than eleven had been arbitrarily removed in the course of eight years.[89] The judiciary was now servile to the king and was to remain so under James. As chief justice, Jeffreys in particular became notorious for the 'Bloody Assize' and the trial of Dame Alice Lisle for high treason in 1685, but he was fully encouraged by James.[90]

Owing to his policy of re-introducing the Roman Catholic religion into England, James was rapidly losing support. Matters were then made worse when his second wife, the Catholic Queen Mary of Modena, gave birth to a son in the early summer of 1688 and thus raised the possibility of a Catholic dynasty. Unconcerned about the brewing storm, James set up an ecclesiastical commission and in April endeavoured to force the Anglican clergy to read from the pulpit his second Declaration of Indulgence, giving toleration to Catholics.[91] The archbishop of Canterbury, William Sancroft, and six other bishops petitioned the king against this, saying it was illegal. Apart from the archbishop the others were: Ken (Bath and Wells); White (Peterborough); Turner (Ely); Lloyd (St. Asaph); Trelawney (Bristol); and Lake (Chichester). James had them imprisoned in the Tower and charged them with publishing a seditious libel in what became known as the *Seven Bishops' Case*.[92]

As seditious libel was a misdemeanour and not a felony the defendants were allowed counsel and were well represented. As a consequence, at the hearing the judges of the King's Bench were evenly divided and they allowed the jury to find in favour of the bishops on the question not only of publication of the petition but also on the legal issue of whether or not it was libellous, thus anticipating Fox's Libel Act[93] by more than a century. The verdict of 'not guilty' was seen as having saved the country from tyranny. It caused scenes of tumultuous enthusiasm in London and, together with concern at the birth of the prince, led directly to the Glorious Revolution. The bishops offered the jury fees and a dinner, estimated to cost between 150 and 200 guineas, but they declined the offer.[94]

James again dismissed a number of judges but as the situation became more and more precarious he finally fled abroad at the end of 1688. Jeffreys tried to follow him, disguised as a seaman with his eyebrows cut off. He managed to get safely to Wapping where he was to join a ship bound for Hamburg. Hiding temporarily in the Red Cow Inn Jeffreys was recognised by a scrivener who had once experienced his venom. On that earlier occasion the scrivener had told his friends, 'I am escaped from the terror of that man's face, which I would scarcely undergo again to save my life; and I shall certainly have the frightful expression of it as long as I live.'[95] And so he did, to the Lord Chancellor's ruin. Jeffreys was captured and taken to the Tower where he died and was buried, aged 43.

JURIES IN SEVENTEENTH-CENTURY LONDON

In regard to both trial juries and grand juries, London was a special case since it had a central urban influence on its jurors quite distinct from that of the counties, and the busiest of the criminal courts were to be found there.[96] It was also the venue of the political trials during the reigns of the later Stuarts towards the end of the seventeenth century and of the criminal libel cases and treason trials of the next century.[97]

It has been said that the late seventeenth century was the heroic age of the English jury, since in the political and constitutional struggles of the time trial by jury emerged as the principal defence of English liberties.[98] Beattie speaks of the jury as having been seen as 'protecting ordinary individuals from arbitrary power and from malicious and unfounded charges' and he goes on to deal with their selection and composition in London.[99]

Questions about the selection and composition of juries have already been briefly touched upon at various points in the preceding chapters but their significance in the late seventeenth century, and their link with nullification and partial verdicts, justifies separate treatment.

Beattie found that in the late seventeenth century two 12-man juries were called to the Old Bailey from both London and Middlesex, and that in each county the same 12 men would serve through the entire session which lasted several days. When some eight or ten trials were completed for Middlesex the jury would retire to deliberate on them all together and the London jury would then hear their cases.[100] The London and Middlesex juries were each, therefore, composed of the same men throughout.

The situation was different at county assizes where an alternative jury from the same county had to sit when the first jury retired, and indeed a succession of juries was usually impanelled. This often caused practical difficulties in finding enough jurors, with the result that in the second half of the seventeenth century juries in the counties began to deliberate in open court on each case as it concluded and announce their verdict immediately. This practice was not adopted at the Old Bailey until 1738,[101] when the jurors' seats at the Old Bailey were re-arranged so that the jurors who previously had sat divided, on both sides of the courtroom, could sit together and 'consult one another and give in their verdict immediately.'[102]

The custom of hearing several cases before retiring and then determining their verdicts had run throughout the history of trial by jury until the eighteenth century. After the Marian legislation of the 1550s on preliminary hearings, cases were dealt with rapidly because evidence had normally been taken earlier by a magistrate; usually there was no counsel on either side and the judge would indicate his view to the jury very briefly. Nonetheless, the judges in the late seventeenth century frequently dominated jury trials and had no hesitation about telling the juries how they ought to decide, often for acquittal, or leaving them an opportunity for partial verdicts.[103]

It is worth considering how the jurors were selected in the City of London. Eligibility for jury service in the city had been established by a statute in 1512 that set the qualification as the possession of lands, tenements or *goods* (italics added) of a hundred marks in value.[104] Only after the Jury Act of 1730[105] were they required to be inhabitants of the city and the property qualification fixed at £100 in real or personal property. Lists of jurors for the forthcoming year were chosen at the annual meeting of the common council and by aldermen. From these lists men were summoned for jury service by sheriffs' officers known as sergeants of the mace. The number of men involved in the process of jury selection was considerable. Some 1,000 were summoned each year to the eight sessions of the London courts, and of those, close to 800 actually appeared and about 320 were sworn.[106] These would include a number of men with considerable experience of jury service behind them, and they would welcome this as an honour and a reflection of their standing in the community.[107]

Beattie notes that a significant number of those chosen were excused or spared by the sheriff or mayor and that there were assertions at the time that such favours were corruptly available. He concludes that there is perhaps some support for this in the fact that some men were excused frequently.[108]

Tax records of jurors sworn in London in 1692 reveal that they were drawn very largely from the higher range of taxpayers and were generally of relatively high standing. This applied even more with members of the grand jury where, in 1692, 90 per cent paid surtax and nearly 80 per cent were in wholesale or retail trades. London was, however, a special case and, as we have seen, its juries had a disproportionate influence on the political cases in the reigns of the later Stuarts, a trend which was not replicated in the provinces.[109] A similar situation occurred with the seditious libel cases and the treason trials of Thomas Hardy, Horne Tooke and others during the eighteenth century.[110]

CONCLUSION

Soon after the restoration of the monarchy in 1660 Charles II endeavoured to carry out his promise from the Declaration of Breda to introduce a degree of religious toleration but was thwarted by Parliament. Instead, the early years of his reign were dominated by attempts to stifle religious dissent by means which did not appeal to jurors, at least not those in London, who far from being placemen were important figures in their localities. Conflict occurred between the Crown and Parliament, with the names 'Whigs' and 'Tories' appearing for the first time and each side endeavouring to pack juries to support them.

The royalist Lord Chief Justice Kelyng was foremost in coercing juries and, following his censure by Parliament, it was left to Chief Justice Vaughan to establish the principle of the inviolability of the juries' verdicts in *Bushell's Case*. And, although Vaughan said nothing about jury nullification, his judgment caused the issue of jury right to decide law to be raised by the Whigs at the time and it was to the fore in the *Seven Bishops' Case* which led to a great deal of debate in the following century. Seen as protecting the individual from arbitrary executive and judicial power, the judgment confirmed the constitutional right of trial by jury. Although it is correctly said that England has no entrenched constitutional rights, that does not mean that the right to jury trial is not real and worth defending. The popularity of juries with opponents of the late Stuarts arose from the belief that they were a check on the use of the law as an instrument of royal and government despotism.

These struggles resulted in the 'Glorious Revolution' which signalled the partial triumph of the disciplined power of the propertied Whigs over royal despotism and the nobility. At last the common law was to be supreme over the prerogative, and the rule of law, as imagined by a propertied elite, began to replace royal discrimination. Ironically, jury packing was widespread but the jury was also seen as having thwarted tyrannical government to protect ordinary citizens from arbitrary power and malicious and unfounded charges.[111] The cruelty of some earlier judges whose tenure of office had been dependent on pleasing the king had been moderated and significant changes in procedure began to emerge, and also transportation began to develop as an alternative punishment alongside the enlargement of the scope of the death penalty.

ENDNOTES for *Chapter 5*

[1] David Ogg. (1967) *England in the Reign of Charles II.* Oxford, Oxford University Press. p. 27.
[2] Clayton Roberts. (1966) *The Growth of Responsible Government in Stuart England.* Cambridge, Cambridge, University Press. p. 144.
[3] 14 Car. II, c. iv.
[4] 16 Car.II. c. 4.
[5] Thomas Andrew Green. (1988) 'A Retrospect on the Criminal Jury Trial, 1200-1800.' In J.S. Cockburn and T.A. Green. (eds.) *Twelve Good Men and True: The Criminal Trial Jury in England, 1200-1800.* New Jersey, Princeton University Press. p. 384.
[6] Green. (1985) *Verdict According to Conscience. Perspectives on the English Criminal Trial Jury 1200-1800.* Chicago, University of Chicago Press. p. 200.
[7] Ibid.
[8] Ibid. p. 249.
[9] Pauline Gregg. (1986) *Free-Born John, A Biography of John Lilburne.* London, J.M. Dent & Sons Ltd. p. 344.
[10] Ogg. Op. cit. p. 216.
[11] 14 Car. II, c. 1.
[12] Green. *Verdict.* Op. cit. p. 202.
[13] Ibid. p. 203.
[14] Ibid. p. 373.
[15] 6 Howell's *State Trials.* (1816). col. 993.
[16] Sir Matthew Hale. (1736) *The History of the Pleas of the Crown.* London, E. & R. Nutt and Others. vol. ii. pp. 160 and 312-3.
[17] 9 Journals of the House of Commons. 35, col. 2.
[18] Notes and Comments. (1964) 'The Changing Role of the Jury in the Nineteenth Century.' 74 *The Yale Law Journal.* New Haven, The Yale Law Journal Co. Inc. p. 171.
[19] 6 *State Trials.* cols. 951-69.
[20] Ibid. 955, 958-9.
[21] Ibid. 957.
[22] Ibid. 959.
[23] Ibid. 960.
[24] Ibid. 961.

[25] Ibid.

[26] Ibid. 964.

[27] Ibid.

[28] Ibid. 966.

[29] Ibid. 968. A mark was worth two-thirds of a pound.

[30] Sir Samuel Starling. (1671) *An Answer to the Seditious and Scandalous Pamphlet, entitled, The Trial of W. Penn and W. Mead*. London. p. 2. British Library. C. 110 e. 3. (6).

[31] William Penn. (1671) *Truth Rescued from Imposture*. London. British Library. T. 407. (17).

[32] 6 *State Trials*. cols. 999-1026.

[33] Ibid. 1007.

[34] Ibid. 1011.

[35] L.O. Pike. (1876) *A History of Crime in England*. London, Smith, Elder & Co. vol. ii. pp. 368-9.

[36] 6 *State Trials*. 1012.

[37] Steven M. Warshawsky. (1996) 'Opposing Jury Nullification: Law, Policy, and Prosecutorial Strategy.' 85 Washington, *Georgetown Law Journal*. p. 198.

[38] Ibid. 1008.

[39] J.P. Kenyon. (1986) *The Stuart Constitution 1603-1688: Documents and Commentary*. Cambridge, Cambridge University Press. p. 406.

[40] John H. Langbein. (1978) 'The Criminal Trial before the Lawyers'. Chicago, 45 *The University of Chicago Law Review*. pp. 285-6.

[41] See *post*. p. 134.

[42] Simon Stern. (2002) 'Between Local Knowledge and National Politics: Debating Rationales for Jury Nullification After *Bushell's Case*.' New Haven. 111 (7) *Yale Law Journal*. pp. 1823-4.

[43] John Hawles. (1680) *The English-Man's Right*. London, Richard Janeway. p. 11.

[44] Stern. Op. cit. p. 1833.

[45] Hawles. Op. cit. pp. 10-11.

[46] Green. *Verdict*. Op. cit. p. 252.

[47] Stern. Op. cit. p. 1815.

[48] Ibid. p. 1840.

[49] Cf. Warshawsky. 'Opposing Jury Nullification. Op. cit. p. 199 where he also discusses the reasons for this.

[50] Richard Vogler—University of Sussex. (Unpublished paper).

[51] 10 *State Trials*. col. 824.

[52] Ogg. Op. cit. pp. 602-3.

[53] Alfred F. Havighurst. (1950) 'The Judiciary and Politics in the Reign of Charles II.' 66 *The Law Quarterly Review*. London, Stevens & Sons. pp. 62-78.

[54] Ibid. pp. 230-31.

[55] 8 *State Trials*. cols. 550-746.

[56] Ibid. col. 724. Remarks on Colledge's trial by Sir John Hawles, Solicitor-general in reign of William III.

[57] Ibid. col. 552.

[58] Green. *Verdict*. p. 251.

[59] Stern. Op. cit. p. 1841.

[60] 8 *State Trials*. cols. 552 and 556.

[61] Langbein. (2003) *The Origins of Adversary Criminal Trial*. Oxford University Press. p. 75.

[62] James Fitzjames Stephen. (1883) *A History of the Criminal Law of England*. London, Macmillan. p. 406.

[63] 8 State Trials. col. 588.

[64] Ibid. col. 694.

[65] Ogg. *England in the Reign of Charles II*. Op. cit. p. 627.

[66] 3 Modern Rep. 52.

[67] Henry Care. (1682) *English Liberties: Or, The Free-born Subject's Inheritance*. London, G. Larkin. p. 209. Cited by Stern. Op. cit. p. 1849.

[68] Care. Ibid. pp. 216-221. Stern. Ibid.

[69] Havighurst. 'The Judiciary and Politics in the Reign of Charles II.' Op. cit. pp. 241-2.

[70] Ibid. p. 242.

[71] Ibid. p. 244.

[72] Eaton Hall Grosvenor MSS. Quoted by Cynthia B. Herrup. (1987) *The Common Peace, Participation and the Criminal Law in Seventeenth-century England*. Cambridge, Cambridge University Press. p. 95.

73 J. S. Cockburn. (1972) *A History of English Assizes, 1558-1714.* Cambridge, Cambridge University Press. p. 115.
74 G. W. Keeton. (1965) *Lord Chancellor Jeffreys and the Stuart Cause.* London, MacDonald. p. 97.
75 Roberts. Op. cit. p. 208.
76 16 & 17 Chas. II, c.3, s. 1.
77 7 & 8 Wm. III. c. 32.
78 3 Geo. II, c. 25.
79 Cynthia B. Herrup. (1987) *The Common Peace: Participation and the Criminal Law in Seventeenth-century England.* Cambridge, Cambridge University Press. p.134.
80 Green. *Verdict.* Op. cit. p. 106.
81 Cockburn. *History of English Assizes.* Op. cit. p. 120.
82 Quoted by James C. Oldham. (1983) 'The Origins of the Special Jury.' Chicago, *The University of Chicago Law Review.* p. 142.
83 Havighurst. (1953) 'James II and the Twelve Men in Scarlet'.*The Law Quarterly Review.* London, Stevens & Sons. p. 528.
84 J.S. Cockburn. (1988) 'Twelve Silly Men? The Trial Jury at Assizes, 1560 –1670.' In Cockburn and Green. (eds) *Twelve Good Men and True.* Op. cit. p. 161.
85 Cockburn. *History.of English Assizes.* Op. cit. p. 118.
86 Cockburn. 'Twelve Silly Men? Op. cit. pp. 160-1.
87 Douglas Hay. (1988) 'The Class Composition of the Palladium of Liberty.' Cockburn and Green. '*Twelve Good Men and True?* Op. cit. pp. 327-8.
88 Havighurst. 'James II and the Twelve Men in Scarlet.' Op. cit. p. 522.
89 Havighurst. 'The Judiciary '. Op. cit. p. 246-7.
90 Keeton. *Lord Chancellor Jeffreys.* Op. cit. p. 330.
91 David Ogg. (1969) *England in the Reigns of James II and William III.* Oxford, Oxford University Press. p. 198.
92 12 *State Trials.* cols. 183-522.
93 32 Geo. 3, c. 60.
94 George Hilton Jones. (1990) *Convergent Forces: Immediate Causes of the Revolution of 1688 in England.* Iowa State University Press. p. 43.
95 Keeton. Op. cit. p. 453.
96 Ibid.
97 For these cases see chapter 6.
98 J.M. Beattie. (1988) 'London Juries in the 1690s.' In Cockburn and Green (eds.) *Twelve Good Men and True.* Op. cit. p. 214.
99 Beattie.'London Juries in the 1690s'. Op. cit. p. 214.
100 Ibid. pp. 218-19.
101 Ibid. p. 221.
102 Langbein. *The Origins of Adversary Criminal Trial.* Op. cit. p. 21.
103 Langbein. 'The Criminal Trial before the Lawyers'. Op. cit. pp. 285-6.
104 4 Henry VIII, c.3.
105 3 Geo. II, c. 25.
106 Beattie. 'London Juries in the 1690s' Op. cit. p. 229.
107 Ibid. p. 234, 247.
108 Ibid. p. 228.
109 Beattie. 'London Juries in the 1690's.' Op. cit. pp. 242-4.
110 See *post. Chapter 6.*
111 Beattie. 'London Juries in the 1690s'. Op. cit. pp. 214-15.

CHAPTER 6

Jury Influence at its Zenith: The 18th Century

INTRODUCTION

The Waltham Black Act of 1723[1], which was passed to prevent the stealing or killing of deer in royal forests and succeeded in adding 50 new capital offences to England's 'Bloody Code', exemplified a considerable extension of the use of the death penalty at the beginning of the eighteenth century. In a sense the government was seeking to use juries for political purposes and in response 'pious perjury' by juries became more common. At the same time, exclusionary rules of evidence were being introduced by the judges to restrict juries and interference with the selection of jurors grew.

Later in the century, in a number of cases of seditious libel, vigorous defence advocates appeared on the scene and helped generate jury opposition to judicial attempts to deflect them from finding whether a publication was or was not libellous. Indeed, by the law of the day they could merely decide whether it had been published, but in these trials the issue of whether the jury could determine questions of law as well as fact became paramount. Counsel, although not yet fully able to represent prisoners, were coming to the fore and played a striking role in some of the seditious libel cases and, more generally, with their impact in the origin of the adversarial system of trial.[2]

As Green has argued 'the seditious libel trials of the eighteenth century constitute an important chapter in the history of freedom of the press and the growth of democratic government.'[3] Towards the end of the century the government, fearful of revolution spreading from France, attempted to introduce a reign of terror and juries, assisted by counsel for defendants, played a role of some significance in treason trials in England that contributed to the development of constitutional protections of liberty.

There were two essential pre-conditions of modern jury nullification. The first was a jury free from intimidation, which largely came about as described in *Chapter 5*. The second was the establishment of a free Bar, with lawyers able to operate in an adversarial confrontation as in the libel and treason trials, a process that will be outlined in this chapter.

The chapter also deals with special juries, the growth of partial verdicts in face of the increasing incidence of the death penalty, and the selection and composition of juries in Essex and the Home Counties in the eighteenth century.

INCREASE IN ACQUITTALS

After the Glorious Revolution the tenure of the judges was made dependent on good behaviour under the Act of Settlement of 1701[4] and they could be removed only upon the address of both Houses of Parliament. Nothing was said in the Act about juries.

During the eighteenth century the proportion of acquittals increased in Essex and the Home Circuit and this was not untypical.[5] For example, King found that '[l]ess than half those indicted for major property crimes in southeastern England were found to be guilty as charged.'[6] The extension of the death penalty, along with the removal of benefit of clergy for numerous offences,[7] focused jurors' minds and produced more partial verdicts where the circumstances of the defendants or the offences appeared to justify them.

The unanimity rule for juries was also a factor in increasing acquittals in the eighteenth century. The jury would want to avoid delay in reaching a verdict which resulted in their being held overnight without food or water, and often without light. Hence, if one or two jurors were holding out against a majority in favour of acquittal it was easier for them to bend towards mercy than to continue the argument. The influential Doctor of Divinity, William Paley, wrote that 'in criminal prosecutions [the unanimity rule] operates considerably in favour of the prisoner; for if a juror find it necessary to surrender to the obstinacy of others, he will much more readily resign his opinion on the side of mercy than of condemnation.'[8]

Errors in indictments could also help secure acquittals. Indictments were lengthy documents and had to be precise. If a date was incorrect the prosecution could fail. The misspelling of a name would cause the case to be thrown out, unless the defendant answered to the indictment initially in ignorance of the mistake,[9] which probably explains why, in political cases at least, the prisoner was not allowed to see the indictment until after he had pleaded. Even before counsel were appearing more often for defendants, Hale had written that 'more offenders escape by the over-easy ear given to exceptions in indictments, than by their own innocence.'[10]

GROWTH OF RULES OF EVIDENCE

As a consequence of juries being repelled by the 'Bloody Code', judges attempted to curb them with new rules of evidence. Hearsay evidence became frowned upon as being dangerous in its effect on the jury, and likely to be misused or overestimated. Even lawyers could often be confounded by its difficulties, although these have normally been judge-made. As Lord Chief Justice Mansfield declared, 'In England, where the jury are the sole judges of the fact, hearsay is properly excluded, because no man can tell what effect it might have upon their minds.'[11]

This view is contested by one modern writer who claims that the theory 'should be considered as nothing more than an unsupported rationale accepted unquestionably in a bygone era.'[12] But to Thayer it was this sort of thing, the rejection on practical grounds of what was really probative, which was characteristic of the law of evidence—'stamping it as the child of the jury system.'[13]

On one hand, the exclusion of hearsay evidence, and other evidential rules such as that excluding previous convictions, can be seen as a means of controlling the jury by limiting what the judges decided it could and could not hear. Alternatively, such exclusions can be considered to be of the essence of a trial system that protects defendants with the presumption of innocence. This presumption, or something akin to it, had existed for some time but was probably first expressed in an English court by the celebrated defence counsel, William Garrow, in 1791 and became commonplace by 1820, when it was placed as sixth in Sir Richard Phillips's *Golden Rules for Jurymen.*[14]

CLASS COMPOSITION OF JURIES

Unlike today, in the eighteenth century most criminal prosecutions were dealt with by jury trial. And a grand jury, hearing prosecution evidence *in camera* to decide if there was a case to go to trial, was required for all prosecutions on indictment. For the petty jury, according to Langbein, 'the occupations of farmer, artisan and tradesman typify the eighteenth-century juror. The jury was, therefore neither aristocratic nor democratic.'[15] However, the 1692[16] requirement of ownership of freehold land rated at £10 per annum still operated as a property qualification for jury membership.[17] The importance of this freehold qualification in the eyes of the judiciary was shown by the reassurance Lord Chief Justice Pemberton felt it necessary to give to Lord Russell, in his trial for High Treason in 1683, about its absence for London jurors:

> I must tell you, you will have as good a jury, and better than you should have had in a county, of £4 or 40 shillings a year freeholders. The reason of the law for freeholds is that no slight persons should be put upon a jury, where the life of a man, or his estate, come in question; but in the city, the persons that are impaneled are men of quality and substance, men that have a great deal to lose.[18]

The names of persons who satisfied the property requirement were compiled annually in each county in a book of freeholders prepared under the supervision of justices of the peace.[19] Later, it was widely suggested that owing to inflation the real value of the qualification was seriously reduced and as a consequence many more relatively poor men who were not competent for the duty, and were subject to corruption, sat on juries than the authorities intended.[20]

However, Hay argues from his research in the counties of Northampton and Stafford that this was emphatically not the case since 'inflation ceased to reduce the jury qualification in the eighteenth century.'[21] In 1730 Parliament enacted that land tax returns were to be the test of jurors' qualifications[22] and this remained the procedure in the late eighteenth and early nineteenth centuries.[23] But whilst land rentals declined in that period land tax assessments remained fixed at the 1692 level and this meant that the jurors selected as jurors were men with higher and higher rental values.[24] As a consequence, Staffordshire in the 1780s and Northamptonshire in the 1770s registered 8.5 and 10.4 jurors per thousand of the population, respectively and by 1823 they had only risen to 9.4 and 10.5 per thousand.[25]

Furthermore, the qualification had a significant effect as shown by a sample year in Staffordshire (1783) when in theft cases (the most common crime) none of those accused was qualified to be a juror whereas one-third of prosecutors in such cases were.[26] In another sample year in Staffordshire in the 1780s a mere two per cent of the accused were men who were qualified to be jurors, whereas 21 per cent of all prosecutors in that year appeared on the freeholders lists. In theft cases, one-third of all prosecutors were qualified and eligible to be jurors.[27]

Three-quarters of adult males were too poor, even if their entire wealth were in land, to qualify as jurors.[28] Hay concludes that the jury was a 'site of significant class power in the legal system rather than a neutral institution broadly representative of all of English society' and that this followed from a 'deliberate, conscious policy.'[29] Nevertheless, and somewhat undermining the conclusion, farmers constituted almost half the jurors at assizes and fully three-quarters at quarter sessions with tradesmen and artisans making up the balance.[30]

Hay found juries were generally more sympathetic to the prosecution than King had found in Essex. They were, he says, a class apart from most of the people who appeared before them. That was also true elsewhere including Essex where King's jurors of the middling sort, who 'saw their interests as often very separate from those of the gentry'[31] and from the higher reaches of society, were often repelled by harsh penalties.[32]

INTERFERENCE WITH SELECTION OF JURORS

Corruption in the selection of jurors still existed in the eighteenth century and, as already indicated in *Chapter 5*, an Act for the Better Regulation of Juries was passed in 1730,[33] referring to 'many evil practices ... used in corrupting of jurors' and 'many neglects and abuses ... in making up the lists of freeholders, who ought to serve on such trials.'

E.P. Thompson has traced the accounts of Baptist Nunn, the gamekeeper of Windsor, who, on several occasions in the 1720s after the notorious Black Act[34] introduced the death penalty for many new offences, scrutinised and altered jury lists with the connivance of the under-sheriffs responsible for the selection of jurors. For instance, his accounts included the following items,[35]

	£	s	d
July 25. Attended again in London desired pannells of Jury to be altered, with Under Sherriffs	1	16	8
26 & 27. Waited upon Mr Walpole to obteyn Perryman's Tryal respited. Promised amendment of Jury Spent With Under Sherriffs	0	11	9

And in the case of James Barlow, indicted in 1724 for breaking the head of a fish-pond and speaking seditious words, it was noted that the king's counsel involved for the Crown 'thought it proper to deferr the Tryal, the Jury having in some Tryals given Verdicts contrary to Evidence.'[36] On the other hand, when, in 1723, the king took an interest in a case at the Old Bailey and told the attorney-general to take the case in hand and prosecute, at the trial the jury were untainted and acquitted the defendants.[37]

In December 1748 a special commission was to be set up to try a number of captured smugglers in Sussex. The Duke of Richmond, who was personally involved, petitioned the chancellor that the commission should be held at Chichester, rather than Horsham, since it was only a few miles from his estate at Goodwood and would be 'more convenient for all of us in this part of the country, where the murders were all committed and all the evidence live, most of the Grand Jury live, and where a sheriff can get a Petty Jury whose probity can be depended upon.'[38]

On 22 July 1749 the under-sheriff at Lewes in east Sussex wrote to the same Duke of Richmond on the coming assizes. 'I am', he said, 'favoured with your Grace's letter and have sent enclosed a copy of the jury, which I have made out as well as I can, and have returned a great part of them out of West Sussex, that your Grace may be the easier informed about them, and if they should not be the proper persons, they may be challenged by the Crown at the assizes.'[39]

According to Thompson, most of the important political trials of the late eighteenth century took place in London where shopkeepers and tradesmen made up the juries. Lists of possible jurymen, he says, are preserved in the Treasury solicitor's papers showing how the Crown sought to eliminate Jacobin sympathisers from juries: 'On one such list, the names from which the jury was to be drawn were marked G. (good), B. (bad), and D. (doubtful). The many B.s included such tradesmen as a scale-maker, a glass-seller, grocers, a sailmaker, and brewers (one Southwark brewer being marked "very B.").'[40]

Juries were not generally trusted to deal with game cases and excise prosecutions[41] both of which were generally taken before magistrates despite their lower sentencing powers. As one steward complained while preparing to prosecute a poacher for assault, 'there is no answering for a Common Jury (who must Try the Indictment) as they have in general a Strong Byass upon their Minds in favour of Poachers, being professed Enemies to all Penal Laws that relate to the Game.'[42] Thus,

> By removing the judicial process to their own parlours, the gentry avoided the expense and possible humiliation of a jury trial and made the prosecution of game offenders, more convenient, but the price they had to pay was considerable since the summary conviction laws usually allowed only relatively minor punishments of a fine or imprisonment.[43]

ADVANCE OF COUNSEL AND ADVERSARIAL TRIAL

The importance of defence lawyers in the criminal courts commenced in the early 1700s when the rule forbidding counsel to the accused, except to argue points of law, had begun to weaken. Then the practice sprang up of judges allowing counsel to do everything for prisoners accused of felony except to address the jury for them.[44] In effect, this meant they could seek to enforce rules of evidence and examine and cross-examine witnesses. 'Cross-examination in particular developed as the century wore on into a means of commenting on the evidence, refuting or discrediting the prosecution case, and aggressively battling for the accused.'[45] They were innovations described by Stephen as the 'most remarkable change' in the character of criminal trials.[46] One reason for the change was the Treason Trials Act of 1696 which encouraged defence counsel, and allowed defence witnesses to testify on oath, in cases of treason. Another was the increasing use of counsel in prosecutions by the state and by the growing number of private associations for the prosecution of felons. These were voluntary bodies, of which there were thousands in the eighteenth century, to spread the cost of investigating and prosecuting crime. As they frequently instructed counsel to prosecute they [47] appear to have led judges to endeavour to assist disadvantaged defendants.

As defence counsel became more involved in the courtroom, the judges and juries took a less active part in proceedings and, except in cases of murder, the presumption of innocence and the beyond-reasonable-doubt standard began to be forcefully applied.[48] With murder, the presumption was not fully established until 1935.[49]

Green has suggested that the second great watershed in the history of trial practice was the increasing recourse to counsel and the development of a true law of evidence in the late eighteenth and early nineteenth centuries.[50] Defence counsel had, however, begun to appear at the Old Bailey and the Surrey assizes in the 1730s.[51] At this time the 'judge and accused—who a century earlier were playing the main forensic roles in the criminal trial—were yielding the centre stage in the courtroom to the lawyers for prosecution and defence.'[52] By the end of the eighteenth century,

counsel had had an immense impact on the conduct of criminal trials. They had ushered into criminal procedure the divisions between examination-in-chief and cross-examination and between evidence and argument, nourished the growth of the law of evidence, changed the nature of the judicial involvement in the trial and supplemented the haphazard efforts of prisoners to defend themselves with professional advocacy.[53]

Nevertheless, defence counsel were still unable to address the jury until the Prisoners' Counsel Act 1836.

Successful criminal counsel like Thomas Erskine, later Lord Chancellor, and William Garrow, later a judge of the court of exchequer, intruded into the criminal trial and began to forge links with juries that had a large impact upon them, often to the discomfort of the judges. This certainly increased the number of acquittals, as will be seen, and led to the adversarial trial system of today. The change is described by one commentator in the following words:

[t]he parties, or more accurately, highly skilled advocates on their behalf assumed ever greater responsibility for interrogation, while the judges retreated from inquisitorial activism and accepted a far more neutral and passive role. Rules of evidence and procedure multiplied and a contentious mechanism arose. Directed by the litigants, emphasising bi-party examination and regulated by a strict set of forensic prescriptions, the structure clearly conformed to an adversarial pattern.[54]

In the eighteenth century the growth of numerous local prosecuting societies meant that barristers were appearing more frequently to conduct prosecutions. In many cases they acted unscrupulously and perjury by prosecution witnesses was widespread. The judges appear to have recognised this and that prosecution evidence at the Old Bailey in the 1730s was often prompted by rewards and was unreliable.[55]

Moreover, the judges perceived that the balance in the courtroom between defendant and prosecutor was shifting to the detriment of the defendant.[56] As a consequence, it was not Parliament but the judges themselves who gradually relaxed the long-standing ban on defence counsel, although they probably did not foresee the consequences of the lawyers taking over the courtroom. However, they did endeavour, with some success, to curtail lawyers' license by tightening the law of evidence.

Nevertheless, King found that:

> Between the 1730s and the early 1780s defence counsel were involved in a minimum of around 10 per cent of London cases. After 1780 this rose rapidly so that by 1800 between a quarter and a third of London prisoners had counsel, as did about a fifth of prosecutors. Provincial practice is more difficult to evaluate but a similar change was taking place … All these figures are considerable underestimates since counsel's presence was only noted if they made decisive interventions.[57]

As Langbein has said, 'some of the most fundamental attributes of modern criminal procedure for cases of serious crime emerged in England during the eighteenth century: the law of evidence, the adversary system, the privilege against self-incrimination, and the main rules for the relationship of judge and jury.'[58] Rules of evidence to avoid prejudicing the jury included the rule against it hearing about someone's previous convictions (if any) and the hearsay rule, the benefit of which Langbein declines to accept.[59] In his latest writing, he strongly confirms his preference for the continental inquisitorial system, which he says seeks the truth, to the adversarial system which he considers suppresses or evades it.[60]

Instead, in the eighteenth century, '[r]ather than undertaking an exercise in finding the truth for the case as a whole, English criminal procedure developed the dialectic method of cross-examination to establish whether a case could be proved against a specific defendant.' In other words, 'the focus of the criminal trial became the defence of the individual against the power of the state, rather than the state finding the offender on behalf of the victim.'[61]

SEDITIOUS LIBEL

The charge of seditious libel in the eighteenth century was a serious obstacle to the growth of a free press and democratic government. The crime, which was a misdemeanour and not a felony (and thus enabled the defendant to engage counsel in any event), involved the intentional publication of a writing that it was alleged scandalised and tended to bring into contempt the government of the day.[62] Truth was not a defence and once the jury found that there had been publication then it followed as presumption of law that there was a seditious intent. As seen in *Chapter 5*, in the *Seven Bishops' Case* the judges were divided on whether the bishops' petition constituted a libel and, in effect, left the question to the jury. This was viewed by some as a useful precedent but in seditious libel cases in the eighteenth century Chief Justice Holt ignored it and followed the practice of the defunct Star Chamber in requiring the jury to find a general verdict of guilty if it found the accused published the writing and it bore the meaning alleged by the prosecution.[63]

This was, in effect, taking a special verdict whereby the judge would ask for an answer by the jury to specific questions, reserving the right to require the jury subsequently to give the general verdict that appeared to follow in law from their answers on the questions of fact.[64] Juries, however, were often unhappy about this, perhaps because it ignored the issue of intention—normally an essential element in crime—which to jurors distinguished 'not only accidents from crimes, but also offenders from real criminals.'[65] In striking similarity to the Quaker cases mentioned in *Chapter 5*, if publication was established the criminal intent was implied.

In 1752 William Owen, a bookseller, was indicted for a libel on the House of Commons.[66] He had published a pamphlet in which he argued that an Alexander Murray had been unjustly and oppressively committed to prison by the House for riotous conduct during the Westminster election of that year. The defendant's counsel urged the jury not to convict unless they thought Owen had a guilty intent. Lord Chief Justice Lee directed them to convict if they thought simply that publication had been proved but the jury persisted in acquitting the defendant.

Twelve years later came a new tract on the role of juries by the prolific writer, Joseph Towers.[67] In this he said that all judges had to do was to advise, whilst it was for the jury to determine law as well as fact. He also wrote that,

It is notorious, that, in many cases, juries do consistently judge on matters of law, as well as fact. When persons are indicted for murder, it is a matter of law, whether the action committed, provided the fact be proved, falls under the denomination of murder, manslaughter, etc. and the jury themselves apply these general principles of law to the particular fact which they are appointed to try, and then bring in their verdict according to their own judgment.[68]

The mid-eighteenth century also saw the emergence of John Wilkes as a national figure. On 23 April 1763 he published what became his famous No. 45 of the *North Briton* paper in which he branded the King's Speech of the Grenville government as dishonest.[69] A general warrant was issued, not against a named person, but for the arrest of all concerned in the production of the *North Briton* and the seizure of their papers. Wilkes appeared in the Court of Common Pleas on 3-6 May 1763 and was set free under the privilege of a Member of Parliament.[70]

When he later sued Under-secretary Robert Wood for trespass for entering his house and seizing papers the case was heard before Charles Pratt (later Earl Camden) Lord Chief Justice of the Court of Common Pleas, and a special jury. Large crowds invaded Westminster Hall crying, 'Wilkes and Liberty!' and the jury may have been influenced by them. Whether they were or not, they found a general verdict in his favour with surprisingly large damages of £1,000. More importantly, the judge ruled that general warrants, which did not name the person to be arrested, were illegal, as they have remained ever since.[71] At one point, in Westminster Hall, Wilkes cried out:

My Lords, the liberty of all peers and gentlemen, and, what touches me more sensibly, that of all the middling and inferior set of people, who stand most in need of protection, is in my case this day to be finally decided upon a question of such importance as to determine at once whether English Liberty shall be a reality or a shadow.[72]

In 1770 John Almon was tried for selling in his shop Junius's celebrated letter to the king on the American colonies.[73] His defence was that the letter had been sold not by him but by his servant in the shop. However, he was found guilty, the law being clear on his responsibility. In the same year John Miller and Henry Woodfall were tried for printing and publishing the same libel.[74] In the case of Miller there was no question as to publication, for the letter had been reproduced in the *Evening*

Post published by him. After Lord Mansfield had told the jury they had to determine nothing except the question of publishing and the innuendoes, they found Miller not guilty. In Woodfall's case the jury returned a verdict of 'guilty of publishing only.' These two cases were clear examples of jury nullification.

THE DEAN OF ST. ASAPH

1783 saw the spectacular trial of William Shipley, the Dean of St. Asaph.[75] This reflected in part the social composition of juries at the time. It also provided a significant example of the nexus between the defence advocate, now becoming more active in adversarial trials, and the jury. This link was central to the case, as well as those mentioned in the previous section, and could not have occurred even 50 years beforehand.

Shipley had published a tract[76] which was alleged by the Honourable Mr Fitzmaurice to be a seditious libel, for which he preferred an indictment against the dean at Shrewsbury after both the attorney-general and solicitor-general had declined to prosecute on behalf of the government.[77] Edward Bearcroft, leading counsel for the Crown, described the tract as a libel and argued that this was not a question for the jury since they were bound to convict the defendant simply if he caused it to be published[78]—which was not denied.

Bearcroft said that the object of the dean's pamphlet was 'to persuade every man of age that he has a right to choose his own representative [to Parliament].' But, he continued with supreme assurance, 'I have no difficulty to say that the man who maintains this proposition is either a fool or a knave. If he believes it himself he is an idiot; if he does not he is a dishonest man.'[79]

Thomas Erskine appeared for the dean and insisted that it was the right of the jury to decide whether the tract was or was not a libel. He pointed out to the jurors that the prosecution had ventured to charge the dean with the seditious purpose of exciting disloyalty to the king and an armed rebellion against the state. Yet all the prosecution evidence amounted to was just publishing the *Dialogue* which contained nothing seditious and had the dean's preface which contained a solemn protest against all sedition.[80]

Erskine said that the dean had published, but was not guilty of publishing since that was not in itself a crime. Reminding them of their consciences he told the jury, 'if you say he is guilty then you say he is guilty of seditious libel and seditious intent.' You are asked, he continued,

> To deliver over the Dean of St. Asaph into the hands of the Judges, humane and liberal indeed, but who could not betray *their* oaths, because you had set them the example by betraying *yours*, and who would therefore be bound to believe him criminal, because *you* had said so on the record, though in violation of your opinions—opinions which, as ministers of the law, they could not act upon—to the existence of which they could not even avert.[81]

Erskine knew that the judge, Mr Justice Buller, would take the (at the time) correct legal position that it was for the judge to decide whether or not a book was libellous and that the jury should decide only if it had been published. In order therefore to forestall judicial reproof at what he was proposing to argue to the contrary, he mischievously said to the jury, 'When I reflect upon the danger which has often attended the liberty of the press in former times, from the arbitrary proceedings of abject, unprincipled, and dependent judges ... I cannot help congratulate the public that you are to try this indictment with the assistance of the learned judge before you, much too instructed in the laws of this land to mislead you by mistake, and too conscientious to misinstruct you by design.'[82]

The jury, he added, should preserve their independence by judging the *intention* which was the essence of every crime.[83] And a man's motives 'only an English jury shall judge. It is therefore impossible, in most criminal cases, to separate law from fact; and consequently whether a writing be or be not a libel, *never can be an abstract legal question for judges.*'[84]

It is interesting that Erskine's rival at the Bar and the other great advocate of the time, Sir William Garrow, took a different view and fully accepted that it was for the judge, and not the jury, to decide the law. In a criminal case at the Old Bailey in 1784 he told the jury:

> Gentlemen, I shall now proceed to state the facts which I shall submit to you in evidence, which I shall do with some particularity, as it will be necessary for the Court to attend to them, and to determine on the law resulting from those facts. And, Gentlemen, I am very much relieved in stating to you my imperfect notions of the law of the case, by feeling that I do it in the hearing of Judges eminent for their learning and integrity, under whose correction it is impossible that I should lead you into error.[85]

Erskine now explained the general law of libel and returned to the question of who was to decide whether a book was libellous or not. If the judge told them that the pamphlet was in the abstract a libel, he would not agree that they had to find the defendant guilty unless they also thought so. As expected, Mr Justice Buller told the jury in his summing up that, there being no doubt as to the libel, the only question they had to decide was whether the defendant had or had not published the pamphlet. The jury retired for half an hour. On their return, they found the dean guilty of publishing only. After bruising exchanges between the judge and Erskine around the word 'only', the judge seemed nonplussed about what to do and the jury, confused by what had taken place, withdrew and eventually returned to enter a verdict of 'Guilty of publishing, but whether a libel or not we do not find.' The judge then declared the dean to be guilty on all counts.

Erskine subsequently moved the King's Bench to set aside the verdict on the ground that the judge had misdirected the jury. He was granted an order to show cause why there should not be a new trial and the matter came before Lord Mansfield, the Lord Chief Justice. Here Mr Bearcroft conceded that it was the *right* of the jury to judge of the whole charge when Mansfield interrupted to say he meant the *power* and not the *right*. Interestingly, Bearcroft demurred saying, 'I did not mean merely to acknowledge that the jury have the *power*; for their power nobody ever doubted; and, if a judge was to tell them they had it not, they would only have to laugh at him, and convince him of his error, by finding a general verdict which must be recorded: I meant, therefore, to consider it as a *right*, as an important privilege, and of great value to the constitution.'[86] Lord Mansfield then quoted, from memory, from a ballad of 1754,

For Sir Philip well knows,
That his *innuendos*
Will serve him no longer
In verse or in prose;
For twelve honest men have decided the cause,
Who are judges of fact, though not judges of laws.

In fact, in what was perhaps a Freudian slip, he was mistaken. The last line actually reads:

Who are judges alike of the facts, and the laws.[87]

Eventually the court found the indictment against the dean to be defective and the case against him was dropped.[88]

FOX'S LIBEL ACT

The Dean of St. Asaph's case had widespread repercussions and led to the moving in the House of Commons in 1792 of a Libel Bill by Charles James Fox. When enacted, the Bill became known as Fox's Libel Act[89] and fully established the right of juries to decide as a matter of law whether or not a writing was libel and not merely that it had been published. They could reach a general verdict of guilty or not guilty without any requirement that they give their reasons for so deciding. It was enacted despite all the judges in the House of Lords declaring that it was inconsistent with the common law—which was, of course, the point of it. As the Act said, in trials for seditious libel the 'jury sworn to try the issues may give a general verdict of guilty or not guilty upon the whole matter put in issue ... and shall not be required or directed ... to find the defendant or defendants guilty, merely on the proof of the publication.' It underlined trial by jury as a form of defence against executive tyranny, with the jury as lawmaker—in effect Sir Patrick Devlin's 'little Parliament'.[90] Paradoxically, because it made the law more certain it also became easier to get convictions since juries no longer had to circumvent it.[91]

LIBERTY SAFEGUARDED

On 5 November 1794 a verdict was awaited in the trial of one Thomas Hardy—a shoemaker charged with High Treason in 'compassing the death of the king.' *Habeas corpus* had been summarily suspended. On the same day in 1688, William of Orange had landed at the small fishing village of Brixham claiming to restore the liberties of England and the Protestant religion.[92] Now, in 1794, according to the radicals, these liberties were again in peril.

The eminent Victorian historian, J.R. Green, described the government's excesses in prosecution and attacks on freedom at this time as the 'English Terror.'[93] In similar vein Lord John Campbell called the frenzied attempts at repression 'a Reign of Terror.'[94] There was, indeed, a good deal of bloodletting in both England and Ireland but English juries played an important part in undermining the political trials by which the government sought to legitimise its assault on liberty.

Economic distress in the early 1790s had brought into existence a number of Corresponding Societies which between them undoubtedly enjoyed widespread support. The London Corresponding Society was founded by a small group of skilled workmen and its secretary was Thomas Hardy, a shoemaker. Its object was to secure Parliamentary reform and manhood suffrage and its subscription was a penny a week. It disavowed violence and branches sprang up all over England, and made contact with the middle-class Constitutional Society in England and revolutionary clubs in France.[95]

Fearful of revolution spreading across the Channel from France, Pitt the Younger and his government arrested 12 members of these societies including John Horne Tooke, a philologist, Thomas Hardy and John Thelwell, an avowed Jacobin.[96] As a measure of Pitt's arrogance, when a prosecution witness, William Sharpe the celebrated engraver, was examined by the Privy Council prior to the trial but refused to be intimidated, Pitt said in front of him with a gesture of despair, 'Well, we can do without his evidence. Let him be sent to prison and hanged with the rest of them in the Tower.'[97] And, that the lives of the accused were at risk was reinforced when Parliamentarian Edmund Burke accused them of being assassins and urged that the disease of the body politic demanded the 'critical terrors of the cautery and the knife.'[98] At the same time the government announced the discovery of a huge revolutionary plot.

Notwithstanding their political moderation the prisoners were charged with High Treason in 'compassing the death of the king' although it was never suggested that they actually threatened the life of the king or intended to use any force whatever. What they were interested in was reform of the corrupt Parliamentary franchise[99] and they called a convention to seek means of securing it. In similar trials held earlier in Scotland, the government had succeeded[100] but what Pitt, who called in Parliament for a Special Powers Act, failed to take into account were the defence barristers, Thomas Erskine and Vicary ('Vinegar') Gibbs, and the independence of the English jury.

The defendants declined to be tried together and the attorney-general, Sir John Scott, selected Thomas Hardy to be dealt with first as the one against whom he could make the strongest case.[101]

The trial commenced at the Old Bailey on 28 October 1794 before Lord Chief Justice Eyre, several other judges and a jury.[102] Sir John Scott, prosecuting with William Garrow and others, produced an enormous mass of documents which covered the whole of his table and his opening speech lasted for nine hours. It is noteworthy that until this time criminal trials could not be adjourned and there had never been a trial for High Treason that had lasted longer than a day. This one was to continue for eight. When midnight approached on the first day Erskine suggested an adjournment in order that the jurors might be permitted to go home for the night. This was objected to by the prosecution as unprecedented and the request was refused, but the court did rise and the jurors were locked up in a tavern near the courthouse.[103]

The case for the prosecution, but not the evidence, was that Hardy wanted a revolution in England similar to that in France. Erskine tackled the defence courageously and, referring to the prosecution allegation about the possibility of meetings leading to disorder, said, 'I protest in his [Hardy's] name against all speculations respecting *consequences* when the law commands us to look only to *intentions.'* Pointing out that Prime Minister Pitt had once been a franchise reformer, not only like his father before him but also like Hardy, Erskine declared, 'It would be the height of injustice and wickedness to torture expressions, and pervert conduct into treason and rebellion which had recently lifted others up to love of the nation, to the confidence of the sovereign and to all the honours of the state.'[104] Despite all the preparation and pressure of the government the jury found Hardy not guilty.[105]

With hope outpacing experience, after the acquittal of Hardy the government persisted with the charge of High Treason against Horne Tooke.[106] This case is of interest for the light it sheds on the mode of seriously disputed criminal trials in the reign of George III. Apart from Tooke's irreverence towards the court with his constant arguments, interruptions and questions to witnesses and the judges, the courtroom often resembled a bear garden with the judges, the jury, the lawyers and the witnesses all joining in when the mood took them.[107] Jurors could ask for additional witnesses to be called, and they also volunteered information relating to the trial.[108] With an expression of jury right, and an indication of the new relations of authority in the eighteenth-century courtroom, in an earlier action brought against him by Charles James Fox, Horne Tooke had begun his address to the jury, 'Gentlemen, there are here three parties to be considered—you, Mr Fox and myself. As for the judge and the crier, they are sent here to preserve order, and they are both well paid for their trouble.'[109]

In his speech to the jury Erskine poured scorn on the government's attempts to link Tooke with an armed rebellion. This brought about intense applause in the courtroom and it took the jury only eight minutes without leaving the jury box to return a verdict of not guilty. Outside the court Erskine's horses were taken from his carriage amidst bonfires and blazing tableaux and he was drawn by the crowds to his home in the Temple. Here, from a window he declared that injured innocence still obtained protection from an English jury and then asked the people to disperse peacefully.[110]

The Crown now blindly proceeded with the prosecution of Thelwell who, a government spy alleged, had cut the froth from a pint of porter and advocated the same fate for the heads of kings.[111] Thelwell was advised by the political theorist William Godwin who had earlier told Joseph Gerrald, one of the defendants in the trials in Scotland, not to forget that the jury, although no doubt carefully packed by the authorities, were men, 'and that men are made of penetrable stuff: probe', he said, 'all the recesses of their souls.'[112] Thelwell too was found not guilty and the government finally had to cancel 800 warrants of arrest which had been prepared for immediate use following the anticipated convictions.[113]

If these trials were the tip of the iceberg of a prospective reign of terror then, in defence of liberty, the acquittals were prime examples of the spirit of the English jury system in action in defence of liberty for all. After all, in the Scottish cases the juries proved subservient to the uncouth Lord Braxfield[114] and there was a great deal more repression at lower levels of society in England by magistrates. For example, after the massacre of Peterloo in 1819 an outwardly Christian clerical magistrate used his position on the bench to tell a defendant, 'I believe you are a downright blackguard reformer. Some of you reformers ought to be hanged, and some of you are sure to be hanged—the rope is already round your necks.'[115]

WATSON AND HONE

Jury nullification was also strikingly manifest near the start of the nineteenth century in the trial in 1817 of Dr James Watson and others on charges of High Treason in levying war against the king.[116] They had called a meeting in Spa Fields in London about economic distress in the capital, at which Watson's excitable son and John Castle, a government spy, endeavoured to cause a riot.[117]

Owing to the reluctance of juries to convict in cases of constructive treason (i.e. the extension of the law of treason to cover actions or events which were not originally envisaged by that law, principally by the judges and in relation to any perceived attempt to undermine the King), the Treasonable Practices Act[118] had been passed in 1795 to incorporate such treasons into the statute law as substantive offences. Indeed, Lord Chief Justice Ellenborough observed in Watson's trial that the statute 'did not so much introduce any new treasons, as declare to be substantive treasons those acts which had been, by successive constructions of the Statute of Treasons [1352], determined to be the strongest and more pregnant overt acts of the several treasons specified in that statute.'[119] Having expressed the view that juries in state trials were perverse, he had welcomed this extension of the meaning of treason and was now, with justices Bayley, Abbott and Holroyd, to try the prisoners. John Castle turned king's evidence and claimed that Watson and others had planned insurrection but he was totally discredited in cross-examination. There were, however, other witnesses and in addressing the jury Lord Ellenborough told them,

> You cannot but feel that you have before you a body of cogent evidence in proof of the design charged against the prisoner, to overset the laws and government of the country and to introduce anarchy and disorder attempted to be carried into effect by means of open rebellion and force directed against His Majesty's government.

He then virtually directed the jury to convict but after retiring for an hour-and-a-half they returned a verdict of not guilty against Dr Watson. The attorney-general then told the court that no evidence would be offered against the other accused and they too were acquitted.[120]

Although law reformer Samuel Romilly appeared to believe the prisoners could have been tried at the Old Bailey and convicted of riot, he wrote that, 'instead of this they are declared innocent, and they escape all punishment, except, indeed, a long and close imprisonment previous to trial, which, as they have been finally acquitted, has the appearance of a great injustice done to them.'[121] The same year, 1817, saw three trials of William Hone in December, described by E.P. Thompson as 'some of the most hilarious legal proceedings on record.'[122] Hone was a poor bookseller and former member of the London Corresponding Society who was indicted for blasphemous libel in parodying the Lord's Prayer:

> Our Lord who art in the Treasury, whatsoever be thy name, thy power be prolonged, thy will be done throughout the empire, as it is in each session. Give us our usual sops, and forgive us our occasional absences on divisions; as we promise not to forgive those that divide against thee. Turn us not out of our places; but keep us in the House of Commons, the land of Pensions and Plenty; and deliver us from the People. Amen.[123]

Lord Ellenborough pronounced this to be 'a most impious and profane libel' but the jury refused to convict, with the consequence, it is said, that the judge retired to his sick-room never to return.[124] From that time forward all parodies were immune from prosecution.[125] However, Hone's victory was in part a consequence of his attorney, Charles Pearson, challenging the selection of some jurors and the rejection of others by the master of the Crown office and winning the support of London's Common Council, for a more honest and random selection of jurors.[126]

If the verdicts in the eighteenth century English treason trials were perverse then they confirm that as Lord Devlin later put it, though juries have no legislative power, 'they can decisively influence those who have. For it is no use making [or continuing with] laws which juries consistently fail to enforce.'[127]

SPECIAL JURIES

On 8 May 1816 Henry Brougham claimed in the House of Commons that in all cases of libel prosecuted by information *ex officio*, the Crown 'never went to trial without a special jury. All other crimes and misdemeanors, felony, and even the highest crime known to the law, High Treason,' he said, 'were always tried before a common jury.' He saw no reason 'for giving to the Crown, in the instance of libel, a right of selection which it did not possess in any other case.'[128] In the same debate, the attorney-general, Sir William Garrow, argued that, in trials for libel prosecuted by the Crown, the defendant had the option of a special jury. This seems an odd claim, however, since the Crown apparently always used a special jury and such juries were not generally favoured by those who were accused and it might be useful here to consider how they were composed.

Essentially, special juries were of three kinds each having different functions. The first, employed from the thirteenth century onwards, were judges of facts requiring knowledge of some special non-legal field. There are medieval cases recorded of self-informing juries of cooks and fishmongers in London summoned to try people accused of selling bad food, and many instances of mercantile disputes being settled by merchants of the trade in question.[129] As Cornish says, 'this was natural in a system under which jurors were expected to decide the case by applying their own knowledge.'[130] And, where a female defendant found guilty of a capital crime claimed to be pregnant she could have an all-female jury 'inspect her belly' and if her claim was proved, execution would be delayed to permit the child to be born and, occasionally, she might be allowed to live.[131]

The second type of special jury involved jurors of higher social status than those who made up petty juries. According to Blackstone, such special juries were originally introduced when causes 'were of too great nicety for the discussion of ordinary freeholders; or where the sheriff was suspected of partiality' in choosing trial jurors.[132] The first reason appears to reflect a clear case of government special pleading.

The third type of special jury, which came to prominence in the latter half of the seventeenth century, and was sometimes known as a 'struck jury', was formed, according to Sir William Garrow, by the sheriff attending the master of the Crown-office, with an agent for each party and selecting 48 names of prospective jurors. Each party was then allowed to strike out the names of 12 of them.[133] To an extent this allowed the parties to pick the jury and the procedure was regularised by an Act of 1730.[134]

A feature of special jurors, whose names appeared on special lists, was that they had to be paid a fee.[135] They were used frequently by the Crown, particularly, although not exclusively, in state and political trials and, following *Bushell's Case* which prevented judges from punishing jurors for their verdicts (see *Chapter 5*), in cases of felonies and of misdemeanours such as seditious libel. There is little doubt that hand picking went on with a court official collaborating with the Crown solicitor for the purpose.[136] Quite well known were 'guinea-men' who were regular special jurors who lived off the fee in each case, commonly a guinea but sometimes as much as five guineas or more, and who knew that continuance of this income depended on bringing in verdicts for the Crown.[137]

As Oldham has confirmed, their members were almost always of a much higher social status than the common jurors and in the counties they were composed of wealthy landed gentlemen, many of whom may have been justices of the peace.[138] Indeed, the County Juries Act of 1825 provided that they should be persons 'who shall be legally entitled to be called an esquire, or shall be a person of higher degree or shall be a banker or merchant.'[139] Then, in 1870, property qualifications were added which prescribed certain minimum rateable values above those for common jurors.[140]

Nevertheless, such men were not always happy to be kept away from their businesses and pursuits and in the City of London in 1867 it was found that a Charles Mayhew who had access to the jury list, ran a lucrative business in getting men excused from jury service. In return for paying him a guinea a year, any man not wanting to serve could send him the summons, and he would swear a false affidavit to get him excused. Although Mayhew was uncovered and put on trial at the Old Bailey, he died before the case came to court.[141] What is surprising is that special juries were not abolished until the Juries Act of 1949.[142]

'PIOUS PERJURY'

The reigns of William and Anne saw the extension of capital punishment to a large number of relatively minor offences. As a consequence, jury discretion became very common with the jurors reaching their judgments on assessments of the character and disposition of defendants[143] and reducing capital penalties to non-capital sentences by partial verdicts in order to save the lives of prisoners, often with the assistance of the judges.[144] Indeed, it has been said that at the time, 'the entire legal fabric, from prosecution to punishment, was shot through with discretion.'[145] Certainly, pious perjury had the effect of making the criminal law of the time less harsh than had previously been supposed.

In some types of cases, such as burglary and aggravated (i.e. more serious forms of) larceny, King concludes that a partial verdict 'effectively limited the range of sanctions available by preventing the judge from passing a capital sentence.' He adds that 'trial before the petty jury was the principal public moment in the long chain of individual and collective choices and interactions that determined the fate of the accused.'[146]

King finds that around 'one-seventh of those indicted for property crimes in the major courts of Essex between 1740 and 1805 had the indictments dismissed as "not found" by the grand jury.' The trial jury acquitted almost a third of the remainder and brought in partial verdicts, reducing the charge and effectively lessening the sentence, in a further ten per cent.[147] These figures are highly significant and between 1782 and 1787, similar figures were to be found in the counties of Surrey, Hertfordshire, Kent and Sussex.[148]

Beattie found that petty juries acquitted in 33.9 per cent of capital cases in which grand juries had indicted in Surrey in the period from 1736 to 1753 and returned partial verdicts in 29.4 per cent of cases.[149] In the Old Bailey, Langbein shows that 171 cases produced 203 defendants, of whom 84 were acquitted. He did not calculate the frequency with which juries down-valued or convicted of lesser offences for the whole of his sample, but in October 1754, of 31 guilty verdicts 14 involved those two types of partial verdict.[150] He concludes, therefore, in his polemic against Douglas Hay, that in 'Property, Authority and the Criminal Law'[151] Hay developed a theory of ruling-class conspiracy against the lower orders and, whilst exaggerating the extent of prosecutorial discretion, he 'underemphasised the importance of jury discretion.'[152]

Langbein argues that acquittals and partial verdicts receive short shrift from Hay and that his theory of ruling-class conspiracy is impossible to reconcile with the reality of jury discretion.[153] Beattie, as we have seen, computed that petty juries acquitted in a third of capital cases and returned partial verdicts in another 30 per cent.[154] Langbein's says his own Old Bailey figures were in accord. One hundred and seventy one cases produced 203 accused, of whom 84 were acquitted.[155]

In all, adds King, who gives little support to the conspiracy theory, 'less than half those indicted for major property crimes in south eastern England were found to be guilty as charged.'[156] These were principled decisions, he suggests, and juries applied what should be called a strong presumption against capital verdicts.[157] There was also evidence indicating that females, the young and those with families to support were the most likely to be given partial verdicts.[158]

As Green puts it,

> The 'selection' of offenders by Crown, bench, and jury for one or another level of punishment became a complex and, at times, an awe-inspiring ritual. Authorities were all the readier to share the power of mitigation with juries in a system in which most of the beneficiaries of mitigation suffered some substantial punishment.
>
> As the jury's role in this evolving system of mitigation became formalised, and in a sense tamed, that role expanded accordingly; but the jury was now more than ever just one part of the system, and the scope of its role in practice depended increasingly upon surrounding institutions and procedures.[159]

In capital cases partial verdicts and the tradition of jury nullification assumed great importance with 'pious perjury' being resorted to frequently by criminal trial juries. On theft in particular, the oft-quoted words of Blackstone may be recalled when he wrote that 'the mercy of juries often made them strain a point, and bring in larceny to be under the value of twelve pence, when it was really of much greater value ... a kind of *pious perjury*.'[160] Blackstone thought such under-valuation was largely a response to inflation over the centuries and achieved justice by preventing from being condemned to death a person whom the legislature had not originally had in mind.[161]

This led Milsom to suggest that 'So far as justice was done throughout the centuries, it was done by jurors and in spite of savage laws.'[162] It does not mean however that people facing trial were tried by their peers who might have been sympathetic to their problems. The property qualification made this impossible in most cases and, as we have seen, detailed studies of criminal juries in individual counties suggest that they were almost always comprised of the fairly well-to-do who would have very little contact with most of those brought before the courts.[163] The cottager who appeared in court charged with theft, saw 12 men sitting opposite him who were the equals and neighbours of the prosecutor; they were employers, overseers of the poor and propertied men.[164]

So, the point, says Hay, 'is not that such juries convicted against the evidence, but rather that a more democratic jury might not have convicted at all.'[165] And, as the number of capital offences increased, the judges themselves began to interpret the penal law in an increasingly narrow manner that sometimes encouraged the jury to leniency.[166] As Hay continues,

> Many prosecutions founded on excellent evidence and conducted at considerable expense failed on minor errors of form in the indictment ... prosecutors resented the waste of their time and money lost on a technicality ... But it seems likely that the mass of Englishmen drew other conclusions from the practice. The punctilious attention to forms, the dispassionate and legalistic exchanges between counsel and the judge, argued that those administering and using the laws submitted to its rules. The law thereby became something more than the creature of the ruling class—it became a power with its own claims, higher than those of prosecutor, lawyers, and even the great scarlet-robed assize judge himself.[167]

Pious perjury, Hay claims, enjoyed at least tacit official acquiescence, 'not least because the reduced charge still meant that the offender was transported, a serious punishment in itself.'[168] Despite all this, however, the frequent refusal of juries to convict in order to save defendants from the gallows when hanging was the automatic penalty for over 200 offences, some of them minor, was exercising their nullification power of mercy to a considerable extent. Not that everyone approved. In 1751 the novelist Henry Fielding, who was a Bow Street magistrate, had written that valuing goods at less than a shilling left the thief to be whipped and able to return immediately to his trade. This, he complained, perjured the jury and injured the public.[169]

Partial verdicts did not, however, occur at random across various types of offences. According to King, 'the most important function of partial verdicts [was] to prevent capital sentences in burglary, housebreaking, and aggravated larceny cases.[170] And juries distinguished, first, according to the seriousness of the offence, and secondly, according to the conduct and character of the accused in a particular case.[171] According to Langbein, in his sample of cases at the Old Bailey partial verdicts were not returned in any cases of livestock theft or highway robbery but in pickpocket cases the juries almost invariably reduced the value of the property stolen to below a shilling to make them non-capital. They would not, however, reduce the value where the evidence indicated that the offenders were professional thieves or gang members.[172] In the end, in Essex in the second half of the eighteenth century trial juries acquitted one-third of defendants and reduced charges by partial verdicts in a further ten per cent of cases.[173]

JURIES IN EIGHTEENTH-CENTURY ESSEX

Peter King has made an engrossing study of juries in Essex from 1735 to 1815. [174] Moreover, looking more widely at the use of discretion and partial verdicts he has concluded from his research that the Essex and Home Circuit patterns are similar and do not appear to be untypical of other counties. His conclusions, therefore, are more significant than just for Essex.

In so far as eligibility in the counties is concerned, it was established in 1692 that 'every juror shall have in his own name or in trust for him within the county, £10 a year of freehold or copyhold lands or tenements.'[175] Just below 'ten per cent of non-exempt households in Essex were listed as having a sufficient estate to serve on a jury in 1734, the equivalent figure after mid century being about eight per cent.'[176] In fact, nearly half the eligible jurors were farmers,[177] although, according to King, they could in different cases share attitudes with those below them socially as well as above. But apart from eligibility what we do not know is whether, when he felt it necessary, the lord lieutenant of the county interfered in the choosing of jurors to sit in certain cases. If so, the jury in those cases could not be said to be representative even of the small percentage of the population qualifying to be chosen.

Essex was alone in introducing in 1784 a policy based on recalling *en bloc* almost all those jurors who had been impanelled three years earlier. Only those who had moved, died or reached the age of 70 were excluded. They were chosen quite deliberately, the requirement of random selection being ignored.[178] This meant that many jurymen had experience from serving on earlier occasions and, as a consequence, may have heard not dozens but hundreds of cases. They also knew many of their fellow jurors. All this appears to have had little effect on acquittal levels, however it does show that contemporary assessments of juries as being illiterate and easily misled were wide of the mark.[179]

On acquittals, verdict patterns in Essex at the time do not support the theory that older and more experienced juries were less likely to acquit than young and inexperienced ones.[180] During the first 15 years of the new triennial system in Essex described above acquittal rates increased steadily from 27 per cent in 1780-84 to nearly 37 per cent by 1795-99. Yet, after 1800 this rising trend was reversed and by 1815-19 fewer than a quarter of those indicted were found not guilty. Nevertheless, this was the time when the Napoleonic Wars came to an end and disgorged numerous former soldiers into unemployment, hunger and possibly crime.

A comparison of acquittal levels in 1782-87 and 1799-1800 with those of the Home assize circuit reveal no substantial deviation even though most of the other counties had no method similar to the triennial system to ensure that a high proportion of their jurors were experienced.[181]

There was also a distinction between grand juries serving at assizes and those for quarter sessions. King shows that 'the assize grand jury in Essex, as elsewhere, was confined to the county elite'[182] (although this had not been the case in the seventeenth century). By contrast, the quarter sessions grand jurors appear to have been composed almost entirely of farmers, artisans, and tradesmen 'with an occasional smattering of individuals of rather higher status, who were styled "gentlemen."'[183]

As far as the composition of grand juries generally in the sixteenth and seventeenth centuries is concerned, Cockburn concludes that:

Surviving lists indicate that Blackstone's contention that grand juries in his day usually consisted of 'gentlemen of the best figure in the county' is not true of earlier centuries. Respected local freeholders—those 'sufficient inhabitants' on whom community service as tithingmen, constables, and coroners rested so heavily—with a leavening of junior magistrates and lesser gentlemen would perhaps describe more adequately the composition of sixteenth- and seventeenth-century grand juries.[184]

King's later book[185], dealing with property crimes, describes the second half of the eighteenth century and early decades of the nineteenth as '... the golden age of discretionary justice in England. The whole criminal justice system was shot through with discretion.'[186] He shows that, with attitudes varying according to the type of offence involved, in Essex assizes and quarter sessions in that period over 90 per cent of assize trial jurors and grand and trial jurors at quarter sessions were of the 'middling sort' namely, professionals, farmers, artisans and tradesmen who were in the top third of English society and were leaders in the local communities. However, they cannot be defined solely in class terms. They acted within constraints when deciding on life or death of which they were often unaware.[187] 'The participation of the landed gentry was very small, that of the landless poor was non-existent.'[188] Similarly, in Surrey assizes the majority were tradesmen and craftsmen including chandlers, blacksmiths, bakers, glaziers, tailors, bricklayers and shoemakers with some yeomen and farmers.[189] As research by King has shown, these counties were probably typical of many others.

King shows that many jurors were called upon to sit on a number of different occasions so that they became quite experienced. By law parish constables had to return annual lists to the quarter sessions of inhabitants qualified to serve on juries and include their names, addresses and titles. Further, by tradition in Essex there were also returned the age of the potential juror, the value of his estate and the parish in which the largest proportion of his holdings were situated.[190] Such details confirm that the jurors were not the peers of the poor many of whom were brought before them for trial. But although if there had been poor jurors they might not have convicted cottagers, especially in cases of theft, nevertheless, perhaps because punishments were harsh, jurors appear to have been anxious to use their discretion in favour of the accused in many cases—those appearing triennially often revealing an expertise greater than that of assize judges who did not serve regularly in the county.[191] This was a situation mirrored in Kent in the mid-seventeenth century as outlined by Cockburn.[192]

The selection and composition of juries is vital to an understanding of the history of the jury since it assists comprehension of why they sometimes defended liberty and in many cases came to use their discretion to defeat the use of capital laws. In the background it is important to remember that until the latter half of the twentieth century juries in England were not representative of the people. The property qualification saw to that and research has shown that, in the main, juries favoured the prosecution rather than the defence.

It has been suggested, however, that because the stated sums required for the property qualification were eroded by inflation many jurors were relatively poor men and, overall, 'the freehold requirements were, if not a complete failure as a method to ensure honest and intelligent jurymen, of very limited value.'[193] But, as Hay has commented, it is not clear why men without sufficient freehold 'must be presumed unintelligent or incapable of dealing with what was a wholly oral procedure.'[194] He then goes on to show that in Northampton and Stafford in the sixteenth and seventeenth centuries at least jurors were of a much higher social standing than most of the men and women whom they tried, or indeed, than the general population.[195] This is given support in the seventeenth century in London where Beattie has shown that jurors were drawn from high tax payers and were generally of high standing.

The position in Essex and the Home Counties was different with juries composed of farmers, artisans and tradesmen prepared to exercise their discretion, but this means they were still composed of relatively wealthy people. Nevertheless, as King shows, they appear to have been prepared in certain cases to exercise their discretion against harsh and oppressive laws.

Conversely, Hay powerfully argues that Parliament excluded the poorest three-quarters of the adult male population and all women from juries in order to sustain the structure of power in eighteenth-century England. He concludes that 'the juries so carefully created by Parliament, sheriffs, constables, and wealth, were the procedural corollary to the inequality embodied in the substantive criminal law and in English society itself.'[196] As a result, 'probably jurors rarely decided entirely against the evidence, rarely perverted the course of English justice in overtly class-biased ways in the eighteenth century. They had no need to.'[197]

It is worthy of note, however, that the last of these conclusions from research in Northampton and Stafford differs from those arrived at by King in Essex where partial verdicts appear to have been quite common in the same period. Juries comprising farmers, artisans and tradesmen were by no means afraid to use their power of mercy to avoid sending defendants to the gallows for minor offences. Further, there were the political cases such as seditious libel and those of Thomas Hardy, Horne Tooke and others where the jury were prepared to defy the government. And, despite a diminution in nullification following the abandonment by stages of capital punishment it has survived, as will be seen, to the present day.

CONCLUSION

As both Green and King have shown, the scope and use of partial verdicts and pious perjury to avoid capital punishment increased in the eighteenth century and Jerome Hall has argued in an influential book that 'By the middle of the eighteenth century the practice of returning fictitious verdicts was so widespread that it was generally recognised as a typical feature of English administration of criminal justice.'[198] In addition, the century witnessed real changes in the criminal justice system, such as stricter rules of evidence and the beginnings of the presence of lawyers for the defence in criminal trials, which, alongside the extension of the scope of the death penalty, was to have wide influences on jury trial and the discretion of jurors.

The 'trials of liberty', from Wilkes through the seditious libel trials to the treason trials, form a sequence of political cases that reveal the extent to which in the eighteenth century courageous counsel, like Erskine and Garrow, had established the position of counsel for the defence, and juries were not intimidated by government propaganda which they may have considered to be aimed at repression.

One of the great changes in this period came with criminal libel and Fox's Libel Act which gave juries the right to decide if a writing was defamatory in law. But, although this was very important, 'jury right' was not extended to other types of cases. However, in his judgment in the *Dean of St. Asaph's* appeal case Lord Mansfield had said that the judge would tell the jury how to do right, but they had it in their power to do wrong,[199] and this recognition of the consciences of jurors has persisted to the present day.

In an endeavour to reduce the impact of that power the Crown gave prominence in some cases to the special jury which, for a time, assumed an important role in the criminal justice system. However, in addition to these 'higher class' juries, tampering with the selection of jurors, and the fact that Catholics, women and others were not eligible to serve on juries, the property qualification alone made it clear that jurors were not representatives of the people before the twentieth century. Nevertheless, juries were popular with the 'middling sort' as a means of taking part in public affairs and, interestingly, they were quite prepared to bring in partial verdicts in certain cases.

Nevertheless, Green has said that in the eighteenth century,

> authorities brought jury practices further under control even as they conceded the principle of the inviolability of the general verdict … When legal reform dismantled … much of the capital law of felony, jury deference to the letter of the law in criminal cases became standard practice for the first time in English history.[200]

This view may account for Green's book *Verdict According to Conscience* ending at the year 1800. The quotation shows clearly that Green accepts that jury nullification was practised throughout the centuries, and that is demonstrably true, but whether deference became standard practice may be a questionable proposition and is difficult to prove. In fact, this period gave rise to a quite radical new form of nullification based on the procedural advances which permitted a free jury and the adversarial system of trial.

ENDNOTES for *Chapter 6*

[1] 9 Geo. I. c. 22. See E.P. Thompson. (1975) *Whigs and Hunters: The Origin of the Black Act.* London, Allen Lane.

[2] John H. Langbein. (2003) *The Origin of Adversary Criminal Trial.* Oxford University Press. p. 167.

[3] Thomas Andrew Green. (1985) *Verdict According to Conscience. Perspectives on the English Criminal Trial Jury 1200-1800.* Chicago, University of Chicago Press. p. 318.

[4] 12 & 13 W. & M. c. 2.

[5] *Cf.* P.J.R. King. '"Illiterate Plebeians, Easily Misled"': Jury Composition, Experience, and Behaviour in Essex, 1735-1815.' In Cockburn & Green. (eds) *Twelve Good Men and True. The Criminal Trial Jury in England 1200-1800.* New Jersey, Princeton University Press. pp. 254-5.

[6] Ibid. p. 255.

[7] J.M. Beattie. (1986) *Crime and the Courts in England 1660-1800.* Oxford, The Clarendon Press. p. 420.

[8] W. Paley. (1785) *The Principles of Moral and Political Philosophy.* In *The Works of W. Paley* (1825) vol. vi. Edinburgh, Peter Brown and T & W Nelson. p. 130.

[9] Sir Matthew Hale. (1736) *The History of the Pleas of the Crown.* London, E & R Nutt and Another. vol. ii. p. 175.

[10] Quoted by Peter King. (2000) *Crime, Justice, and Discretion in England. 1740-1820.* Oxford University Press. p. 240.

[11] Re: Berkeley. [1811] 4 Camp. p. 415.
[12] Richard D. Friedman. (2002) 'No Link: the Jury and the Origins of the Confrontation Right and the Hearsay Rule.' In *The Dearest Birth Right of the People of England": The Jury in the History of the Common Law*. Oxford, Hart Publishing. p. 100.
[13] J.B. Thayer. (1898) *A Preliminary Treatise on Evidence at the Common Law*. Boston, Little, Brown and Company. p. 266.
[14] J.M. Beattie. (1991) 'Scales of Justice: Defense Counsel and the English Criminal Trial in the Eighteenth and Nineteenth Centuries.' 9 (2) *Law and History Review*. University of Illinois Press. p.249.
[15] John H. Langbein. (1987) 'The English Criminal Trial Jury on the Eve of the French Revolution.' In Padoa Schiappa, A. (ed) *The Trial Jury in England, France, Germany, 1700-1900*. Berlin, Durcker & Humblot. p. 25.
[16] 4 W. & M. c. 24.
[17] Douglas Hay. (1988) 'The Class Composition of the Palladium of Liberty; Trial Jurors in the Eighteenth Century.' In Cockburn and Green. *Twelve Good Men and True*. Op. cit. pp. 309-10.
[18] Howell. (1818) 9 *State Trials*. col. 594.
[19] Langbein. 'The English Criminal Trial Jury.' Op. cit. p. 25.
[20] See James C. Oldham. (1983) 'The Origins of the Special Jury.' Chicago University Press. 50 *The University of Chicago Law Review*. p. 145.
[21] Hay. 'The Class Composition of the Palladium of Liberty.' Op. cit. p. 314.
[22] 3 Geo. II, c. 25, s.1.
[23] Hay. 'The Class Composition of the Palladium of Liberty.' Op. cit. p. 314.
[24] Ibid.
[25] Ibid. p. 321.
[26] Ibid. pp. 350-1.
[27] Ibid. pp. 350-1.
[28] Ibid. p. 315.
[29] Ibid. p. 311.
[30] Ibid. p. 330.
[31] King. 'Illiterate Plebeians' Op. cit. p. 304.
[32] Ibid. p. 255.
[33] 3 Geo. II, c. 25.
[34] Geo. I. c.22.
[35] Thompson. *Whigs and Hunters*. Op. cit. p.78.
[36] Ibid. p. 79.
[37] Old Bailey Sessions Papers. (April 1723). Cited by John H. Langbein. 'The Prosecutorial Origins of Defence Counsel in the Eighteenth Century: The Appearance of Solicitors.' 58 *The Cambridge Law Journal*. Cambridge. p. 333.
[38] West Sussex Record Office. Goodwood MSS, 155/H 42. Cited by Cal Winslow. (1975) 'Sussex Smugglers.' In *Albion's Fatal Tree: Crime and Society in Eighteenth Century England*. London, Allen Lane. p. 138.
[39] Winslow. Ibid. p. 165.
[40] E.P. Thompson. (1968) *The Making of the English Working Class*. London, Penguin Books. p. 509.
[41] King. *Crime*. Op. cit.. pp. 247-8.
[42] Douglas Hay. (1975b) 'Poaching and the Game Laws on Cannock Chase.' In *Albion's Fatal Tree*. Op. cit. p. 211.
[43] King. *Crime*. Op. cit. p. 248.
[44] James Fitzjames Stephen. (1883) *A History of the Criminal Law*. London, Macmillan. vol. i. p. 424.
[45] King. *Crime*.Op. cit. p. 228.
[46] Stephen. Op. cit. The process is dealt with in detail by Langbein (2003) *The Origins of Adversary Criminal Trial*. Oxford, Oxford University Press.
[47] Déirdre Dwyer. (2003) Review of John Langbein. 'The Origins of Adversary Criminal Trial' 66 *The Modern Law Review*. Oxford, Blackwell Publishing. p. 941.
[48] John H. Langbein. (1978) *The Criminal Trial before the Lawyers*. Chicago, 45 The University of Chicago Law Review. p. 266. Contrast the view of Barbara Shapiro that the beyond-reasonable-doubt test in effect existed in the seventeenth century as a 'satisfied conscience' standard. (1983) *Probability and Certainty in Seventeenth-Century England: A Study of the Relationships Between Natural Science, Religion, History, Law and Literature*. New Jersey, Princeton University Press. p. 168.
[49] *Woolmington v. DPP*. [1935] AC. 462.

[50] Green. *Verdict*. Op. cit. p. 267.

[51] David J.A. Cairns. (1998) *Advocacy and the Making of the Adversarial Criminal Trial 1800-1865*. Oxford, Clarendon Press. p. 30.

[52] Langbein. 'The Criminal Trial Before Lawyers'. Op. cit. p. 307.

[53] Cairns. *Advocacy*. Op. cit. p. 3.

[54] Stephan Landsman. (1990) 'From Gilbert to Bentham: The Reconceptualization of Evidence Theory.' In 36 *The Wayne Law Review*. University of Oregon School of Law. p. 1150.

[55] John H. Langbein. (1999) 'The Prosecutorial Origins of Defence Counsel in the Eighteenth Century: The Appearance of Solicitors.' 58 *Cambridge Law Journal*. Cambridge. p. 364.

[56] Beattie. 'Scales of Justice:' Op. cit.. p. 224.

[57] King. *Crime, Justice and Discretion in England*. Op. cit. p. 228.

[58] John H. Langbein. (1983b) 'Shaping the Eighteenth-Century Criminal Trial: A View from the Ryder Sources.' Chicago, 50 *The University of Chicago Law Review*. p. 2.

[59] Langbein. *The Origins of Adversary Criminal Trial*. Op. cit. p. 178. *et. seq.*

[60] Ibid. pp. 342-3.

[61] Dwyer. Review of Langbein's ' Origins'. Op. cit. p. 943.

[62] Green. *Verdict*. Op. cit. p. 318-19.

[63] Ibid.

[64] Glanville Williams. (1963) *The Proof of Guilt, A Study of the English Criminal Trial*. London, Stevens and Sons. pp. 264-5.

[65] See Cynthia B. Herrup. (1985) 'Law and Morality in Seventeenth-Century England.' 106. *Past & Present*. Oxford, The Past and Present Society. p. 110.

[66] 18 *State Trials*. cols. 1203-1230.

[67] Joseph Towers LLD. (1764) *An Enquiry into the Question, whether juries are, or are not, judges of law as well as of fact; with a particular reference to the case of libels*. London. J. Debrett.

[68] Quoted in 21 *State Trials*. cols. 851-52.

[69] 19 *State Trials*. cols. 1075-1138.

[70] J. Steven Watson. (1960) *The Reign of George III 1760-1815*. Oxford, The Clarendon Press. p. 99.

[71] 19 *State Trials*. cols. 1154-1176. And see Raymond Postgate. (1956) *That Devil Wilkes*. London, Dennis Dobson. pp. 51-58.

[72] George Rudé. (1962) *Wilkes and Liberty: A Social Study of 1763 to 1774*. Oxford. Clarendon Press. pp. 26-7.

[73] 20 *State Trials*. cols. 803-868.

[74] Ibid. cols. 870-895.

[75] 21 Ibid. cols. 847-1044. Lord Devlin has said that this case is the most important in English law not to be discussed in the textbooks. Devlin. (1991) 'The Conscience of the Jury'. 107 *The Law Quarterly Review*. London. Stevens & Sons. p. 401.

[76] William Shipley. (1783) *The Principles of Government in a Dialogue between a Gentleman and a Farmer*. London, John Stockdale.

[77] Lord John Campbell. (1847) *Lives of the Lord Chancellors*. London, John Murray. vol. vi. p. 427.

[78] 21 *State Trials*. col. 891.

[79] Lloyd Paul Stryker. (1947) *For the Defense: Thomas Erskine, The Most Enlightened Liberal of his Times, 1750-1823*. New York, Doubleday & Company, Inc. p. 129.

[80] 21 *State Trials*. col. 899.

[81] James Ridgway. (1847) *Speeches of the Rt. Hon. Lord Erskine at the Bar and in Parliament*. London, J. Ridgway. vol. i. pp. 138-40.

[82] Campbell. Op. cit. p. 430.

[83] Ibid.

[84] 21 *State Trials*. col. 924.

[85] Old Bailey Proceedings Online. (www.oldbaileyonline.org 2003) January 1784. trial of John Henry Aikles. (tr17840114-80).

[86] 21 *State Trials*. col. 973.

[87] 21 *State Trials*. cols. 1037-8.

[88] Ibid. col. 1044.

[89] 32 Geo. 3. c.60. (1792).

[90] See *post* p. 176.

[91] Sir William Holdsworth. (1966) *A History of English Law*. London, Methuen & Co. Ltd. vol. x. p. 693.

[92] As the legend on his statue in Brixham proclaims.

[93] J. R. Green. (1874) *A Short History of the English People*. London, The Folio Society. p. 818.

[94] Campbell. Op. cit. p. 460.

[95] G.D.H. Cole. (1966) *A Short History of the British Working-Class Movement: 1789-1947*. London, George Allen and Unwin Ltd., p. 29.

[96] Alan Wharam. (1992) *The Treason Trials, 1794*. London, Leicester University Press. pp. 91-101.

[97] John Hostettler. (1996) *Thomas Erskine and Trial by Jury*. Chichester, England, Barry Rose Law Publishers Ltd. p. 121.

[98] Thomas Hardy. (1832) *Memoir*. London, James Ridgway. pp. 42-3.

[99] As Pitt had actively been before the French Revolution.

[100] Wharam. Op. cit. pp. 59, 64.

[101] Campbell. *Lives*. Op. cit. p. 471.

[102] 24 *State Trials*. cols. 199-1408.

[103] Wharam. *Treason Trials*. Op. cit. pp. 151-2.

[104] Hostettler. *Erskine*. Op. cit. p. 114.

[105] Ibid. p. 118. The tension of the trial so affected the foreman of the jury, a Thomas Buck from Acton in west London, that on the jury's return to the court he delivered the verdict in a whisper and promptly fainted on the spot.

[106] 25 *State Trials*. cols. 1-748.

[107] Langbein. 'The Criminal Trial Before Lawyers.' Op. cit. pp. 282-3.

[108] Langbein. '*Origins*'. Op. cit. p. 319.

[109] Hostettler. *Erskine*. Op. cit. p.120.

[110] Stryker. Op. cit. p. 335.

[111] Ibid. p. 340.

[112] James Epstein. (1996) 'Our real constitution: trial defence and radical memory in the Age of Revolution.' In James Vernon (ed.) . *Re-reading the constitution, New narratives in the political history of England's long nineteenth century*. Cambridge, Cambridge University Press. p. 27.

[113] E.P. Thompson. (1968) *The Making of the English Working Class*. Op. cit. p. 150.

[114] Wharam. *Treason Trials*. Op. cit. p. 50. Robert Louis Stevenson based his *Weir of Hermiston* on Lord Braxfield.

[115] *The Times*. 27 September 1819.

[116] 32 *State Trials*. col. 579.

[117] Ibid.

[118] 36 Geo. 3, c. 7.

[119] 32 *State Trials*. Op. cit.

[120] Ibid.

[121] Romilly. (1840) *Memoirs of the Life of Sir Samuel Romilly*. London, John Murray. vol. iii. p. 298.

[122] Thompson. *The Making of the English Working Class*. Op. cit.. p. 792.

[123] Ibid.

[124] Ibid. p. 793.

[125] Ibid.

[126] Harriet Harman and John Griffith. (1979) *Justice Deserted: The Subversion of the Jury*. London, National Council for Civil Liberties. p. 12.

[127] Devlin. 'The Conscience of the Jury'. Op. cit. p. 398.

[128] Hansard. (April-July 1816). First series. vol. xxxiv. col. 393.

[129] W.R. Cornish. (1968) *The Jury*. London, Allen Lane. pp. 31-3.

[130] Ibid. p. 31.

[131] Oldham. 'The Origins of the Special Jury'. Op. cit. p. 171.

[132] Sir William Blackstone. (1830) *Commentaries on the Law of England*. London, Thomas Tegg. vol. iv. pp. 357-8.

[133] Hansard. (April-July 1816) First series. vol. xxxiv. col. 395.

[134] 3Geo. II. c, 25.

[135] Oldham. 'Origins'. Op. cit. p. 204.

[136] Cornish. *The Jury*. Op. cit. p. 131.

[137] Ibid. pp. 131-32.

[138] Oldham. 'Origins.' Op. cit. 209.

[139] 6 Geo. 4, c. 50.

[140] Cornish. *The Jury*. Op. cit. p. 32.

[141] Michael Lobban. (2002) 'The Strange Life of the English Civil Jury, 1837-1914.' In Cairns and McLeod (eds) "*The Dearest Birthright of the People of England*": *The Jury in the History of the Common Law*. Oxford, Hart Publishing. p..200.

[142] 12 & 13 Geo. 6. c. 27.

[143] J.M. Beattie. (1977) 'Crime and Courts in Surrey 1736-1753.' In J.S. Cockburn (ed) *Crime in England 1550-1800.* London, Methuen & Co. Ltd. p.171.

[144] Beattie. (1988) 'London Juries in the 1690s.' Op. cit. p. 251.

[145] John Brewer and John Styles. (1980) (eds) *An Ungovernable People: The English and their law in the seventeenth and eighteenth centuries.* London, Hutchinson. p. 18.

[146] King. '"Illiterate Plebeians, Easily Misled"': Op. cit. p. 254.

[147] Ibid. pp. 254-5.

[148] Ibid. p. 255.

[149] Beattie. 'Crime and Courts in Surrey, 1736 –1753.' Op. cit. p. 176.

[150] Langbein. (1983a) 'Albion's Fatal Flaws.' 98 *Past & Present.* Oxford, The Past and Present Society. p. 106.

[151] Hay. *Albion's Fatal Tree.* Op. cit. p. 52.

[152] Langbein. 'Albion's Fatal Flaws.' Op. cit. p. 105.

[153] Ibid. p. 106.

[154] Beattie. 'Crime and Courts in Surrey.' Op. cit. p. 155.

[155] Langbein. 'Albion's Fatal Flaws.' Op. cit. p. 106.

[156] King. '"Illiterate Plebeians"'. Op. cit. p. 255.

[157] Langbein, 'Albion's Fatal Flaws.' Op. cit. p. 106.

[158] King. '"Illiterate Plebeians"' Op. cit. p. 255.

[159] Green. *Verdict* Op. cit. p. 267.

[160] Blackstone. *Commentaries* Op. cit. vol. iv. p. 248.

[161] Ibid. p. 239.

[162] S.F.C. Milsom. (1981) *Historical Foundations of the Common Law.* London, Butterworths. p. 403.

[163] See Essays by Post, Powell, Lawson and Cockburn in Cockburn and Green. *Twelve Good Men and True.* Op. cit.

[164] Hay. 'Property, Authority and the Criminal Law.' Op. cit. p. 38.

[165] Ibid. pp. 38-9.

[166] Ibid. p. 32.

[167] Ibid. pp. 32-3.

[168] Philip Handler. 2002. 'The Limits of Discretion: Forgery and the Jury at the Old Bailey, 1818-21.' In Cairns and McLeod. (eds) *"The Dearest Birthright of the People of England"*: Op. cit . p. 162.

[169] Henry Fielding. (1751) *An Enquiry into the Causes of the Late Increase of Robbers.* London, A. Millar. p. 73.

[170] King. 'Crime.' Op. cit. p. 233.

[171] John H. Langbein. (1983) 'Eighteenth-Century Criminal Trial.' Chicago, 50 *University of Chicago Law Review.* p. 53.

[172] Ibid. pp. 53-4.

[173] King. 'Crime.' Op. cit. p. 231.

[174] King. 'Illiterate Plebeians.' Op. cit. pp. 254 -304.

[175] 4 & 5 W. &. M. c.24, ss. 15. 18. See King. Ibid. p. 267.

[176] King. Ibid. p. 261.

[177] Ibid. p. 265.

[178] Ibid. p. 286.

[179] Ibid. p. 283.

[180] Ibid. p. 290. But modern research appears to indicate the contrary. Cf. D.W. Broeder. (1965) 'Previous Jury Trial Service affecting Juror Behaviour.' 506 *Insurance Law Journal.* pp. 138-43. Cited by Hay. 'The Class Composition of the Palladium of Liberty.' Op. cit. p. 347.

[181] King. 'Illiterate Plebeians.' Op. cit. p. 291.

[182] Ibid. p. 278.

[183] Ibid. pp. 279.

[184] Cockburn. *English Assizes.* Op. cit. pp. 112-113.

[185] King. 'Crime.' Op. cit.

[186] Ibid. p. 1.

[187] See Green. *Perspective.* Op. cit. p. 386.

[188] King. 'Crime.' Op. cit. p. 243.

[189] Beattie. 'Crime and Courts in Surrey.' Op. cit. p. 164.

[190] King. 'Illiterate Plebeians.' Op. cit. p. 258.

[191] Ibid. p. 292.

[192] See *ante* p. 58.
[193] Oldham. 'Origins'. Op. cit. pp. 146-47.
[194] Hay. 'Class Composition of the Palladium of Liberty:' Op. cit. p. 310.
[195] Ibid. pp. 310-11.
[196] Ibid. pp. 356-7.
[197] Ibid. p. 356.
[198] Jerome Hall. (1935) *Theft, Law and Society.* Boston, Little, Brown & Co., p. 143.
[199] *R. v. Dean of St. Asaph* [1784] 4 Dougl. p. 173.
[200] Green. *Verdict.* Op. cit. pp. 267-8.

CHAPTER 7

Criminal Law Reform: The 19th Century

INTRODUCTION

As outlined in the last chapter, the eighteenth century saw a substantial increase in the number of capital crimes. Along with a statutory weakening of the opportunity of defendants to plead benefit of clergy (see *Chapter 3*), this caused a growth in the exercise by juries of pious perjury. By this time and in the following century jury nullification was exercised in a number of cases of treason and forgery but there were also a large number of partial verdicts where the defendant was found guilty but the value of goods stolen by theft or in burglary was reduced to make the crime non-capital, particularly for females, the young and those with families to support.[1]

In fact, not just capital laws but the whole structure of criminal justice was in need of far-reaching reform. At the commencement of the nineteenth century it contained a mass of strange technicalities, curious anomalies and barbarous penalties. It lacked any certain principles of reason or justice. According to Milsom, 'the criminal law had by the eighteenth century reached an incoherence which seemed to defy even the modest order of the alphabet ... nothing worthwhile was created. There is no achievement to trace.'[2]

Modern research has modified Milsom's verdict. For example, Cynthia Herrup, in a book which she claims is a social history of criminal process in early modern England, has written that, '[r]ather than a subject with but a "miserable history," the criminal law appears now as a responsive mechanism of considerable flexibility.'[3] However, that may be because, as recent research on the jury has shown, jury nullification exercised to avoid sending minor offenders to the gallows made the law more merciful than was once believed.

In any event, in 1833 Lord Brougham, as Lord Chancellor, felt obliged to advise the king to appoint the criminal law commissioners of that year to review and codify the entire criminal law.[4] Working at the task for many years they found it both difficult and time-consuming because of the disordered condition of the law. However, in time they achieved a great deal in helping to reform the law, but, unlike the alternative of summary jurisdiction, they had little to say about juries although they sent questionnaires to those in, and connected with, the courts and the legal profession asking for suggested improvements on, among other things, grand juries and the unanimity rule. They did, however, have an indirect influence on jury trial by proposing that juveniles should be dealt with by magistrates, although the idea was rejected at the time. Nevertheless, Jeremy Bentham, who inspired the commissioners, gave intellectual repute to the idea of replacing jury trial with summary trial.

How far the effects of jury discretion and the efforts of the commissioners to reduce the incidence of the death penalty changed the criminal law is discussed in this chapter alongside the significant advent of either-way cases. It was in this period that defendants indicted to appear in the higher courts were first given the choice of summary trial instead of trial by jury if intending to plead not guilty. This choice of summary trial was to have a profound effect in reducing criminal jury trial and the rights of those accused of crimes.

IDEOLOGIES OF CAPITAL PUNISHMENT

As Cornish has written, 'during the first forty years of the nineteenth century, capital punishment was the issue around which every other aspect of the penal system turned.'[5] On this question, the divergence of views on the use to be made of capital punishment expressed by the Rev. Martin Madan, a barrister and influential publicist, on the one hand and William Paley, doctor of divinity and archdeacon of Carlisle on the other, had a considerable influence. In 1785, Madan demanded that all capital laws should be rigidly enforced holding that punishment ought to be inflicted not so much with a view to the offence already committed, but to prevent future crimes.[6] The influence that his book exercised on the judges produced a considerable, though temporary, increase in sentences of death which stung Sir Samuel Romilly to reply in an essay in the following year.[7] It culminated later in Romilly introducing Bills to repeal certain statutes which imposed the death penalty for larceny.[8]

Paley, was not a lawyer, but he was intellectually more formidable than Madan. In Chapter 9 of his *Principles of Moral and Political Philosophy* in 1785[9], he gave to the practice of discretion an ideological blessing that was to have a profound influence for nearly a century. He proposed that capital punishment should be the penalty for numerous kinds offences but should be inflicted upon only a few examples of each kind. As Professor Leon Radzinowicz has said, it is impossible to over-estimate the importance of Paley's book, 'which for many years exercised a potent influence on the trend of English criminal legislation.'[10] It exemplified what Herrup has observed in regard to an earlier period: 'the discretion once dismissed as inefficiency was in fact one of the strengths of the legal system.'[11]

This suited the small but powerful aristocracy which, with its large scale property interests and long memories of the Stuarts and Cromwell, would not tolerate the idea of a regular police force and continued to rely instead on its own power in the counties and on the abundance of capital laws to protect its interests. According to Cornish :

> The landed aristocracy chose to increase the gamut of capital offences, with a particular eye on the protection of their own kinds of property. But they did not move so extravagantly in the direction of other forms of repression. True they did something to by-pass the trial jury, that 'bulwark of liberty', by increasing summary trial before justices. True also that some new policing arrangements were beginning to develop where robbery and theft were most prevalent. But in these matters, as in the actual execution of capital felons, they stopped at a certain point.[12]

The trade and manufacturing classes, on the other hand, felt their kinds of property to be far less secure. The crimes from which they generally suffered were not dealt with summarily but went for trial before a jury with the outcome often uncertain. The intricacies of the laws of theft and embezzlement left them widely exposed and they felt a need for more certain penal laws to secure their property. Again, according to Cornish, 'the case against capital property offences was quickly supported by middle-class interests, anxious to protect their own typical forms of wealth—merchandise and money, rather than land and game.'[13]

BENTHAM AND THE EARLY 19TH CENTURY JURY

In 1825 Sir Robert Peel, as home secretary, included in his reforms of the criminal law the Juries Act[14] of that year. First, he denounced the petty constable who was responsible for returning the lists of men in each parish who were qualified for jury service by describing him as:

> An individual who was frequently unable to read or write, and too often open to seduction. Thus he had ascertained that the petty constable, in consideration of some trifling gratuity, often omitted the names of persons who were best qualified to serve on juries, and inserted the names of others who were less qualified to discharge that duty.[15]

So, ignoring the failure of earlier statutes to correct similar iniquities, Peel provided by his 1825 Act that churchwardens and overseers of the poor would replace the constable. And, henceforth, a man aged between 21 and 60 years became liable to serve as a trial juror if he occupied a dwelling of at least £20 annual value for rating (£30 in London and Middlesex) or if he owned freehold land with an annual value of £10 or more, or had a tenancy for 21 years or more with an annual value of at least £20.

Although they ensured that there was an increase in the number of men qualifying and entering the jury pool, these property qualifications remained in force throughout the nineteenth century and, significantly, continued to confine jury membership to a limited section of society. Even with that 'safeguard' against poorer people serving on criminal juries, early in the nineteenth century the composition of those juries continued to suffer severely from handpicking. This was particularly so in political cases when packing juries was felt to be desirable in the interests of the state or local notables.

In 1821 Jeremy Bentham, in an onslaught on packing, cutting and bribing jurors, had noted that the packing of juries 'is now become a *regular*, a *quietly established,* and *quietly suffered* system. Not only is the yoke already about our necks; but our necks are already *fashioned* to it.'[16] According to Douglas Hay, 'Packing and vetting in state trials was undoubtedly a refined, recondite art.'[17]

In general Bentham had a curious attitude to the jury. He considered it to be an 'occasional body of non-professional and non-official judges, employed to constitute and apply a check to the power of a professional or official judge, or body of judges.'[18] Yet his proposals for it seemed likely to diminish that role. For example, he wanted to make the jury's verdict not binding on the judge, thus producing what he called an 'unimpowered jury.' He also suggested smaller juries and majority verdicts. Having sought to emasculate the power of the jury he thought it would then be safer to provide the manpower for juries from the 'lower orders'. Moreover, 'if a decision was reached by votes it could be made without discussion immediately the trial ended.'[19]

Bentham had the visionary idea that such a body of men, unable to discuss the case before them or reach a binding verdict, would 'raise the state of society from the lowest level to the highest.' Another innovatory alternative to the established jury that he proposed was the introduction of a quasi-jury to sit with the judge to help him with advice and act as a check upon him. In effect it would be a small body of assessors, but with no power to outvote the judge. It could however be drawn at random from the 'promiscuous multitude' as part of the process of self-government.[20] On the other hand, among his many schemes, Bentham also favoured a system of stipendiary magistracies to cover the entire country, i.e. summary justice administered by a state magistracy.[21] And, in advocating the summary jurisdiction of magistrates, preferably stipendiary, over juries he gave intellectual standing to the crucial changes towards summary, instead of jury, trial later in the century, and those in the twentieth century dealt with in the next chapter.[22]

WIDESPREAD NULLIFICATION

That nullification had widespread public support is shown by perhaps the most significant petition to Parliament at the time (1830). This was from 214 cities and towns asking for the abolition of death for forgery. It included the signatures of some 1,000 bankers who claimed they suffered most from the crime, but had found from experience that the possibility of infliction of the death penalty for it prevented the conviction and punishment of the criminal and thus endangered the very property which it was intended to protect.[23] In this connection Forsyth wrote:

> When ... the difficulty of obtaining convictions is at all general in England ... such conduct in juries is the silent protest of the people against [the law's] undue severity. This was strongly exemplified in the case of prosecutions for the forgery of bank-notes, when it was a capital felony. It was in vain that the charge was proved. Juries would not condemn men to the gallows for an offence of which the punishment was out of all proportion to the crime; and as they could not mitigate the sentence they brought in verdicts of Not Guilty. The consequence was, that the law was changed; and when secondary punishments were substituted for the penalty of death, a forger had no better chance of an acquittal than any other criminal.[24]

Little over a year later, seven foremen of Old Bailey juries, joined by upwards of 1,100 merchants, traders, etc. from London who either had served on juries or were liable to serve as jurors, petitioned the House of Lords saying:

> That in the present state of the law, juries feel extremely reluctant to convict where the penal consequences of the offence excite a conscientious horror on their minds ... hence in Courts of Justice, a most unnecessary and painful struggle is occasioned, by the conflict of the feelings of a *just* humanity with the sense of the obligation of an oath.
> That witnesses also are very frequently reluctant to give evidence ... lest they might bring upon their consciences the stain of blood, and thus criminals ... escape with *complete impunity.*[25]

This was from a group of men who suffered most because the notes of the Bank of England were easy to forge.[26] In 1797 there had been 'an epidemic of forgeries and an avalanche of prosecutions.'[27] And, in the period 1818-21 the situation reached a crisis point. Two juries at the Old Bailey refused to convict any of the prisoners charged with the capital offence of uttering forged notes. The evidence was clear, the judge had given instructions to convict and yet the jurors, using their discretion to mitigate, acquitted.[28]

Nevertheless, the use of discretion must not be exaggerated. In the period 1812-18, out of a total of 131 capital trials for forgery at the Old Bailey there were 84 convictions and 47 acquittals, which means that roughly two out of every three defendants were convicted.[29] Even this rate of acquittals was sufficiently significant, however, to ensure that in 1819 an Act was passed which authorised the Bank of England to print notes that were much more difficult to forge.[30]

CRIMINAL LAW COMMISSIONERS

Following the enactment of the Great Reform Act in 1832, after a long period of repression during and following the French Revolution, there exploded an enormous surge for Benthamite reform of many aspects of life including the criminal law.[31] The government responded with a number of measures and, on the advice of Lord Chancellor Brougham, in 1833 King William IV appointed five law commissioners to review and codify the criminal law. This was the first commission of its kind in the country's history and the commissioners were appointed:

> For the purpose of digesting into one statute all the statutes and enactments touching crime, and the trial and punishment thereof, and also of digesting into one other statute all the provisions of the common or unwritten law touching the same, and for inquiring and reporting how far it may be expedient to combine both those statutes into one body of the criminal law. [32]

The first positive help the commissioners gave to the home secretary, Lord John Russell, was in framing a measure to enable counsel fully to represent defendants. The Prisoners' Counsel Act of 1836[33], as it became known, allowed those accused of felony to have counsel address the jury on their behalf.[34] This was already the position in trials for misdemeanour. Nevertheless, the Bill was strongly opposed by 12 of the 15 judges of the time, with Mr Justice Park threatening to resign if it were enacted, although in the event he did not do so.[35]

The whole issue had been raised by Bills in Parliament in 1821, 1824, 1826 and 1834—all of which were defeated, largely by lawyers in both Houses of Parliament who were unable to see what advantages lay in store for the profession if they were enacted.[36] In an effort to win lawyer support Lord John Russell sought a report from the criminal law commissioners and this was published on 9 June 1836.[37] Russell's move proved to be shrewd and the report helped to swing over the lawyers and secure the safe passage of his Bill. In fact, Lords Lyndhurst and Denman 'ensured the postponement of the second reading of the Bill in the Lords to enable the report to be printed and read.'[38]

The Bill was soon seen as a golden opportunity for work by the more powerful members of the legal profession and whilst the Law List of 1800 showed 598 barristers, by 1900 the figure had risen to 9,457.[39] Another consequence was an expansion of the complicated law of evidence, which the defence lawyers required to keep extraneous matters from the minds of the jurors, and the fixing of the burden of proof on the prosecution. The adversarial system of trial was finally fully established with counsel as its forensic giants dominant in the courtroom.[40]

At the request of the home secretary, Lord John Russell, the commissioners gave him influential backing in considerably reducing the incidence of the death penalty in 1837.[41] During the course of that year Russell, armed with drafts prepared by the commissioners, sponsored Bills in the House of Commons[42] for the removal of the death penalty from 21 of the 37 offences still capital and for restrictions in the use of such punishment in the 16 remaining. As a measure of the success of this climax to the crusade commenced by Romilly, whereas in 1831 over 1,600 persons were sentenced to death (although many of them were not executed) by 1838 the number sentenced had been reduced to 116. Before long, the death penalty was inflicted only in cases of murder and treason. It is interesting that capital punishment was thus abolished for the very offences for which juries had for centuries been inclined to invoke mercy.[43]

This reduction in the incidence of capital punishment, together with the Prisoners' Counsel Act 1836, were to have a profound impact on the criminal law in general and jury trial in particular. Mitigation of sentence in serious cases by juries was no longer seen by jurors as so necessary as before and it declined accordingly, although remaining to some extent. Nonetheless, the commissioners' reports, published over 12 years from 1833 to 1845, with over two million words in 2,324 large folio pages, are largely forgotten despite including much that remains of great interest today. They included four reports comprising a complete criminal code and a draft Act of Crimes and Punishments. The latter defined particular offences and set forth general principles governing, for instance, the effects of insanity, intoxication, age, duress and marital coercion on criminal liability.[44]

Green has argued that reform of sanctions, along with transportation replacing the gallows in many cases, 'brought to an end a long phase in the history of the English criminal trial jury.'[45] The role of the jury in using discretion to temper the use of capital punishment would continue but at a greatly reduced level with the jury usually adhering to the letter of the law.[46] As Sir Samuel Romilly pointed out, the jury had been in the awkward situation of having had to choose in each trial between imposing a penalty that it believed to be far too cruel, in the hope that the Crown would then exercise mercy, or committing an act of perjury.[47] Removing this dilemma from the responsibilities of the jury not only reinforced respect for the law but also facilitated reform of the law which may well have been held back over a long period of time by jury discretion, as it had been in the past by benefit of clergy.

As already suggested, after the Reform Act 1832, this was 'one manifestation of the claims of the newly rich to a stouter share of political power,'[48] as they now wanted certainty in a less harsh system of law rather than the discretion which suited, and was exercised by the landed interests. Nonetheless, owing to the secrecy surrounding the deliberations of the jury, discretion has been able to continue to the present day.

Two of the topics the criminal law commissioners raised in 1845 when dealing with criminal procedure in their eighth report were grand juries and the unanimity rule for petty juries. In both cases they took evidence by questionnaire from interested parties although they gave no reasons for doing so. They sent the questionnaire to members of the legal professions and others who were involved in criminal administration. It was answered by 30 barristers,[49] 13 clerks of the peace, 41 clerks to magistrates and four other attorneys or firms, three coroners, three police magistrates and Lord Denman, chief justice of the Queen's Bench. As can be seen, 'the sector of opinion canvassed is accordingly narrow, but by no means uninfluential. It is a record of opinions sufficiently numerous to suggest which views were generally shared in such circles, and which were idiosyncratic.'[50] The answers make fascinating reading.[51]

GRAND JURIES

Mention should be made of the grand jury which, until the twentieth century, played a prominent sifting role among those accused of crimes. Unlike the trial jury it could have up to 23 members; it met in secret; it heard only the prosecution without the defendant being present; and it reached a decision on whether an accused should go to trial by a majority if its members could not all agree.[52]

Members of grand juries were meant to be—and usually were—men of substance although they were not always willing to accept unpaid responsibility. There was no bar on their being related to the accused and, according to John Bellamy, in Tudor times some definitely were.[53] Through the centuries there is little evidence of grand juries asserting independence in the way trial juries often did, although Lambarde drew attention to the tendency of grand jurors in Kent in the sixteenth century to 'usurp the functions of both trial jury and judge, and to the criticism of this development by both local magistrates and assize judges.'[54] Moreover, he was critical of them as being 'wont to pass over the huge heaps of offences, that they may seem rather to have conspired with evildoers … than to have come with prepared minds to have wicked men made good by deserved punishment.'[55]

And Zachary Babington, an Oxford Circuit associate, in his *Advice to Grand Jurors in Cases of Blood* in 1677 wrote of grand jurors '(as if they were judges both of law and fact) … finding the indictment sometimes manslaughter, when they should find it murder, contrary to the sense and direction of the learned judge … whereby a murderer many times escapes.'[56] Furthermore, according to Herrup, 'Grand jurors represented the legal conscience of the shire; their very presence could be a restraining influence on local malice and on magisterial highhandedness.'[57] Nevertheless, too much should not be made of their independence.

Throughout the Middle Ages, grand jurors were chosen by two men nominated in each hundred or town by the bailiffs except when a powerful magnate or the government decided to deal with the selection themselves. For an example of the latter, in May 1537 the Duke of Norfolk told Henry VIII that he had appointed two grand juries at York and had declared his mind to them. This probably meant telling them that since he and the king believed in the truth of the Bills of indictment before them, they should also.[58] And, Bellamy says that 'In the sixteenth century, when the government felt it to be necessary, it did not hesitate to appoint the jurors itself.'[59] As has been seen, by the late seventeenth century they were frequently used by the monarchy in a purely political role although this proved counter-productive in fuelling the desire for change that produced the Glorious Revolution.

Originally the presenting jury, the grand jury came in time to receive indictments and its task was to determine whether there was a sufficient case for the accused to answer at assizes or quarter sessions. That function was intended to protect falsely accused persons against the stigma, risk, and expense of a criminal trial. However, it was alleged in evidence given to the commissioners, for instance, by R. Leigh[60] clerk of the peace for the borough of Wigan, and Pitt Taylor,[61] that the grand jury was often abused by deliberately being given too little of the available evidence (after bribery of witnesses) with the result that guilty people were set free. The secrecy of the proceedings, it was said, prevented such misconduct from coming to light.

As can be seen from the evidence given, some of the respondents saw the grand jury resulting in greater respect for the criminal justice system by the 'lower orders'. Others thought it was pointless in view of the magistrates' preliminary enquiries; that it protected liberties but jurors could be tampered with; that it was an instrument of oppression; and that jurors often exhibited a class position.

The Lord Chief Justice, Lord Denman, well known as a law reformer, in his reply to the commissioners expressed the view that grand juries produced no benefit other than the co-operation of the higher and middle classes in the administration of justice.[62] This opinion was supported by Sir G.A. Lewin, recorder of Doncaster, who believed the grand jury, as he condescendingly put it, showed 'the humbler classes that the first people in their county take an interest in the administration of justice ... and that they will not be put upon their trial by persons of their high station without an impartial inquiry.'[63] Others, including Leigh, thought the grand jury to be pointless since a magistrates' preliminary inquiry was sufficient to establish whether someone should be sent to trial.

Leigh took a middle view. Grand juries were a great protection of the liberties of Englishmen, he said, and should not on any account be abolished. However, witnesses could be tampered with or kept back, or have their evidence changed, to ensure that a bill was thrown out. As a consequence, he believed prisoners should be put on trial on an indictment framed on the depositions returned by magistrates unless the judge directed that a grand jury be summoned. This might be necessary where material facts turned up after the preliminary hearing.

J. Pitt Taylor answered the commissioners' questions in a critical article in *The Law Magazine*[64] which appeared as Appendix C of the commissioners' report. He wished to abolish grand juries not only because they were 'utterly useless' but also because they defeated the ends of justice, were instruments of oppression, were expensive and created inconvenience. After the public proceedings before magistrates, the prosecutor and his witnesses had to go, one by one, before a secret tribunal, composed of 23 gentlemen unacquainted with the law, to repeat their accusation in the absence of the accused. Neither the depositions nor lawyers were available and if 12 out of the 23 jurors considered a *prima facie* case of guilt was established a true bill was found.

It was idle, continued Pitt Taylor, to suppose frauds were not daily practised on the grand jury and witnesses were often tampered with. Moreover, a prosecutor who preferred a bill before a grand jury, was not compelled to proceed to trial in the event of a true bill being found, nor were his witnesses bound over to appear and testify in court. Thus a bill found by perjury could be used as a means of extortion against an innocent man or, if founded on truth, against the guilty.[65]

J.P. Cobbett, a barrister, detected a class attitude in gentlemen on grand juries. He wrote that he had attended assizes and quarter sessions over 12 years during which he had witnessed the trials of thousands of prisoners. Although in general he did not approve of abolishing what had been long established, he thought that the grand jury had outlived its usefulness. He claimed that grand juries were prone to endorse 'No bill' on whatever was presented to them against people of their own class. He knew an instance where a crowd of labouring men were indicted at assizes for having, during an election riot, committed the then capital offence of demolishing a house. At the same assizes, bills were also preferred against a number of gentlemen for a misdemeanour in having hired and abetted the same rioters and made them drunk for the purpose. The grand jury found all the bills against the labourers 'True', but found 'No bill' for each of the gentlemen. Yet he presumed they had no strong evidence against the former since at their trial they were speedily discharged.[66]

Charles Sprengel Greaves Q.C. was not only a distinguished writer on criminal law as editor of *Russell on Crimes* but also a barrister, a magistrate and co-author of the important 1861 Criminal Law Consolidation and Amendment Acts.[67] He thought grand juries might be abolished with advantage if a suitable substitute could be found. Failing to find one, he said they should have their procedure improved by having witnesses sworn immediately before giving their evidence and having a legal officer peruse the depositions whilst each witness was giving his evidence, with power to put any questions arising.[68]

Other respondents also argued that frauds were practised daily and witnesses were often tampered with. Nonetheless, a majority of 42 to 36 of the witnesses favoured retention of the grand jury although it should be remembered that the quality, experience, and force of argument of the witnesses varied considerably. In the event grand juries were not abolished until 1933.[69]

UNANIMITY OF JURIES

By the nineteenth century the need to prove guilt beyond reasonable doubt in criminal trials was becoming fully established and this can be said to have reinforced the requirement of jury unanimity. Nevertheless, commissioners appointed to inquire into the practice and proceedings of the superior courts of common law thought it absurd that the rights of a party in a complicated case should depend upon his ability to satisfy 12 individuals that one set of facts was the true one. Such a body of men, it said were often found to have irreconcilable views and requiring them to be unanimous could only lead to improper compromises. They recommended that after 12 hours of deliberation, if no agreement was reached the verdict of a majority of nine should be accepted.[70] This proposal was, however, not acted upon.

The question asked by the criminal law commissioners was whether the time had come for a change to majority verdicts either in the case of an acquittal or in the case of a conviction or both, and 71 of their respondents out of 95 on the whole questionnaire expressed an opinion either way. Although the respondents divided fairly equally it is interesting that a number of them favoured the Scottish method of permitting a 'not proven' verdict whilst even a simple majority also found some favour. One barrister thought that in political cases a simple majority would raise fears of corruption.

Lord Denman and others were briskly in favour of all verdicts of juries remaining unanimous.[71] On the other hand E.E. Deacon, a barrister, thought three-quarters of the jury should be able to find a verdict of guilty and that if less than that number were against the prisoner the verdict be 'not proven' as in Scotland, provided that if the majority were not in favour of a conviction there should be an acquittal.

Quite a number, like Messrs Philcox and Baldock, who were magistrates' clerks at Hastings, thought a simple majority would be sufficient as it was difficult to expect 12 men to agree.[72] But although this has been proposed by such an authority as the Law Society,[73] the presumption of innocence and the necessity of proving guilt beyond reasonable doubt would clearly be at risk. J. P. Cobbett also wanted to adhere to unanimity. In ringing tones he demanded that the commissioners should not countenance the slightest tampering with that 'palladium of our liberties, the most transcendent privilege we can enjoy or wish for, the sacred bulwark of the nation, all inroads upon which, though begun in trifles, are ... fundamentally opposite to the spirit of our constitution.'[74]

Anticipating the modern practice. S.R. Bosanquet, barrister, argued that ten (or perhaps nine) out of 12 would be a proper majority. In many neighbourhoods, he asserted, there were two or three well-known persons who made it their pleasure to differ from other people and impede business. Their pertinacity fettered and compromised the good sense and consciences of the majority and thus prevented justice. Greaves claimed that his experience had taught him that the minority, and sometimes a very small minority, were more frequently right than the majority and the great advantage of the necessity of unanimity was that it unavoidably compelled real consideration which would never take place where a majority alone was sufficient.[75]

J. Stuart Roupell, barrister, indicated that majority verdicts would be hazardous, if not dangerous, in decreasing the strong reliance which all Englishmen had in the propriety of every verdict and lessening the deep-rooted and universal respect for the jury as an institution. There had to be evidence of guilt so strong as to leave the jurors in no reasonable doubt of it. If ten could convict, notwithstanding the doubts of two, the principle of the law was lost.

In the event the respondents were equally divided on the unanimity principle (38 to 38), yet despite the obvious interest in the matter, since more respondents replied on this question than any other except grand juries, the commissioners chose not to touch upon it in their report. Nevertheless, they obtained, and published, the views on aspects of jury trial and other topics of a large section of those involved in the criminal justice system, which was in itself a unique exercise.

CHOICE OF SUMMARY TRIAL

In the early nineteenth century crimes were either serious indictable offences, tried before a judge and a jury at assizes or quarter sessions, or minor non-indictable offences, tried summarily before magistrates sitting without a jury. Hence, when a statute of 1827[76] recast the law of larceny and allied offences, the more serious were made indictable whilst jurisdiction over some less serious offences was given to justices of the peace.[77] In all cases the accused had no choice in the matter and if the charge was at all grave he had jury trial by right.

The first inroad upon this system where an indictable offence necessarily meant jury trial was made in the case of young offenders. Against a background of growing concern at the severity of punishments for children including death, in 1836 the criminal law commissioners were asked to consider the desirability of distinguishing between modes of trial of juvenile and adult offenders. They presented their report[78] a year later, after examining numerous witnesses, and concluded that it would not be advisable to make any distinction in the mode of trial between adults and juveniles. However, they deprecated the holding of juveniles in prison for months awaiting trial at quarter sessions or assizes and proposed an exception to their general conclusion by suggesting an increase in the summary jurisdiction of magistrates over young people and allowing them to dismiss a defendant altogether if his or her offence were considered to be trivial. In other cases, bail should be granted for juveniles on remand and the length of prison sentences should be lower for young people.

The government refused to implement the report, with Lord John Russell saying that 'it would violate the principle of trial by jury,'[79] as indeed it would have done. However, the commissioners' suggestion did come to fruition in 1847 with the Juvenile Offenders Act[80] which provided that simple larceny by any child aged 14 or less should be tried summarily if the justices saw fit and the parent or guardian of the child consented. The purpose of the statute, following the thinking of the commissioners, was to ensure a speedy trial to avoid the contamination of children in custody awaiting trial with adult offenders. In 1850 the age was raised to 16.[81] Although it was correct that juveniles should be treated differently from adults, in this way the commissioners may be said to have unwittingly started the process whereby magistrates gradually took over most cases from the jury.

In 1848 the Summary Jurisdiction Act[82] (commonly known as Jervis's Act after the attorney-general, Sir John Jervis) was passed. It both clarified and enlarged the powers and duties of magistrates and granted them power to issue a summons or warrant for every indictable offence committed within their area, or elsewhere if the suspect had entered the area of their jurisdiction. This paved the way for a huge expansion of the public judicial work of justices during the nineteenth and twentieth centuries which eventually was to result in their disposal of nearly 98 per cent of all prosecutions in England and Wales[83] and severely lessened trial by jury.

An even more significant change for adults then occurred a few years later with the enactment of the Criminal Justice Act of 1855.[84] What the Act did was to enable magistrates to deal with simple larceny, or attempted larceny, where there was a theft of money or goods not over ten shillings in value, if the justices agreed and the accused consented. Previously the cut-off point had been 12 pence. This marked a turning point in the history of the criminal process. Prior to the Act, 'the distinguishing feature of the criminal process had been trial by jury: henceforth, there was to be a steadily increasing erosion of that "palladium" of the liberties of the subject.'[85] The immediate effect of the Act was a sharp reduction in the number of jury trials upon indictment.[86] In 1854 the number of such trials was 29,359, whilst for 1856 the figure was 19,437. Comparing the average of the five years preceding 1855 with the five years following, the decrease amounted to 34.9 per cent.[87] No doubt, the government was suitably pleased with the financial savings involved.

It is interesting that such a fundamental change in criminal trial was treated with indifference by most Members of Parliament. The Criminal Justice Bill was introduced in the House of Lords by Lord Chancellor Cranworth in 1854.[88] Lord St Leonards rose to say that he did not trust magistrates in quarter sessions and he did not see why he should do so in petty sessions. Furthermore, as someone could suffer two years in prison for committing a trivial offence his lordship considered he was entitled to a jury. Having thus unburdened himself, St Leonards went on to say that he would not oppose the Bill. Only one other peer spoke to the Bill and in a short statement said he supported it.

On 26 March 1855 the Bill received its second reading in the House of Commons where it was introduced by Sir George Grey who outlined its provisions.[89] Here, Seymour Fitzgerald, the Member for Horsham, expressed 'great doubts as to the principle of the Bill, which would transfer the trial of one half' of cases before the judge and jury at assizes or quarter sessions to magistrates in petty sessions. With some prescience he asked that once the policy was in force what was to prevent it being taken further? We must not, he concluded, 'infringe on the great safeguard of our liberties—trial by jury.' Robert Palmer, Member for Berkshire, thought the Bill should cover only trivial offences such as 'stealing a couple of turnips'. Only two other members spoke in the debate and, expressed a view repeated by governments today, that the Bill should be supported because of the heavy financial costs of trial by jury.

When the Bill reached its third reading,[90] an alert T. Chambers, Member for Hertford, said that although the Bill dealt with a great constitutional question it had reached the third reading without any discussion of its principle. It would abolish the 'great constitutional tribunal for trying criminals' and set up an entirely new tribunal in its place. No one could say why, and the Bill gave no answer for it had no preamble. He denied that there was any considerable degree of delay and expense with trials and said that to the extent that there were, for the offences covered, people should be allowed bail. The attorney-general, Sir A.E. Cockburn,[91] endorsed the Bill that he believed would be of 'great benefit to criminals, magistrates and the country.' Three other members agreed with him and the Bill received the royal assent on 14 August 1855. Thus was this great constitutional change introduced by parliament, with only a handful of members bothering to discuss it.

In line with Seymour Fitzgerald's foreboding, this policy of replacing juries with magistrates was extended by the Summary Jurisdiction Act of 1879. If the justices saw fit and the accused, or his parent or guardian, consented summary trial was considered appropriate for a child under 12 for any offence other than homicide. There was summary trial also for offenders between 12 and 16 for a wide variety of offences, and for adults charged with larceny to a value not exceeding 40 shillings. Once again there was a decline in the number of jury trials. Taking the annual average for five years preceding and following the statute, the number of indictable offences tried summarily increased by 8,764 a year, or 23.3 per cent.[92]

Thus did the most significant assault on criminal trial by jury in English history commence in the nineteenth century and it should be borne in mind that,

when a defendant exercises his election between summary trial and trial on indictment the choice he has to make will be influenced by more than a preference for a mode of trial. Committal for trial involves waiting (perhaps in prison) and the possibility of a longer sentence if convicted. The scales are weighted in favour of summary trial.[93]

Furthermore, the country had by now been transformed into an industrialised and more democratic society; it was believed that with new kinds of disputes there was a need for simpler and speedier processes to deal with the growing volume of work.[94] Also behind the attack lay the perceived view that summoning juries caused inconveniences and delays, was costly, impeded the desire to keep court timetables flexible and cut down the length of trials.[95] This clearly involved, however, less democratic processes before magistrates rather than juries.

Jury conditions

Another jury reform of the nineteenth century was in regard to keeping the jury without meat, drink or fire until they had reached their verdict. The responsibility for ensuring this rested with the bailiff in charge of the jury and on one occasion one of the jury asked for a glass of water. 'The bailiff came into court and asked Mr. Justice Maule if he might give the jurymen water. "Well," said the judge, "it is not meat, and *I* should not call it drink; yes, you may."'[96] Then, the rule was abolished by the Juries Act 1870, and Alexander Pope's couplet from *The Rape of the Lock* was no longer applicable:

> The hungry Judges soon the Sentence sign,
> And Wretches hang that Jury-men may Dine.[97]

Despite Green's assertion that jury nullification was declining after the reduction in the incidence of the death penalty,[98] another example of juries acting according to conscience is shown by the cases of women who killed their newborn babies while suffering the after-effects of childbirth. In law such women were guilty of murder and were so charged but there was a long tradition of juries exercising mercy in order to avoid the death penalty by substituting the offence of concealing a birth, which was non-capital. The Royal Commission on Capital Punishment of 1866[99] tried to find a compromise as did Sir James Fitzjames Stephen in his Criminal Law Code of 1878 as well as a number of MPs, but to no avail. Jury nullification had its effect, however, and eventually an Infanticide Act was passed in 1922 which created a non-capital offence of a mother causing the death of her child.

CONCLUSION

At the beginning of the nineteenth century the criminal law still bore marks of its feudal origin with capital punishment as its most significant feature. By 1832 the new reforming Whig government was determined upon its reform and to this end the criminal law commissioners were appointed. As a consequence of their labours, and although their Bills codifying the law were not enacted, considerable reform of the criminal law was effected during the century.[100] To this should be added the civilising effect of the clear formulation of the presumption of innocence and the beyond-reasonable-doubt standard of proof in criminal trials.[101]

In the early part of the century a Jurors' Petition to the House of Lords in 1831 revealed the strong feeling among jurors that they were being made accessories to judicial murder. However, the abolition in 1838 of the death penalty for most crimes diminished the future need for nullification, although jury discretion did not disappear and could still influence the law as its effect in helping to produce the

Infanticide Act early in the twentieth century was to show. No alteration occurred with regard to the grand jury or the unanimity rule for petty juries despite severe misgivings about the former being expressed by many influential witnesses to the criminal law commissioners.

The Prisoners' Counsel Act 1836 gave the final fillip to the dominance of lawyers in the criminal courts, entrenching the adversarial system and the replacement of the judge as the most active participant in trials.

So far as the role of the criminal jury is concerned, the most portentous change came with the introduction of either-way cases in the 1850s. Whether this is considered to be a reform, in the sense of an improving change, or not, it was a startling innovation that made serious inroads into the system with the criminal trial jury suffering a considerable diminution in its scope as many types of cases were transferred to the magistrates' courts. It represented the first systematic, statutory reduction in the role of the criminal jury in its history and set the tone for future attacks which will be considered in the next chapter.

ENDNOTES for *Chapter 7*

[1] P.J.R. King. (1988) '"Illiterate Plebeians, Easily Misled": Jury Composition, Experience, and Behavior in Essex, 1735-1815.' In Cockburn and Green (eds.) *Twelve Good Men and True: The Criminal Trial Jury in England, 1200-1800.* New Jersey, Princeton University Press. p. 255.

[2] S.F.C. Milsom. (1969) *Historical Foundations of the Common Law.* London, Butterworths. pp. 365, 353.

[3] Cynthia Herrup. (1987) *The Common Peace: Participation and the Criminal Law in Seventeenth-century England.* Cambridge, Cambridge University Press. pp. 1, 2.

[4] See *Parliamentary Papers.* (1834) vol. xxvi.

[5] W.R. Cornish, (1978a) 'Criminal Justice and Punishment.' In *Crime and Law in Nineteenth Century Britain.* Dublin, Irish University Press. p. 14.

[6] Martin Madan. (1785) *Thoughts on Executive Justice, with Respect to Our Criminal Laws, Particularly on the Circuits.* London, J. Dodsley.

[7] Samuel Romilly. (1786) *Observations on a late Publication Intituled, Thoughts on Executive Justice.* See *Memoirs of the Life of Sir Samuel Romilly.* (1840) London, John Murray. vol. i. p. 90.

[8] *Hansard* [15] cols. 366-374. (9 February 1810).

[9] William Paley. (1785) *The Principles of Moral and Political Philosophy.* In *The Works of W. Paley.* (1825) Edinburgh, Peter Brown and T. & W. Nelson. Chap. 4 and 9. p. 526.

[10] Leon Radzinowicz. (1948) *A History of English Criminal Law and its Administration from 1750.* vol. i. *The Movement for Reform.* London, Stevens and Sons Ltd. pp. 248-9.

[11] Cynthia Herrup. (1985) 'Law and Morality in Seventeenth-Century England.' 106. *Past and Present.* Oxford, The Past and Present Society. p. 123.

[12] Cornish. 'Criminal Justice and Punishment.' Op. cit. p. 19.

[13] Ibid.

[14] 6 Geo. IV. c. 50.

[15] *Hansard.* [12] (Second ser.). col. 968.

[16] Jeremy Bentham. (1821) *Elements in the Art of Packing as applied to Special Juries etc.* London, Effingham Wilson. pp. 61-186.

[17] Douglas Hay. (1988) 'The Class Composition of the Palladium of Liberty: Trial Jurors in the Eighteenth Century.' In Cockburn and Green (eds) *Twelve Good Men and True.* Op. cit. p. 352.

[18] Bentham. (1843) *Principles of Judicial Procedure. Works.* ii. Edinburgh, William Tait. p. 118.

[19] Ibid.

[20] Ibid.

[21] Richard Vogler. (1991) *Reading the Riot Act. The Magistracy, the Police and the Army in Civil Disorder.* Milton Keynes, Open University Press. p. 126.

[22] I am indebted on this point to an unpublished paper by Dr Richard Vogler, Senior Lecturer of the Law School the University of Sussex.

[23] *Journals of the House of Commons.* (24 May 1830) vol. 85. p. 463.

[24] W. Forsyth. (1852) *History of Trial by Jury.* London, John Parker. p. 431.

[25] Radzinowicz. *A History of English Criminal Law.* Op. cit. pp. 731-2. The petition is given in full from *Journals of the House of Lords.* (1830-1831) vol. 63. p. 964.

[26] Cairns and McLeod. (eds) (2002) *"The Dearest Birthright of the People of England": The Jury in the History of the Common Law.* Oxford, Hart Publishing. p. vi.

[27] Philip Handler. (2002) 'The Limits of Discretion: Forgery and the Jury at the Old Bailey 1818-21.' In Cairns and McLeod (eds) *The Dearest Birthright of the People of England.* Op. cit. p. 155.

[28] Ibid.

[29] Ibid. p. 158.

[30] 1 Geo. IV. c. 92.

[31] Cornish. *Criminal Justice and Punishment.* Op. cit. p. 8.

[32] *Parliamentary Papers.*(1834) First Report. xxvi. p. 105.

[33] 6 and 7 Will. IV. c. 114.

[34] J. A. Hostettler. (1982) 'Counsel for the Defence.' 11 *The Anglo-American Law Review.* Chichester, England, Barry Rose Law Periodicals Ltd. p. 76.

[35] Sir Harry B. Poland, Q.C. (1900) 'Changes in Criminal Law and Procedure since 1800.' In (1901) *A Century of Law Reform.* London, Macmillan and Co., Limited. p.50.

[36] Hostettler. 'Counsel'. Op. cit. p. 86.

[37] *Parliamentary Papers.* (1836). vol. xxxvi. p. 123.

[38] Cairns. Op. cit. p. 75.

[39] Blake Odgers. (1901) *A Century of Law Reform.* Op. cit. p. 30.

[40] John H. Langbein. (1978) 'The Criminal Trial before the Lawyers.' Chicago, 45 *University of Chicago Law Review.*

[41] P.P. (1836) Second Report. xxxvi. p. 183. See also David J.A. Cairns. (1998) *Advocacy and the Making of the Adversarial Criminal Trial 1800—1865.* Oxford, Clarendon Press. pp. 73, 90.

[42] [37] *Hansard.* (third series) col. 709. (1837).

[43] See Green. (1985) *Verdict According to Conscience: Perspectives on the English Criminal Trial Jury 1200-1800.* Chicago, University of Chicago Press. p. 356.

[44] Criminal Law Commission. Fourth Report 1839 [168], xix; Fifth Report 1840 [242], xx; Sixth Report 1841 [316], x; Irish University Press Criminal Law 3; Seventh Report 1843 [448], xix; IUP Criminal Law 4. See Cornish 'Criminal Justice and Punishment.' Op. cit. p. 53.

[45] Green. *Verdict.* Op. cit. p. 356.

[46] Ibid.

[47] Sir Samuel Romilly. (1810) 'Observations on the Criminal Law of England'. London, *Monthly Review.* pp. 22-3.

[48] Cornish. 'Criminal Justice and Punishment.' Op. cit. p. 19.

[49] Including three QCs, one Serjeant, four Recorders and one chairman of quarter sessions.

[50] Cornish. (1978b) 'Defects in Prosecuting—Professional Views in 1845.' In *Reshaping the Criminal Law: Essays in honour of Glanville Williams.* (ed. P.R. Glazebrook), London, Stevens & Sons. p. 307.

[51] Grand Juries and Unanimity are dealt with in *Parliamentary Papers.* 8th Report. (July 1845). Appendix A to vol. 4. Irish University Press (1971) Dublin, Ireland. pp. 209-343.

[52] Radcliffe & Cross. (1964) *The English Legal System.* London, Butterworths. p. 199.

[53] John Bellamy. (1979) *The Tudor Law of Treason: An Introduction.* London, Routledge & Kegan Paul. p. 128.

[54] Conyers Read. (ed.) (1962) *William Lambarde and Local Government .His "Ephemeris" and Twenty Nine Charges to Juries and Commissions.* Ithaca. New York, Cornell University Press. pp. 119-20.

[55] Ibid. p. 112.

[56] Cockburn. *Introduction to Calendar of Assize Records.* Op. cit. pp. 51-2.

[57] Herrup. *The Common Peace.* Op. cit. p. 93.

[58] Bellamy. *The Tudor Law of Treason.* Op. cit. p. 128.

[59] Ibid.

[60] *Parliamentary Papers.* Commissioners' 8th Report. Op. cit. pp. 226-7.

[61] Ibid. Appendix C. pp. 357-69.

[62] Ibid. p. 507.

[63] Ibid. pp. 516-18.

[64] (1844) vol. 131. pp. 245-75.

[65] Re-printed in Parliamentary Papers. Op. cit. pp. v653-65.

[66] Ibid. pp. 589-96.

[67] 24 and 25 Vict.
[68] Ibid. pp. 542-47.
[69] Administration of Justice (Miscellaneous Provisions) Act, 1933. 23 & 24 Geo. 5, c. 36.
[70] Common Law Commissioners' Third Report. (1831) No. 92. pp. 69-70.
[71] Parliamentary Papers. Op. cit. p. 507.
[72] Ibid. pp. 535-6.
[73] *Law Society's Gazette.* (22 December 1976). London, Law Society. p. 1073.
[74] Parliamentary Papers. Op. cit. pp. 589-96.
[75] Ibid. pp. 542-47.
[76] 7 & 8 Geo. IV, c. 29.
[77] R.M. Jackson. (1937) 'The Incidence of Jury Trial During the Past Century.' 1 *The Modern Law Review.* London, Stevens & Sons Limited. pp. 132-3.
[78] P.P. (1837) xxxi. p. 1.
[79] *Hansard.* [37] 3rd. ser. col. 926. (April 1837).
[80] 10 &11 Vict. c. 82.
[81] 13 & 14 Vict. c. 37.
[82] 11 & 12 Vict. c.43.
[83] Skyrme, Sir Thomas. (1991) *The History of the Justices of the Peace.* Chichester, England, Barry Rose Publishers. vol. ii. p. 177.
[84] 18 & 19 Vict. c.126.
[85] A.H. Manchester. (1980) *A Modern Legal History of England and Wales 1750-1950.* London, Butterworth & Co. Ltd. p. 161.
[86] Ibid. p. 94.
[87] Jackson. 'Incidence of Jury Trial'. Op. cit. p.136.
[88] *Hansard.* [136] col. 1871.
[89] Ibid. [137] col. 1167.
[90] Ibid. [139] col. 1866. (6 August 1855).
[91] Ibid. col. 1879.
[92] Jackson. 'Incidence of Jury Trial. Op. cit. p. 136.
[93] Ibid. p. 138.
[94] W.R. Cornish. (1968) *The Jury.* London, Allen Lane. p. 22.
[95] Ibid.
[96] Poland. 'Changes in Criminal Law and Procedure since 1800.' Op. cit. p. 51.
[97] Canto III, lines 19-20. (1714) In *Five Cantos Written by Mr. Pope.* London, Bernard Lintot. p. 20.
[98] Green. *Verdict.* Op. cit. p. 356.
[99] Parliamentary Papers. xxi. (1866).
[100] See John Hostettler. (1992) *The Politics of Criminal Law: Reform in the Nineteenth Century.* Chichester, Barry Rose Law Publishers.
[101] Langbein. 'The Criminal Trial before the Lawyers.' Op. cit. p. 266. However, Shapiro considers the beyond-reasonable-doubt standard existed in the seventeenth century. See *ante* p. 64.

CHAPTER 8

Attacks on the Jury: The 20th Century

INTRODUCTION

The twentieth century saw a vast increase in the numbers of people made eligible for jury service. Alongside this, and to some extent undermining it, the statutory system created in 1855 which gave magistrates, but more particularly defendants, a choice of summary hearings instead of jury trial grew into an increasingly wide category of 'either-way' cases.

After World War I women in England could be selected as jurors for the first time in recognition of their role in wartime.[1] Then, following the 1965 Morris Report[2] the Juries Act 1974 extended jury service, with certain exceptions, to voters on the electoral register. This, with the reduction of the voting age to 18 years of age, is estimated to have increased the number of potential jurors from eight million to 30 million.[3]

This was the high watermark, however. Since that time there have been more and more piecemeal changes to the jury system. These include the decision to introduce majority verdicts in place of unanimity in certain circumstances, the making of many more offences triable only summarily and a surprising admission by the attorney-general of police vetting of jurors. It is necessary to consider the implications of these changes and whether they were advisable or were introduced in an effort to reduce the scope of the system after it had been democratised.

Although widespread criticism of the middle class nature of juries[4] resulted in the 1974 Act extending general eligibility for jury service to those on the electoral register, it is true to say that since that time there has been considerable pressure from the government and some judges to gain support for trimming the wings of the jury system. So far as governments are concerned the main motivation is said to be to reduce the costs of trial by jury in the Crown Court. This process culminated in December 1999, when the Lord Chancellor, the home secretary and the attorney-general joined together to invite Lord Justice Auld to undertake a review of, and to advise on, the structure of the criminal courts including trial by jury. The Auld Report was published in 2001.[5] Although not accepted in full in the subsequent White Paper *Justice for All* (2002),[6] it is useful to examine some of the arguments of both documents. Not only did they inform the Criminal Justice Act 2003,[7] they also set out the leading polemics to be found against the jury system at the commencement of the twenty-first century and these are likely to re-surface. Also to be considered is how far jury nullification exists today and whether it is as widespread as in previous centuries. Certainly, both Auld and the Government have complained that there are far too many acquittals in the Crown Court.

EXTENDING LIABILITY TO JURY SERVICE

The struggle in Britain for universal suffrage in the Parliamentary franchise is an exciting one which led eventually to universal adult suffrage including for women[8] and then for everyone over 18 years of age.[9] A highlight in this struggle was the dedicated campaign of the Suffragettes in the years leading up to World War I. This, and the work of millions of women in the war effort, ensured that once victory was won on the battlefield so it would be at home.[10] That also involved the jury since it would have been illogical to have given women the vote but not allowed them to sit on the jury which was all-male until 1919. In that year the Sex Disqualification (Removal) Act was passed which, by section 1, abolished all the then existing restrictions upon the admission of women into professions, occupations and civic positions including appointment as magistrates and selection as jurors.

It seems curious today that between 1919 and 1971 the trial judge could order that a jury be composed wholly of members of one sex. 'While this power was used reasonably often to secure all-male juries, particularly for the trial of sexual offences, no case is known of an all-female jury being ordered until 1969 when Thesiger J. thought such a step appropriate to the trial of a woman for the manslaughter of her neice.'[11] After the Court of Appeal expressed their disapproval[12] the power was abolished.[13]

After 1919 both men and women could serve as jurors, but only if they met the property qualification. Even when they qualified, working class people were not anxious to sit on a jury since until 1949 there had been no compensation for loss of wages and a jury summons could involve an arduous financial burden,[14] and a threat to continued employment. Moreover, the small number of women householders kept the numbers of female jurors low. As a consequence, in 1956 Lord Devlin (a strong supporter of trial by jury) famously said that the jury was not really representative of the nation as a whole but was 'predominantly male, middle-aged, middle-minded and middle-class.'[15] Despite this reasonable assessment, criticism of the jury system at that time was rare. Today, as will be seen, the situation is different.

In 1965 the Morris Committee on jury service marked a sea change in the approach to the composition of juries by concluding that it was 'inherent in the very idea of a jury that it should be as far as possible a genuine cross-section of the adult community,' and the qualification for service should be 'citizenship as evidenced by inclusion in the electoral register as a parliamentary elector.'[16] The Metropolitan Commissioner of Police and the Association of Chief Police Officers told the committee that the quality of jurors had gone down.[17] This was a subjective view, however, not backed by evidence and it was ignored by the committee.

The committee received no convincing evidence that householders had any special abilities as jurors and chose to prefer to see jury duty based upon the right of citizenship. This was the basis of the Juries Act 1974 when the property qualifications first laid down for jurors under Sir Robert Peel were brought to an end and general eligibility for jury service was extended to all those on the electoral roll.[18] The only qualifications now are: an age of at least 18 and not more than 70; to have been ordinarily resident in this country for a period of at least five years since the age of 13; and registration as a Parliamentary or local government elector.[19]

Reducing ineligibility
Those still ineligible to serve prior to the Criminal Justice Act 2003 included judges, justices of the peace, men and women involved in the administration of the legal system and in professions and occupations concerned with the administration of

justice such as barristers, solicitors, police, prison and probation officers; and also clergymen, the mentally ill and people on bail. In general, ineligibility arose because it was believed that most of the people in these categories might have an undue influence on other jurors. This was overturned by the 2003 Act and, with the exception of mentally disordered people, all those in these categories are now eligible.[20]

The argument that the specialist knowledge and prestige of such people would enable them unduly to influence their fellow jurors was dismissed. As Sir Robin Auld put it, 'I do not know why the undoubted risk of prejudice of that sort should be any greater than in the case of many others who are not excluded from juries and who are trusted to put aside any prejudices they may have.'[21] That does not, however, deal with the difficulty, for those connected with the criminal justice system, of putting in abeyance their knowledge of that system. For instance, although they cannot always be told explicitly, they can often judge from defence counsel's questions when a defendant has previous convictions.

Two groups can no longer claim to be excused from sitting. First: peers, MPs and full-time members of the armed forces; second: medical practitioners, dentists, nurses, midwives, vets and pharmaceutical chemists.[22] People with a criminal record involving particular types of sentence continue to be disqualified.[23]

For a trial, 12 jurors are selected from a panel randomly summoned from the electoral register. They are chosen without regard to any skill and they sit for such short periods that they are unable to acquire judicial experience. They always sit with a judge, in isolation in court and the jury room, and give no reasons for their verdict, which ensures it cannot be challenged other than by a general appeal. For the legal and lay combination to work properly there should be not only an independent and sensible jury but also a skilful and impartial judge.[24]

THE CURTAILMENT OF JURY TRIAL

The late twentieth century saw not only the considerable expansion of eligibility for jury service but also piecemeal but serious legislative and administrative erosions of the scope of jury trial. As early in the century as 1925 a large number of cases which were previously triable only by a judge and jury had been brought within the jurisdiction of magistrates at petty sessions.[25] Fifty years later, in 1975, the James Committee reached the 'firm conclusion' that the choice of venue by the defendant should not be removed because of its long existence and widespread public support.[26] Notwithstanding this decided view, in 1977 the government introduced the Criminal Law Act which, based on the James Committee's own proposals, took away from defendants the right to choose trial by jury in the case of some public order offences and those where criminal damage below £200 was alleged,[27] even though this meant that a new raft of accused persons might be sent to prison without an opportunity to exercise their previous right to elect jury trial.

With the Criminal Justice Act 1988 the powers of magistrates were further extended by increasing summary offences to include, among others common assault and battery, and taking a conveyance without consent.[28] Five years later the Royal Commission on Criminal Justice suggested that the prosecution and defence could agree on the mode of trial but otherwise the magistrates court should decide upon the venue.[29]

Either-way cases

Today there are some 30 main types of either-way offences, comprising about 700 individual crimes including offences of violence, threats to kill, burglaries and thefts, arson not endangering life, and causing death by aggravated vehicle taking.[30] This break with the past has led Sir Robin Auld to conclude, against the historical evidence, that the right to trial by jury is not some 'ancient, constitutional, fundamental or even broad right of the citizen to jury trial.' It began, he says, in the nineteenth century as an elective right to avoid the obligation of trial by jury in a limited number of indictable cases.[31] But this is to turn the right to jury trial into an obligation to avoid if possible, which is not how it is generally perceived.

Similarly, an academic lawyer, Peter Duff, has suggested that many English practitioners and commentators regard the defendant's right of election in respect of either-way offences as fundamental to the very institution of trial by jury, 'despite the fact that it is largely the product of (relatively recent) historical, cultural and political contingencies.'[32] But this ignores the fact that until 1855 indictable offences to which the defendant pleaded not guilty were always dealt with by juries.

Speaking of present trends Duff continues that:

> [I]t does not seem to me that transferring the right to decide the mode of trial for 'either-way' offences from the defendant to the courts represents an unwarranted attack on the institution of trial by jury nor does it amount to an unjustified diminution of the rights of English defendants. The 'right' to trial by jury is already severely limited and to give the courts, rather than defendants, the final say as regards 'either-way' offences is not going to change this significantly.[33]

Perhaps placing the *right* to jury trial in quotation marks is indicative of a negative attitude to the jury and, of course, there has never been a right of election in the author's Scotland.

Expressing another view, the James Committee in 1975 said:

> There is substantial opinion in favour of removing the defendant's right of election [but] this is almost entirely confined to those directly responsible for the administration of justice, whether as judges, court staff or prosecutors. Virtually all of the organizations ... representing a wider interest (including practitioners' organizations) took the contrary view.[34]

According to *Justice for All*, most either-way cases are dealt with by magistrates—'87 per cent in 2000, with 9 per cent going to the Crown Court because the magistrates declined to take the case and 4 per cent because defendants elected.' It adds that 'the proportion of these cases that are heard by magistrates has increased in recent years. In over half of the either-way cases that do go to the Crown Court and in which the defendant pleads or is found guilty, magistrates could have given the sentence.'[35] But, it may be significant that 67 per cent of those pleading not guilty in the Crown Court are acquitted.[36] In the event, the Criminal Justice Act 2003 whilst it altered the qualifications of jurors and introduced certain judge-alone trial scenarios did not interfere with the existing list of either-way offences nor seek to reduce the right of an accused person to choose jury trial - although it did increase the sentencing powers of magistrates' courts so that many more either-way cases are likely to end up being dealt with in this latter court.

JURY CHALLENGES

For most of the twentieth century it was possible for the defence to challenge jurors without giving any reason in an attempt to obtain a sympathetic jury. Such challenges were known as peremptory challenges. In 1925, the number of such challenges allowed was reduced from 25 to 12. In 1949 the number was reduced to seven (or seven for each defendant where two or more were tried together) and in 1977 the number was fixed at three.[37] Section 32 (3) Courts Act 1971 provided that a party to proceedings 'shall be entitled to reasonable facilities for inspecting the [jury] panel.' This enabled the defence to exercise its right of challenge. But by section 31, the Act also gave the Lord Chancellor's office overall control of jury panels, now the Jury Summoning Bureau under his auspices of the Department of Constitutional Affairs. Lord Hailsham, as Lord Chancellor, promptly removed jurors' occupations from the jury list, fearing such information would assist the defence to challenge jurors in 'cases with political overtones.'[38] There is no limit to the number of jurors that can be challenged 'for cause' (i.e. for good reason).

In a conspiracy trial in 1977 at the Old Bailey, involving 17 black defendants, the defence requested that at least six black jurors should be selected. When this was refused, 103 jurors were challenged by defence barristers and the final jury contained five black people.[39] This and similar cases led to the long-standing right to peremptory challenge being abolished altogether in 1988.[40] This has been a setback for efforts to secure a jury of peers and racially mixed juries. A year later, the Court of Appeal held that there is no principle that a jury should be racially balanced, that race should not be taken into account when jurors are selected, and that the judge has no power to interfere with the composition of the jury to achieve a multiracial jury.[41] In fact, the common practice in the USA of extensive use of peremptory challenges produces a jury like the defendant, whereas random selection in the UK produces a jury which reflects the community.

The prosecution, on the other hand, still has the right to 'stand by' a juror, without showing cause and with no upper limit, but subject to restrictive guidelines issued by the attorney-general in the same year.[42] Challenge for cause also remains, but the burden of proof is on the person who seeks to make it and the defence lawyers do not normally have any information on which to mount a challenge, nor are they permitted to gain it by questioning potential jurors.

More worryingly, following counsel's inquiries in the ABC official secrets trial in October 1978, when 93 jurors on the jury panel were vetted, the attorney-general, Sam Silkin, disclosed (not to Parliament but to *The Times* newspaper) that since 1948 a practice had grown up by which the prosecution privately checked the jury list against the records of the police.[43] (It may be significant that 1948 was the year which saw a Bill to abolish the special jury.) It was decided, Silkin said, that in the interests of justice the practice should continue to be handled by the police, but subject to safeguards. Against a general rule that random selection should be observed, the police were advised that the rule could be diverted from 'where strong political motives were involved.' This vague formulation was later changed to cases in which national security was involved and to 'terrorist cases'.[44] The aim was to ensure that jurors were 'well inclined towards their king's and country's service and interest.'[45] In the light of the history of trial by jury this appears to be a case of *plus ça change.*

MAJORITY VERDICTS

At first jurors must still attempt to reach the centuries-old requirement of a unanimous verdict. But if they cannot agree after two hours, or a longer time if the judge thinks it appropriate, they will be instructed that they may return a verdict by a majority of at least ten to two or at least nine when the jury has been reduced to ten or eleven.[46] If the verdict is guilty they will be asked to tell the court whether it was by a majority and what the majority was. This enables the Court of Appeal to take it into account when considering whether it is a safe finding.[47] If the verdict is not guilty, the jury will not be asked if it was by a majority. This is to prevent prejudice to the defendant.

Officially, the change to majority verdicts in certain circumstances was introduced, it was said by the government, to avoid growing intimidation and bribing of jurors although the expense of retrials was very likely also a factor. In fact, the home secretary of the day, James Callaghan, could produce no evidence of intimidation or bribery when questioned in the House of Commons beyond three allegations of intimidation reported to the police in 1966, none of which resulted in a prosecution.[48] No research on the question was carried out by a Royal Commission or anybody else and a 600-year-old rule was simply abandoned. It was, said *The Times,* 'not rational reform but fumbling in the dark.'[49]

It has been argued, in an Anglo-American debate held in an endeavour to secure majority verdicts in the USA, that unanimity is no longer required in England because, although it may have been necessary to ensure a fair trial for a defendant in those times when a defendant had few rights, in modern times he or she enjoys many trial safeguards.[50] It is also suggested that it gives the jury more power and avoids hung juries.[51] These are questionable assumptions (although a rogue juror can sometimes present a problem) and there can be no doubt that the idea of majority verdicts can undermine the presumption of innocence and the necessity of proving guilt beyond reasonable doubt. Jury tampering has occurred but there is no clear evidence that it is widespread. In the Anglo-American debate one participant pointed out that 'the deliberations don't take quite as long if all you really need is ten votes to convict; the view of the dissenters, the two opposing jurors, becomes irrelevant.'[52] There is also the possibility that they may well withdraw from taking an active part in the jury's deliberations.

So far as the 'reasonable doubt' test is concerned, in 1979 Lord Scarman held that it was whether the jury felt sure of the defendant's guilt.[53] It is of interest that when Professor Michael Zander conducted research for the Auld Report among 1,763 members of the public, 1,364 magistrates and 128 criminal justice professionals, he found that 51 per cent of the public and 31 per cent of the magistrates and professionals considered that 'sure' meant 100 per cent proof of guilt.[54] This may explain the higher acquittal rate by juries than by magistrates, although Zander thinks the evidence insufficient to draw that conclusion. However, three-quarters of both the general public sample and of the magistrates' sample said they would need to be at least 90 per cent sure before convicting and that suggests, says Zander, that most people, whatever their role and experience of the system, take the business of convicting very seriously.[55]

Nevertheless, there are, of course, opponents of the jury system. In the nineteenth century Sir James Fitzjames Stephen thought that a jury of 12 was 'a group just large enough to destroy even the appearance of individual responsibility'[56] although in general he was favourable. It is sometimes said that jurors are not capable of dealing with some very complex cases, particularly where fraud is involved. Individual jurors can be intimidated or may be corrupt or biased, which is one of the reasons why, it was said, majority verdicts were introduced by the Criminal Justice Act in 1967. Jury trials are more expensive than trials by a judge sitting alone, as indicated by the James Report.[57] But in spite of these defects, real or otherwise, judges, who have worked with juries over many years have praised the system including Coke, Hale, Blackstone, Stephen, Devlin and Denning. Seemingly, many members of the public are content with the system and many defendants who plead not guilty to a serious charge prefer, when they have the choice, to be dealt with by a judge and jury at the Crown Court rather than by magistrates, even though the range of penalties available in the Crown Court is higher.

THE AULD REPORT

Generally speaking, in his 2001 report Sir Robin Auld put with clarity the arguments of many of those who wish to dilute the jury system, or abandon it altogether, and he made a number of proposals some of which have since been included in the Criminal Justice Act 2003. They therefore bear consideration, particularly as those of his proposals that have not so far been adopted may appear in future legislation, since making inroads into the jury is a continuing process, in the main on the ground of cost.

Dispensing with the jury

Auld considered the possibility of the trial of cases on indictment being heard without a jury and *inter alia* proposed:[58]

- the defendant have the option of being tried by a judge alone. This proposal was dropped from the Criminal Justice Bill by the Government after opposition from the House of Lords;
- with either-way offences—cases triable either on indictment or before magistrates—to empower the magistrates' court, instead of the defendant who pleads not guilty, to decide where and how he or she is to be tried;
- to allow the court to dispense with a jury in cases of serious or complex fraud. Now, the Act enables the prosecution to apply to a judge in such cases for them to be conducted without a jury and also for the judge to order 'judge alone' trial as indicated later in the chapter. In reaching his or her decision the judge must consider whether the complexity or length of the trial makes it so burdensome to the members of a jury that the jury is dispensed with in the interests of justice;
- to extend the provision for trial without jury to young defendants under 18 years of age. This would mean that for the first time young people could be tried for serious offences, including murder, without the benefit of a jury;
- to amend the law to require a judge, instead of a jury to determine the issue of fitness to plead.

There cannot be any doubt, after reading his report, that Sir Robin Auld did not view the jury in a very flattering light and this led him to make certain proposals, many of which have been acted upon by the Government and have reduced the role of the jury further than had occurred in the recent past.

Auld accepted that the jury is often described as the 'jewel in the Crown' of the British (*sic*) criminal justice system and that it commands much public confidence. Judges and lawyers, he said, consider that in general, juries 'get it right' and for most it is also an important incident of citizenship.[59] However, he added that support for it is not universal and he downgraded its importance by stressing on a number of occasions that only about one per cent of criminal cases in England and Wales culminate in trial by jury.[60] That may be correct as a percentage figure (although many of those tried by magistrates plead guilty) but every working day scores of defendants are undergoing jury trial in Crown Court centres across the land and more than 250,000 people serve on juries each year.[61] What Auld did not explain is why, if so few cases reach a jury, it is necessary to reduce that percentage even further by means of proposals which will be considered shortly.

As indicated earlier, Auld claimed that there is no right to trial by judge and jury.[62] This is a view echoed by Penny Darbyshire, a researcher for Auld, who writes that the jury is a symbol to legitimate the criminal justice system and the defendant has no real right to a jury.[63] However, it is a curious symbol that has played such a significant and prominent part in the political and legal history of the country for some nine centuries and it is untrue to suggest that such a right does not exist or is a figment of some people's imaginations. It appears that Auld and Darbyshire are saying that there was no right to claim jury trial until the 'either-way' system was introduced in 1855. In doing so they ignore the fact that prior to that date a defendant did not need to make such a claim as all indictable offences were tried before a jury. In any event, they are glossing over the distinction between the right to a jury trial and the right to *elect for* a jury trial.[64]

Auld also said that sadly juries did not prevent the miscarriages of justice uncovered in the late 1980s and early 1990s (mentioned in *Chapter 9*) that shook public confidence.[65] But nor did the judges in those cases indicate the problems in their directions to the juries and, as Lord Devlin has said, 'in trial by jury the judge may sometimes play a more significant part than the jury itself.'[66] Furthermore, it seems unfair to select the juries alone for Sir Robin's displeasure when both they and the judges were misguided by police and forensic evidence that was subsequently proved to be false.

Ethnic minorities
In 1993 Lord Runciman's Royal Commission on Criminal Justice reported that, nationally, ethnic minority communities were not seriously under-represented on juries.[67] Nonetheless, six years later, Home Office research showed that about 24 per cent of black people, 15 per cent of those from the Indian sub-continent and 24 per cent of other ethnic minorities were not registered on the electoral roll and therefore were not eligible for jury service.[68]

In 1989, the Court of Appeal held that a judge had no power to influence the composition of the jury in cases with a 'racial dimension'[69] and, indeed, to do so would be to deny the principle of random selection. However, earlier there were a number of cases where judges ensured representation of minorities on a jury trying a minority defendant. And for over five centuries members of minorities such as Jews, Germans and Italians had the right to be tried by a jury comprised of half Englishmen and half foreigners (not necessarily of the same nationality of the defendant). For example, in the trial of John Henry Aikles at the Old Bailey on 14 January 1784, he claimed he was a Hessian and a jury were sworn of whom half were Hessians.[70] Such a jury was called a *jury de mediate linguae* (of half tongue).[71] As its existence suggested that the English legal system was prejudiced it was abolished, but not until 1870. Auld recommended that, for cases where the court considers that race is likely to be relevant to an issue of importance in the case, there should be selection of a jury with up to three people from any ethnic minority group.[72] However, this could lead to other minority groups such as homosexuals or feminists demanding similar treatment and was not accepted by government.

Jury to explain its verdict

According to Auld, the jury is unique among decision-makers in the English criminal trial process in not having to explain its decisions, and it is unclear whether the oracular verdict satisfies Article 6 of the European Convention On Human Rights in its requirement of a reasoned decision.[73] But, although the question has not been decided by the Strasbourg Court, it has held in *Condron v. United Kingdom* that 'the fact that the issue of the applicant(s)' silence was left to a jury cannot of itself be incompatible with the requirement of a fair trial.'[74] This, said Auld, 'suggests that the court is amenable to accepting the jury's verdict as the final word in a judgment of which the summing-up furnishes the overt reasoning process.'[75] It was not approved by Auld, however, who cited Sir Louis Blom-Cooper QC., as saying that a publicly unaccountable jury is a 'curiosity' in today's democratic society.[76]

It follows logically that Auld also proposed that section 8 Contempt of Court Act 1981 be amended to permit, where appropriate, enquiry by the trial judge and/or the Court of Appeal into alleged impropriety by a jury, whether in the course of its deliberations or otherwise.[77] This would take us back to the position before *Bushell's Case* (see *Chapter 5*) and, with forcing the jury to answer questions publicly, which he also proposed, might well spell the end of the independent jury as we know it. Finally, by law the judge must sum up to the jury[78] and the Court of Appeal agreed with Auld in considering judges' instructions to be part of the requirements of a fair trial laid down by article 6 of the European Convention On Human Rights.[79]

Modern nullification

The 'dispensing' ability of the jury still obtains and was used, for example, in 1974 when a jury acquitted 14 pacifists charged with conspiracy to contravene the Incitement to Disaffection Act 1934 by distributing leaflets to soldiers. The verdict was in open defiance of a direction by the judge that the defendants had clearly contravened the statute.[80]

The acquittal on a murder charge of O.J. Simpson in the USA in 1995 is perhaps a classic example of jury nullification.[81] And, nearer home, on 18 January 2001 a jury at Manchester Crown Court found two activists who attempted to damage a Trident nuclear submarine not guilty of conspiracy to commit criminal damage.[82] There have also been some noteworthy examples of trials carefully confined to the magistrates' courts by a charging policy that reduced the value of criminal damage to an amount below the level at which defendants could elect for jury trial. Such cases occurred during the miners' strike of 1984-5 and on one occasion at Greenham Common when one million pounds worth of criminal damage was reduced to criminal damage to a fence in order to avoid jury trial.

Nullification has also been famously exercised in recent times in the cases of Clive Ponting, and Randle and Pottle, and shown by a number of acquittals in cases of alleged criminal damage to jet aircraft by anti-war and environmental campaigners where juries have ignored directions from the bench. In one such case, in 1996, four women were acquitted of damaging a British Aerospace Hawk jet in protest against the sale of such jets to foreign countries.[83]

Ponting's case from 1985 is of particular interest. He was a senior civil servant in the Ministry of Defence, tried under section 2(1) of the Official Secrets Act 1911 for leaking classified documents to a Member of Parliament. His defence centred on the argument that the disclosure was permitted by the statute if it was 'in the interests of the state.' However, the judge held that the 'interests of state' were not for the jury to decide. No proof of *mens rea* beyond an intention to commit the *actus rea* was necessary. Nevertheless, apparently following their consciences, the jury acquitted Ponting.[84]

Randle and Pottle were acquitted in 1991 of helping in the escape of the spy George Blake from Wormwood Scrubs prison despite an explicit admission of having done so published three years earlier in their book *The Blake Escape: How We Freed George Blake and Why*.[85] There have also been several examples in England and Wales in 2000-01 of jury acquittals of people charged with possessing cannabis when their defence has been that it relieved the symptoms of the disease multiple sclerosis.[86] Similarly, because the crime of murder involves an intention to kill, in a case before Lord Goff the jury refused to accept that two defendants who killed a man were guilty of murder when they believed they had not intended to kill him. Lord Goff indicates that it must have been plain to the jury that what was intended was serious bodily harm and they declined to find murder and brought in a verdict of manslaughter.[87]

According to Blake, '[t]he importance of juries as a protection against oppression by the state is as important this century as it has been in the past.'[88] Nonetheless, although jury sympathy does still play a part there appears to be no generally comparable situation with the pious perjury and partial verdicts of the eighteenth and nineteenth centuries discussed in earlier chapters. The situation then was different, with the death penalty all-pervading even for minor felonies.

Mode of trial

Auld reported that at the time of his report 'either-way' cases were approximately one quarter of the total workload of the criminal courts and around eleven per cent of them were committed to the Crown Court for trial.[89] The Crown Prosecution Service (CPS) estimates that about 30 per cent of committals for trial occur at the election of the accused. Some 22,000 defendants charged with either-way offences elected to be tried in the Crown court in 1997 even though the magistrates were willing to try them.[90] One researcher concluded from her sample that with such offences, the rate of acquittal was about twice as high in the Crown Court as in the magistrates' courts.[91]

The Lord Chief Justice first revised the *Mode of Trial Guidelines* in 1995, to say that either-way offences should be dealt with summarily, in the absence of aggravating circumstances.[92] Subsequently, the Government has tried twice to reduce further the role of jury trial in such cases. First, in November 1999 with a Criminal Justice (Mode of Trial) Bill[93] to provide that courts, not defendants, should decide where all either-way cases should be tried. The purpose, it was said, was to secure an annual reduction of about 12,000 Crown Court trials, producing a net yearly saving of £105 million. The cost of the justice system is a frequent preoccupation of governments. The Bill was supported by those least inclined to approve of jury trial including some judges, magistrates and police. As the Bill would have meant for those it affected putting one's livelihood and reputation in the hands of a single judge it was vehemently opposed by lawyers involved in criminal work, civil liberties organizations and ethnic minority groups including the Commission for Racial Equality. After all, it can be claimed, any offence serious enough to involve a sentence of imprisonment is serious enough to justify allowing the defendant to choose trial by jury. Following heated debate in the House of Lords the Bill was defeated.[94]

Undaunted, in February 2000 the Government introduced a new Criminal Justice (Mode of Trial) (No. 2) Bill.[95] This reduced the discretionary powers of magistrates in making mode of trial decisions and provided that they should give reasons for their decisions. It passed the Commons after a three-line whip and the guillotine but was also defeated in the Lords, this time even more decisively, partly on the ground that it would have denied jury trial to many who are at present committed to the Crown Court for trial. This time the Government promised not only similar legislation in the future but also, if necessary, the use of the Parliament Act 1911 to secure its enactment. After considering, and rejecting the validity of, reasons why defendants choose jury trial Auld supported the Government's proposals subject to appeal on paper to a circuit judge.

THE WHITE PAPER AND CRIMINAL JUSTICE ACT 2003

The 2002 White Paper, *Justice for All,*[96] contained a good many useful suggestions that are designed to ensure that justice is done both more speedily and more often. However, it contemplated 'fairer and more effective trials' without spelling out what these terms meant. Fairer to whom—the defendants, the victims or the witnesses? Does more effective mean quicker, cheaper, more 'correct' results? Or are these terms a code for more findings of guilt and fewer criminals getting off on technical grounds?[97]

According to the White Paper the quality of the electoral register is to be improved to ensure in particular that more people from minority ethnic communities are registered.[98] In addition, as already indicated, the list of those no longer exempt from jury service includes judges, lawyers, doctors, dentists, vets, nurses, ministers of religion and peers. This reflects the view that the age of deference to professionals and those in positions of authority is past and that denying exemptions will probably improve the quality of juries. Nevertheless, there is a problem with having judges, lawyers and others involved in the criminal justice system on the jury. They may, for instance, know the prosecution and defence barristers, they will know why if the defendant does not put his character in evidence and they will be able to draw conclusions if they know some evidence has been disallowed.

The concern of Government ministers is that acquittal rates are too high in many parts of the country where juries are considered to be unrepresentative. There seems to be an underlying suggestion that in many cases the guilty walk away free. But why, it may be asked, is it wrong for juries to acquit people? Convicting more people is acceptable if it is clear they are guilty, but how clear can it be if a jury is unconvinced? In fact, figures which are very significant have been given by Richard Foster, chief executive of the CPS. He says that the CPS deals with 1.4 million potential prosecutions every year and of those they prosecute in the magistrates' courts 98 per cent are convicted and in the Crown Court 88 per cent are convicted.[99] The question that might be asked on these figures is not how many guilty defendants go free but how many innocent defendants are convicted?

The White Paper dealt with criminal justice generally, not just with juries, and many of its proposals to improve the system, including the police and the CPS, and search for the truth in trials are welcome. Nevertheless its proposals on the jury and rules of evidence needed careful scrutiny. As intimated earlier, certain rules of evidence came into existence precisely to avoid juries being misled.[100] The Criminal Justice Act 2003 contains an extensive reworking of longstanding rules of evidence alongside changes in the jury system. The presumption of innocence has so far been preserved but due to a re-alignment of sentencing powers as between the Crown Court and the magistrates' courts jury trial will effectively end with many defendants wondering whether to risk a sentence above 12 months if they chose trial by jury.[101] The background is the Government's belief that a number of changes on evidence and procedure were needed to strengthen the hand of prosecutors. Why it should be assumed that many acquitted defendants are in fact guilty is not clear. Nevertheless, not all Auld's proposals to reduce the right to elect jury trial were incorporated in the 2003 Act and nor was that for a new 'middle-tier' court.

Under the 2003 Act, judges in the Crown Court are now allowed to hear trials sitting alone where there is a 'real and present' danger of jury tampering and it is in the interests of justice to do so.[102] When the relevant clause in the Criminal Justice Bill was debated in the House of Commons on 19 May 2003 the home secretary said that it would apply to fewer than 100 cases a year and denied this was a 'slippery slope' towards the end of the right to trial by jury. This was challenged in the debate in the House of Commons by Q.C.s Robert Marshall-Andrews MP and Vera Baird MP, who said it was 'the beginning of the end for jury trial' which she predicted would disappear by the end of the decade.[103] Moreover, judges are given powers to dismiss a jury in the course of a trial and sit alone if the jury is being intimidated or possibly where there is a 'serious risk that the jury will be subject to bribery or intimidation'. Although the defendant's existing right to elect for trial by jury will be retained as an issue of principle, it is to be kept under review.

Juveniles are not generally tried by a jury. The 5,000 young offenders who do at present go to the Crown Court for trial each year will in future come before a youth court. For serious charges this will consist of a judge and two lay magistrates.

Double jeopardy

The double jeopardy rule, a basic principle of the criminal justice system which prevents an individual being re-tried for a crime of which he or she had already been acquitted, is some 800 years old. The emphasis is, however, on the words 'for which he or she has already been acquitted.' Because jeopardy 'attaches' at the outset of a criminal trial, in modern times the double jeopardy rule has prohibited the prosecution or the court from interrupting a case that was going badly in order to try it afresh on another day before another jury. Once there is a second trial, the defendant is in jeopardy a second time for the same offence. However, in the seventh century jeopardy did not attach until the jury's verdict was entered.[104] Hale noted that whilst Coke's *Institutes* say that a case cannot be withdrawn from a jury:

> yet the contrary course hath for a long time obtained at Newgate and nothing is more ordinary than after the jury sworn, and charged with a prisoner, and evidence given, yet if it appear to the court, that some of the evidence is kept back, or taken off, or that there may be a fuller discovery, and the offence notorious, as murder or burglary, and that the evidence, though not sufficient to convict the prisoner, yet gives the court a great and strong suspicion of his guilt, the court may discharge the jury of the prisoner, and remit him to the jail for farther evidence, and accordingly it hath been practised in most circuits of *England*, for otherwise many notorious murders and burglaries may pass unpunished by the acquittal of a person probably guilty, where the full evidence is not searched out or given.[105]

Thus, in the case of Hugh Coleman, tried for bigamy, when the court saw that the evidence would be insufficient to convict, it apparently halted the trial short of any verdict and 'advised the wives to provide themselves with better evidence, till which time he was to be secured.'[106]

The principle of double jeopardy has now been withdrawn retrospectively in certain cases. Where someone has been acquitted of a serious offence such as murder, kidnap, armed robbery or rape, the Court of Appeal can quash the acquittal and order a retrial if it is in the interests of justice to do so and there is compelling new evidence that is reliable, substantial and makes it highly probable that the defendant is guilty.[107] It is difficult to see how, notwithstanding the direction of the judge, the second jury will remain untainted, especially in high profile cases.

Both a new police investigation and a re-trial will be subject to the personal consent of the Director of Public Prosecutions, and is, says the Home Secretary, David Blunkett, justified by the development of DNA profiling technology and forensic science.[108] Nevertheless, what is to stop the prosecution or the court from interrupting a case that is going badly in order to get a second opportunity later, as judges once did according to Hale? And introducing '*compelling* new evidence' might well indicate to a jury that the defendant is guilty.

Previous convictions

Before the Criminal Justice Act 2003 a defendant could be cross-examined on his or her previous convictions only if he or she attacked the character of the prosecutor or his or her witnesses.[109] The question of previous convictions is a difficult one as is shown by the convoluted law of similar fact evidence, where it is considered by the judges that similar previous acts can be submitted in evidence. They also decided that evidence of a propensity to commit certain types of crimes is not permissible whereas previous convictions which show a method or habit are.

A case that was worrying to many people was that of Nicholas Edwards heard at the Old Bailey in September 2000.[110] Edwards, aged 39, was found guilty of raping

Miss D, aged 25, after the jury were allowed by a House of Lords ruling to hear evidence (i) from four women who had earlier gone to court claiming Edwards had raped them even though he was acquitted; and (ii) from a woman whom he was jailed for raping. The ruling was based on the ground that the women's testimonies established a pattern of behaviour that was strikingly similar to the evidence in the present case and outweighed any prejudice against the accused, despite the fact that it could be argued that the prejudicial value of four women giving evidence that he had raped them was so overwhelming that it could never be outweighed.

This set a new precedent not only on similar fact evidence but, to some extent, although not in theory, in also overruling the rule of double jeopardy. The law lords held that the rule would not be breached by allowing the women to give evidence since the defendant was not charged with and would not be at risk of conviction of the earlier rapes, but only on the alleged rape for which he was standing trial. Their evidence was relevant and admissible as similar fact evidence despite the previous acquittal.

Nevertheless it remained a principle that in general a verdict should be based on the evidence given in court and not on what the defendant has done on other occasions. Otherwise what had happened to the presumption of innocence? And might not the police arrest suspects on the basis of knowledge of previous offences and hope that the revelation of past convictions (or acquittals) would be a substitute for evidence? But the White Paper proposed that not only the judge but juries also should be told of a defendant's previous convictions and acquittals, 'or anything else suggesting a criminal tendency', if sufficiently relevant in the view of the judge[111] and this approach is included in the Criminal Justice Act 2003 under the rubric, 'evidence of bad character'.[112]

The White Paper conceded that research undertaken for the Law Commission showed that knowledge of previous convictions might prejudice a jury unfairly against the defendant.[113] Nonetheless, in a worrying display, it gave examples of imaginary cases where previous convictions or, what is even worse, anything suggesting a criminal tendency should be admissible. The first two examples go well beyond previous convictions and are particularly disturbing—although the remaining four examples are equally suspect.

Example 1:

A doctor is charged with indecent assault against a patient. He denies that any indecency took place. Two separate patients in the last five years have made similar complaints resulting in separate trials. On both occasions the doctor has been *acquitted.*

The matter in issue is whether the complainant is telling the truth when she says that the indecency took place, or the accused when he says it did not. It *defies belief* that it could only be an unlucky coincidence that *this number of patients* have made this kind of allegation and therefore the previous allegations are of clear probative value. The judge should therefore be able to rule that the jury should hear of the previous *allegations,* taking into account the other evidence in the case and the *risk that undue weight might be put upon them.'* [114] (author's italics)

So here we have not even previous convictions but previous acquittals, a 'defying of belief' and a recognition that a risk exists in putting in this so-called evidence. Does it really defy belief that three allegations in five years is an unlucky coincidence? Doctors are very vulnerable to this kind of allegation and if the possibility of coincidence 'defies belief' it must logically follow that the previous allegations (of which he was acquitted) are not merely of 'clear probative value' but proof of guilt.

Example 2:

D is charged with assaulting his wife. He has a history of violence including a number of convictions for assault occasioning actual bodily harm and there are witness accounts of him striking his wife in the past. D claims she received her injuries falling down [the] stairs. In this case the previous conduct could be thought relevant to determining whether the allegations of violence or D's version of events are true. The Judge should be able to rule whether this is admissible, provided he is satisfied it can be put in its proper context to the jury.[115]

In this example the case against the defendant is clearly that he has a propensity for violence, the inference being that if he has done it before he is likely to have done it again. As with the first example, if the judge allows the evidence of previous incidents to be heard he or she is effectively determining the verdict.[116] This is a long way from trying defendants on the facts of the case alone and with a presumption of innocence.

One recent experiment examining the effects of revealing a previous conviction to simulated jurors concludes that its results clearly confirm that evidence of previous convictions can have a prejudicial effect and that 'If we assume that amongst defendants with similar previous convictions, some are innocent of the current offence, we have good grounds to infer that routinely revealing previous convictions would indeed increase the risk of convicting an innocent man.'[117]

Hearsay

At the same time hearsay evidence—evidence that is second-hand and not given by a witness in court—has also become admissible in some cases[118] having been seen as 'another area ripe for change.'[119] Yet cross-examination is at the heart of our trial system and the change means the loss of the fundamental value of a witness being cross-examined and having his or her veracity assessed by the jury—something that Hale insisted upon four centuries ago.[120] It raises the question: why did these exclusionary rules exist? As Langbein, who on the whole opposes them, has said,

> The danger that inexperienced laymen rendering conclusory and unassailable judgments might err in matters of life and death has led to the development of prophylactic safeguards at the trial stage. The information about the case that is allowed to reach the jurors is filtered through rules of evidence that are meant to exclude types of information whose import the jurors might misapprehend. The hearsay rule and the rule excluding evidence of past criminal convictions typify this exclusionary system.[121]

CONCLUSION

Early in the twentieth century, women became eligible for jury service for the first time but, apart from that important advance, major changes did not occur until the second half of the century. Then the composition of the jury was widened to include, with certain exceptions, all those on the electoral register so that the majority of the people could now take part in the administration of justice. But, because of this democratisation of the jury, there have been continued efforts by both parties in governments of different hues to diminish the range of cases in which juries are involved. The right of the defence to challenge jurors has been reduced almost out of existence, majority verdicts now occur and the vetting of jurors by the police continues in certain cases, subject to guidelines.

It is significant that the bringing of virtually everyone whose name is on the electoral register into the jury system by the Criminal Justice Act 2003 is a radical democratisation which involves a greater change to the whole concept of the jury, as hitherto understood within the constitution, than any change before. It means, that for the first time, the composition of the jury really will reflect the community. The reason for the change in Auld's view was to dispel the impression 'that jury service was only for those not important or clever enough to get out of it.'[122] But, it is ironic that such a fundamental change has occurred just at the time when successive governments have been engaged in reducing the role of the jury.

The jurisdiction of magistrates has seen a remarkable expansion since the mid-1800s until they now deal with some 97 per cent of criminal cases.[123] Juries are rarely used in the High Court, except in libel cases, and in general trial by jury has declined in the last hundred years. As is shown by the foregoing, this has particularly been the case in the second half of the twentieth century but even so there has been a renewed and serious assault on criminal trial by jury in the twenty-first century. The threat to criminal jury trial is clearly an ongoing phenomenon.

Nullification by juries, particularly on what they consider to be serious issues and morality, still continues but in general it is difficult to quantify owing to the secrecy surrounding what goes on in the jury room and what juries may tell afterwards. It might seem unlikely to be on a scale seriously to disturb anyone but Lord Justice Auld took strong exception to it in his report, going so far as to claim that it should be made unlawful.

All this on the basis that jury trial and such rights are harmful to prosecutions and enable too many criminals to go free. But it seems difficult to provide any objective proof of this. Some, like Penny Darbyshire, have argued that it would help if section 8 of the Contempt of Court Act 1988 were amended to enable research into how juries work to be carried out inside and outside the jury room, but the Government have rejected this. In any event, the jury system has the confidence of the public and has:

> a built-in mechanism for sustaining the public trust which supports it. For it continually draws ordinary members of the community into the workings of the courts, instructs them briefly in the processes of the law, and then returns them to their ordinary lives generally well satisfied with the community duty which they have undertaken, and with the functioning of the administration of justice.[124]

As we have seen, to Blackstone in the 1830s the jury of his day was the 'sacred bulwark of the nation'[125] and a foundation stone of liberty, and so it may still be considered. It has been described by Lord Devlin as a lamp of freedom and he went on to say:

Each jury is a little Parliament. The jury sense is the Parliamentary sense. I cannot see the one dying and the other surviving. The first object of any tyrant in Whitehall would be to make Parliament utterly subservient to his will; and the next to overthrow or diminish trial by jury, for no tyrant could afford to leave a subject's freedom in the hands of twelve of his countrymen.[126]

So that trial by jury is more than an instrument of justice and more than one wheel of the constitution: it is the lamp that shows that freedom lives.[127]

Auld, on the other hand, saw it as an obstacle to obtaining convictions in some cases. He claimed—wrongly, it has been argued in this chapter— that there is no such thing as a right to jury trial and that the system should be further restricted. He then proposed, and it has been enacted, that the option of jury trial be taken away from some 6,000 adults and 5,000 young offenders a year. Following his lead and the arguments in the White Paper, *Justice for All*, based upon his report, the Criminal Justice Act 2003 has ensured that the safeguards for defendants of the principle of double jeopardy, and not allowing juries to know of previous convictions or to hear hearsay evidence have all been severely diminished.

It is little wonder that, on 18 July 2002, *The Times* wrote in dismay that 'some of the proposals of the White Paper risked corrupting the justice system. They would deny human rights, increase the chance of miscarriages of justice and lead to sloppier police and prosecution work.' Since then the Act, incorporating many but not all of the proposals of the White Paper, has become law. Moreover, those not included in the Act may well resurface in the future.

ENDNOTES for *Chapter 8*

[1] Sex Disqualification (Removal) Act 1919.

[2] Lord Morris Committee on Jury Service. (1965) Cmnd. 2627.

[3] Nicholas Blake. (1988) 'The Case for the Jury.' In Mark Findlay and Peter Duff. *The Jury Under Attack*. London, Butterworths Property Ltd. p. 142.

[4] See, for example, Lord Devlin post. p. 126.

[5] Sir Robin Auld. (2001) *Review of the Criminal Courts of England and Wales*. (The Auld Report). London, HMSO.

[6] London, HMSO. Cm. 5563.

[7] Eliz. II, c. 44.

[8] Equal Franchise Act 1928.

[9] Representation of the People Act 1969.

[10] See H.H. Asquith. (1928) *Memories and Reflection.1852-1929*. London, Cassell, p. 140. For the impact of the suffragettes see Martin Pugh. (1980) *Women's Suffrage in Britain 1867-1928*. London, The Historical Association and (2001) *The Pankhursts*. London, Allen Lane.

[11] A.P. Sealy & W.R. Cornish. (1973) 'Jurors and their Verdicts.' 36 *The Modern Law Review*. London, Stevens & Sons Ltd. p.499.

[12] *R. v. Sutton* [1969] Crim.L.R. 402.

[13] Sec. 35(7), Courts Act 1971.

[14] W.R. Cornish. (1968) *The Jury*. London, Allen Lane. p.28.

[15] Lord Devlin (Sir Patrick Devlin). (1956) *Trial by Jury*. London, Methuen. p. 20.

[16] Morris Committee. Op. cit. paras. 41-43.

[17] Ibid. paras. 45-48 and 53-64.

[18] Criminal Justice Act 1972.

[19] Juries Act 1974.

[20] Criminal Justice Act 2003. Schedule 33.

[21] *Auld Report*. Op. cit. p. 147.

22 Ibid.

23 Criminal Justice Act 2003. Schedule 33.

24 Devlin. *Trial by Jury.* Op. cit. p. 121.

25 Sir Thomas Skyrme.(1979) *The Changing Image of the Magistracy.* London, The Macmillan Press Ltd. p. 5.

26 The James Committee. (1975) *The Distribution of the Criminal Business between the Crown Courts and the Magistrates' Courts. Report of the Interdepartmental Committee.* Cmnd. 6323. paras. 60-61.

27 Criminal Law Act 1977. ss. 15 and 22, schedule 4.

28 Ss. 37-39.

29 Royal Commission on Criminal Justice. 1993. Cm. 2263.

30 The Magistrates' Courts Act 1980, as amended.

31 The Auld Report. Op. cit. p. 138.

32 Peter Duff. (2000) 'The Defendant's Right to Trial by Jury; A Neighbour's View.' *The Criminal Law Review.* London, Sweet & Maxwell. p. 93.

33 Ibid. p. 94.

34 The James Committee. Op. cit.

35 White Paper. *Justice for All.* Op. cit. c. 4.20.

36 (December 2001) *Home Office Criminal Statistics for England and Wales 2000.* Cm. 5312. p. 20.

37 The Criminal Law Act 1977. Cf. Sally Lloyd-Bostock and Cheryl Thomas. (1999) 'Decline of the "Little Parliament": Juries and Jury Reform in England and Wales.' 62 *Law and Contemporary Problems.* Duke University School of Law. Durham, North Carolina. p. 24.

38 M.D.A. Freeman. (1981) 'The Jury on Trial.' 34 *Current Legal Problems.* London, Stevens & Sons. p. 72.

39 *The Times.* 27 April 1977.

40 Criminal Justice Act 1988, s. 118(1).

41 *R. v. Ford.* [1989] 3 All ER. 445.

42 88 Cr. App. R. 123.

43 Sean Enright & James Morton. (1990) *Taking Liberties. The Criminal Jury in the 1990's.* London, Weidenfeld and Nicolson. pp. 40-41.

44 The guidelines are set out in an appendix to Freeman. 'The Jury on Trial'. Op. cit. pp. 98-101.

45 See E. P. Thompson. (1980) *Writing by Candlelight.* London, The Merlin Press. pp. 103-6.

46 Criminal Justice Act 1967. Juries Act 1974, s. 17.

47 *R. v. Wallett.* [1968] 2 All E.R. p. 296.

48 Blake. 'The Case for the Jury.' Op. cit. p. 143.

49 *The Times.* 4 April 1967.

50 Eugene R. Sullivan and Akhil R. Amar. (1996) 'Jury Reform in America—A Return to the Old Country.' 33 *American Criminal Law Review.* Illinois University Press. p. 1141.

51 Ibid.

52 Ibid. p. 1153.

53 *Ferguson v. The Queen.* [1979] All E.R. 877.

54 Michael Zander. (2000) 'The Criminal Standard of Proof—how sure is sure?' London, 150 *New Law Journal.* p. 1517.

55 Ibid. p. 1519.

56 James Fitzjames Stephen. (1883) *A History of English Criminal Law.* London, Macmillan. vol. i. p. 568.

57 The James Report. Op. cit.

58 *Auld Report.* Op. cit. p. 177.

59 *Auld Report.* Op. cit. p. 135.

60 Ibid . e. g. Appendix IV.

61 Lloyd-Bostock and Thomas. 'Decline of the "Little Parliament": Op. cit.. p. 28.

62 *Auld Report.* Op. cit. pp. 137-8.

63 Penny Darbyshire. (1991) 'The Lamp That Shows That Freedom Lives –Is it Worth the Candle?' *The Criminal Law Review.* London, Sweet & Maxwell. p. 744.

64 Lloyd-Bostock and Thomas. 'Decline of the "Little Parliament". Op. cit. p. 17.

65 *Auld Report.* Op. cit. p. 139.

66 Lord Devlin. (1991) 'The Conscience of the Jury'. 107 *The Law Quarterly Review.* London, Stevens & Sons. p. 398.

67 *Royal Commission on Criminal Justice.* (1993) chap. 8. para. 62.

68 *Research Findings No 102.* (1999) Home Office Research, Development and Statistics Directorate.

69 *R. v. Royston Ford.* [1989] 89 Cr. App. R. 278.

[70] Old Bailey Proceedings Online. (www.oldbaileyonline.org2003). January 1784. trial of John Henry Aikles. (t17840114-80).

[71] Penny Darbyshire and others. (2001) 'What Can the English Legal System Learn From Jury Research Published up to 2001?' Internet. http// www.kingston.ac.uk/~ku00596.elsres01.pdf Commissioned for the Auld Report.

[72] *Auld Report.* Op. cit. p. 159.

[73] Ibid. p. 168.

[74] (2000) 31 EHRR1 at para. 57.

[75] Auld Report. Op. cit. p. 171.

[76] (2001) EHRLR, p. 5.

[77] *Auld Report.* Op. cit. p. 173.

[78] *R. v. Bowerman.* [2000] 2 Cr. App. R. 189 (CA).

[79] *R. v. Francom.* [2000] 1 Cr. App. R. 237. (CA).

[80] Blake. 'The Case for the Jury.' Op. cit. p. 141.

[81] Internet. www.Oj+Simpson+Trial&ac

[82] Internet. www.wcp.gn.apc.org/Jan01.htm

[83] *Financial Times.* 6 August 1996.

[84] *R. v. Ponting.* (1985) Central Criminal Court. And see J.C. Smith and D.J. Birch. (1985) 'Case and Comment—R. v. Ponting.' *Criminal Law Review.* London. Sweet and Maxwell. p. 320.

[85] *Cf. R. v. Central Criminal Court. Ex parte Randle & Anor.* (1992). 1 All ER. 370. And Randle and Pottle. (1989) *The Blake Escape: How we freed George Blake and why.* London, Harrap.

[86] Darbyshire *et al.* 'What Can the English Legal System Learn?' Op. cit. p. 34.

[87] R. Goff. (1988) 'The Mental Element in the Crime of Murder.' 104 *Law Quarterly Review.* London, Stevens and Sons Ltd. p. 30.

[88] Blake. 'The Case for the Jury.' Op. cit. p. 141.

[89] *Auld Report.* Op. cit. p. 193.

[90] Home Office. (1998) *Determining Mode of Trial in Either-way Cases.* p. 2.

[91] J. Vennard. (1985) 'The Outcome of Contested Trials.' in D. Moxon (ed.) *Managing Criminal Justice.* London, HMSO. p. 131.

[92] Ibid. p. 630.

[93] HMSO. AJ1000150.

[94] *Auld Report.* Op. cit. p. 191.

[95] HMSO. AJ1000225.

[96] Cm. 5563.

[97] Brian P. Block. (2002) 'The White Paper and the Rules of Evidence.' *Justice of the Peace.* London, Butterworths. vol. 166. p. 893. See also, particularly, *Chapter 4 of Justice for All.*

[98] *White Paper.* Op. cit. chap. 7. 28.

[99] *The Times.* 26 June 2002.

[100] *Ante.* chapter 6.

[101] *The Times.* 18 July 2002.

[102] Criminal Justice Act 2003. s. 44.

[103] *The Times.* 20 May 2003.

[104] John H. Langbein. (1978) 'The Criminal Trial before the Lawyers.' Chicago, 45 *The University of Chicago Law Review.* p. 287.

[105] Sir Matthew Hale. (1736) *The History of the Pleas of the Crown.* London, E.and R. Nutt and Another. vol. ii. p. 295.

[106] Old Bailey Sessions Papers. [1718] pp. 5-6. See Langbein. 'The Criminal Trial before the Lawyers.' Op. cit. p. 287.

[107] Criminal Justice Act 2003. ss. 75-80.

[108] *The Times.* 18 July 2002.

[109] Criminal Evidence Act [1898] s. 1 (f) (ii).

[110] Reported in *The Times* 22 September 2000 and *The Guardian* 25 September 2000.

[111] *White Paper.* chap. 4. 54.

[112] Criminal Justice Act 2003. Part 11. chapter 1.

[113] *White Paper.* chap. 4. 55.

[114] Ibid. chap. 4. 56.

[115] Ibid. chap. 4. 56

[116] See Block. 'The White Paper and the Rules of Evidence.' Op. cit. p. 893.

[117] Sally Lloyd-Bostock. (2000) 'The Effects on juries of Hearing About the Defendant's Previous Criminal Record: A Simulation Study.' *Criminal Law Review.* London, Sweet & Maxwell. p. 755.

[118] Criminal Justice Act 2003. Part 11. chapter 2.

[119] *White Paper.* Op. cit. chap. 4.60.

[120] Hale. *The History of the Pleas of the Crown.* Op. cit. vol. ii. pp. 276-7.

[121] Langbein. 'The Criminal Trial before the Lawyers.' Op. cit. p. 273.

[122] *Auld Report.* Op. cit. p.140.

[123] Enright and Morton. *Taking Liberties.* Op. cit. p. 2.

[124] Cornish. *The Jury.* Op. cit. p.18.

[125] William Blackstone. (1830) *Commentaries on the Law of England. London, Thomas Tegg. vol. iv.* p. 344.

[126] These words are reminiscent of those of Thomas Erskine in the trial of the Dean of St. Asaph.

[127] Devlin. Op. cit. p. 164.

CHAPTER 9

Conclusion

INTUITIVE POWER

The jury is a form of participatory democracy compared with the representative democracy that obtains in elections. It has direct involvement in decision-making institutions of the state and provides an education for all the participants.[1] It is meant to be an impartial body rather than a purely representative one.[2] Moreover, juries inject community values into the formal legal process, and can bring about a sense of equity and fairness against the cold and mechanistic application of legal rules.[3] At times they can result in the spirit of the law being observed in contrast to a legalistic adherence to the law.

The criminal trial jury in various forms has survived for over 800 years and is deeply embedded in English culture. One reason for its popularity has frequently been its perceived independence and its ability to act intuitively. In the beginning it carried on the community involvement expressing the popular will in the ordeals outlined earlier in *Chapter 2*, and in the early years jurors consciously used their nullification power to produce a high level of acquittals, often around 50 per cent in cases of murder and theft. With homicide they could distinguish between unpremeditated killing and murder and with theft they often reduced the value of the stolen goods.[4]

This was followed with verdicts of not guilty in popular political causes, and with 'pious perjury' to avoid the imposition of the death penalty for non-violent theft under the 'Bloody Code' in the eighteenth century. As a consequence, jury power has generated over the centuries a great deal of respect among sections of the population. From the thirteenth century the criminal jury trial has been public trial participated in by large numbers as either jurors or prisoners. It is seen by many people as of cardinal importance in society since, despite its flaws, it enables accused persons to be judged fairly and, today, a wide range of people to participate in a democratic institution. Nonetheless, in the absence of a written constitution in this country it is vulnerable to attack and has clearly been diminished and is still under assault.

PERVERSE VERDICTS

So-called 'perverse verdicts' have occurred as long as there have been juries, as indicated in the preceding chapters. For many commentators, like E.P. Thompson, they are a glory of our legal system; for others less favourably inclined they are one of the acceptable costs of the jury system. To Lord Devlin they were a protection against laws that the ordinary man might regard as 'harsh and oppressive' and an insurance 'that the criminal law will conform to the ordinary man's idea of what is fair and just.'[5] Auld, however, put it that 'there are many, in particular the Bar, who fervently support what they regard as the right of the jury to ignore their duty to return a verdict according to the evidence and to acquit where they disapprove of the law or of the prosecution in seeking to enforce it.'[6] It is claimed, he said, that unpopular laws have to be obeyed by all so why should juries be exempt?

But, nullification may be considered desirable where a law has changed and become unjust or oppressive. A prime example of the latter is shown by the response of Lord John Russell in abolishing the death penalty for many crimes, including minor offences, in 1838. On the other hand jury equity is often contested as being an example of unelected and unaccountable people overriding the decisions of elected and accountable legislators.

Auld said that juries have no right to dispense with or nullify the law and that to do so is contrary to their oath. He recommended, therefore, 'that the law should be declared, by statute if need be, that juries have no right to acquit defendants in defiance of the law or in disregard of the evidence, and that judges and advocates should conduct criminal cases accordingly.'[7] What the last phrase means and how the demand could be met are unclear and, for the moment, the Government have ignored the suggestion which was not included in the Criminal Justice Act, 2003.

On this issue, Auld ignored some 800 years during which nullification and partial verdicts by juries have often been praised (and often criticised) and thus neglected the true place of the jury in our culture. As Devlin observed, 'While the judge might put the matter very strongly in his summing-up, he cannot direct a verdict of 'guilty' or refuse to accept a verdict of 'not guilty' if returned. In short, there cannot be in law a perverse verdict of acquittal.' Devlin then quoted Lord Sankey, L.C. saying in *Woolmington's Case*[8] that for the judge to say that the jury must in law find the prisoner guilty would be to make him 'decide the case and not the jury, which is not the common law.'[9] The words are reminiscent of those of Lord Chief Justice Vaughan in *Bushell's Case*.

Also emphasising the question of culture, another writer has said, 'juries are there to determine facts but that is not why we have them. Juries are part of our inherited political culture. Just as criminal trial legitimises the entire criminal process, so the jury legitimises the trial.'[10]

JURY DISCRETION

As this book has tried to demonstrate, in a very significant sense, despite property qualifications, the community feeling for moral justice and mercy exhibited in trial by ordeal and by the early trial jury has been an inherent feature underlying criminal trial by jury throughout its long history. And this is the secret of its enduring popularity.

In other words, jury nullification can be said in many periods to have been of the essence of criminal jury trial. It is described by Andrew Leipold, a writer who is largely opposed to it, as 'one of the most potent forces in the criminal law.' Nullification occurs, he says,

When the defendant's guilt is clear beyond a reasonable doubt, but the jury, based on its own sense of justice or fairness, decides to acquit. The nullification doctrine recognises this power to 'acquit against the evidence', even though when a jury nullifies, it ignores the judge's legal instructions and vetoes a legislative definition of culpable conduct. In terms of raw power, nullification has few parallels: rarely can a public entity make such a critical decision with no obligation to justify its action and with no recourse for the aggrieved party.[11]

He further argues that nullification has undesirable collateral effects flowing from procedural rules that have the effect of protecting the nullification power against errors.[12] An example is the unavailability of appeals from jury decisions. And, he considers that for every case where the jury extends mercy to a deserving defendant there may well be other cases where the verdict is based on improper considerations, such as that a victim of a sexual assault was 'asking for it', or prejudice based on race.[13]

Leipold believes that eliminating jury nullification altogether is probably impossible and certainly undesirable. Instead, he proposes that nullification be treated in the same way as affirmative defences such as self-defence, duress, necessity and infancy where the defendant has committed the *actus reus,* and perhaps has the *mens rea,* but is not punished because his or her actions were justified or excused. Parties could raise and present evidence and arguments to the point, and the jury could make a better decision. In return, judges should then be able to overturn an acquittal or the prosecution could appeal an unfavourable verdict.[14]

But that might well be too high a price to pay for circumscribing jury nullification, even if that were desirable. What is the point of the jury if its verdicts can be overturned by a judge or a group of judges?

OPPOSITION TO JURY NULLIFICATION

It must be admitted that there is considerable feeling against the whole idea of jury nullification (and even of the jury itself) among some academic lawyers and senior police officers, for whom it raises problems. For certain academics it is illogical, unlawful and untidy. As for police officers, they sometimes see prisoners go free whom they sincerely believed to be guilty and they believe that jurors are often intimidated.

Professor Glanville Williams wrote that though juries have long had the ability to reach perverse verdicts there was no evidence of their wide use of it. Yet, if that is so, he did not indicate why there is such concern about it. Developing his point, he continued that 'Most of the great pronouncements on constitutional liberty, from the eighteenth century onwards, have been the work of judges … the assumption that political liberty at the present day depends upon the institution of the jury … is in truth merely folklore.'[15] But he gave no examples of liberties arising from the decisions of judges and said instead that,

(j)ury trial did not avail the Chartists, for example. This was because charges of sedition and unlawful assembly were usually tried by special juries, who belonged to the propertied classes and were unlikely to look with favour upon subversive movements.

They were also, he added, specially picked for their 'reliable' opinions, the Crown retaining special panels of jurors for the purpose—'a practice against which the law certainly afforded (as it still affords) no safeguard.'[16]

However this means the Chartists were not tried by the ordinary petty jury so to say that it did not avail them is a *non sequitur*. Not that the jury is always, and historically has always been, on the side of civil liberty. In recent times it found Dennis Lemon guilty of publishing a blasphemous libel in *Gay News*[17] despite blasphemy being outdated in multicultural England. And, of course, the 'Birmingham Six', the 'Guildford Four', 'The Maguire Seven' and other cases in which there were miscarriages of justice all involved defendants being convicted by juries, although it must be said that in those cases named the jury were denied vital material by the prosecution or supplied with false evidence.[18] Nor, historically in the mid-nineteenth century, were juries inclined to assist men on strike for offences vaguely described as 'obstruction' or 'molestation'. As Cornish has said:

> Many [judges] were prepared to widen the law so as to catch participants who did very little in furtherance of a strike. Juries were apparently not offended by these developments in the law, for they rarely refused to convict the defendants. Changes in the law were achieved not by resistance from juries, but by the acquisition of political power by urban workers in 1867. The Conspiracy and Protection of Property Act 1875 provided that strike action should not result in a criminal prosecution except where there had been some form of aggressive picketing or physical danger or annoyance to the public.[19]

Apart from that, Williams was of course a distinguished academic lawyer but on the jury his sources are now often shown by modern research to have been outdated and they led in 1963 to erroneous conclusions on his part, which were sometimes repeated later by Lord Justice Auld.

In the view of the American jurist Steven Warshawsky, because juries are neither elected nor accountable they are 'fundamentally undemocratic institutions … ill-suited to be making public policy' by nullification.[20] For his part, Auld wrote that every person accused of a crime has a right to be tried according to the law as it is and not how a jury interpret it.

SUPPORT FOR JURY NULLIFICATION

What nullification involves can include protecting a person from government persecution, rejecting what the jury sees as an unfair provision of the criminal law, applying mercy, and concluding that even if the case of the prosecution is true it is somehow insufficient to justify a sentence.

Throughout its history the criminal trial jury has at times nullified the law and some people think that jury nullification should be encouraged. A case for this is put in an article by M.D.A. Freeman[21] based on the constitutions of Indiana and Maryland in the United States where the jurors are judges of both law and fact. He argues that it is desirable that juries can reach decisions on their merits, while a judge is constrained by the law.[22] In Lord Devlin's phrase, unlike judges they have a 'sovereign power of acquittal.'[23]

Scheflin and Van Dyke say that 'jurors bring a variety of perspectives to their deliberations that enables them to see beyond the single viewpoint of the judge.'[24] Moreover, 'jury nullification is more than just a price the legal system pays for jury service. Rather, it is a distinct and unique benefit to our system of government that not only brings the community and the law closer together, but also adds a new dimension to the concept of democratic self-rule for all participating in the jury experience.'[25] In addition, 'the jury may not always be right, but neither is any other deliberative body. As the conscience of the community drawn from a representative cross-section of that community, it is the best we have ... because it is us.'[26]

For his part, Lord Denning (then Sir Alfred Denning), in a well-received lecture, declared that,

> The fundamental safeguards have been established, not so much by lawyers as by the common people of England, by the unknown juryman who in 1367 said he would rather die in prison than give a verdict against his conscience, by Richard Chambers who in 1629 declared that never till death would he acknowledge the sentence of the Star Chamber, by Edmund Bushell and his eleven fellow-jurors who in 1670 went to prison rather than find the Quakers guilty, by the jurors who acquitted the printer of the Letters of Junius, and by a host of others. These are the men who have bequeathed to us the heritage of freedom.[27]

And further:

> To this day, when a man accused of serious crime is put in charge of the jury, it is in words which have come down through the centuries: 'To this charge he has pleaded not guilty and puts himself upon his country, which country you are.' All our past struggles are bound up in that one sentence. He entrusts his liberty to a jury of his fellowmen. So in the last resort do we all.[28]

Another indirect effect of nullification is seen when proposed charges, particularly under the Official Secrets Act, are dropped before going to trial for fear that jurors will reject them as they did in the Ponting case in the 1980s. A more direct influence is felt when, in some trials, the prosecution offers reduced charges to the court when it is uncertain of jury sympathy for a defendant's actions. And, as we have seen, the removal of the death penalty in 1838 by Lord John Russell for many offences, including the forgery of bank notes, followed widespread nullification by jurors in some cases. Russell had already put the matter succinctly when he wrote:

> The power which juries possess of refusing to put the law in force has been the cause of amending many bad laws which the judges would have administered with professional bigotry, and above all, it has this important and useful consequence, that laws totally repugnant to the feelings of the community for which they are made, cannot long prevail in England.[29]

Nullification in England today is believed to be quite rare. But since juries deliberate in secret and cannot give reasons for their verdicts no one can really know. Whether it is liked or not it still exists and it can be believed that 'the right of juries to decide in defiance of the law ... is central to the jury's democratic function.'[30] Clearly it still occurs. For example, prior to 1956 motorists who killed while driving dangerously were charged with manslaughter. Juries were reluctant to convict bad drivers of so serious an offence and it was replaced by Parliament with one of causing death by dangerous driving, with a lesser maximum penalty.[31]

As Freeman has put it, 'The fight to preserve the jury may be seen as symbolic, a defence of individual liberty in the wake of a vast increase in the powers of the state.'[32] To that extent, but not so far as in his day, Blackstone's famous dictum that the jury is 'the sacred bulwark of the nation, upholding the liberties of England'[33] may be considered to be true. Even as recently as 1922, and before the jury had become truly democratic, Lord Atkin, in words reminiscent of those of Blackstone, said that trial by jury is 'the bulwark of liberty, the shield of the poor from the oppression of the rich and powerful.'[34]

Nonetheless, it should be borne in mind that, as Green has written:

Juries nullified the law in many instances not out of mercy but out of fear of the defendant's friends or relatives, or for political favour, or even, perhaps, for monetary gain. The bench could not always be certain whether the jury's motives were mercenary or merciful ... some verdicts were corrupt and the bench had to guard against them.[35]

It cannot be denied, however, that the inscrutability principle is inherent in the jury system. It has existed from the beginning and cannot be done away with without destroying the system itself. Although it was a civil case and not quite analagous, what should be made of the Appeal Court judges overturning a libel award to a former Liverpool footballer, Bruce Grobbelaar, on the unprecedented ground in modern times that a jury verdict to acquit in an earlier criminal trial was 'perverse'—that is that the judges did not agree with it? To tamper with juries because they do not return the 'correct' verdict is similar to saying that democracy should be restricted because some people vote for the 'wrong' party. Fortunately for Grobbelaar, the House of Lords ruled that 'the Court of Appeal was wrong to overturn the jury's verdict in a libel case as perverse where the jury's verdict could have been given an alternative explicable interpretation.'[36]

Section 8 of the Contempt of Court Act 1981 made it a criminal offence to 'obtain, disclose or solicit any particulars of statements made, opinions expressed, arguments advanced, or votes cast by members of a jury in the course of their deliberations.' This was aimed at newspapers, researchers and others as likely to render the secrecy of the jury's deliberations invalid. Auld certainly had a serious purpose in mind, but was in breach of the spirit of section 8, when he proposed that the judge should devise a series of questions for the jury which they should answer publicly.[37] Although this is common for all Continental juries (who, in any event, are more subordinate to the judge than their English counterparts), it would revive the idea of a special verdict. And, as Lord Devlin has said, the jury 'are to be told what the law is, but in any case which involves both fact and law no one is to know whether they have followed the law or not, for under a general verdict no one can know how they have distinguished between fact and law.'[38]

Fortunately the current Government saw the danger in Auld's proposal and rejected the idea, adding, 'Nor do we intend to legislate to prevent juries from returning verdicts regarded as perverse where the verdict flies in the face of the evidence, as has happened very occasionally.'[39] It seems clear, therefore, that public opinion in support of the jury system still carries some weight, although the assurance might not prove to be long lasting.

THE JURY A LUXURY?

Darbyshire has written that she is not anti-jury, but she commences the essay in which she asserts this by saying that it is a luxury we cannot afford.[40] She argues that at the present time magistrates determine fact and law and, on her own figures of defendants dealt with by magistrates in 1995, 81 per cent pleaded guilty in person plus ten per cent by post.[41] Although she contends that this does not mean that the Crown Court is the normal trial court,[42] it cannot be denied that clearly the jury in the Crown Court decides the most important cases.

Darbyshire's main point is that *'the jury has already been replaced'* (her italics). 'In Blackstone's time,' she says, 'jury trial was the central criminal forum and probably was a guardian of democracy and civil liberties but over the last three centuries, the jury has been replaced for 99 per cent of the defendants and victims who pass through our criminal courts.'[43] Perhaps that is overstated but unfortunately it is largely true (even if much of the work of magistrates' courts involves relatively minor regulatory offences that would hardly justify costly trial by jury). However, it does not follow that the jury should be replaced altogether—rather that what remains should be treasured.

THE JUROR'S OATH

The judicial oath taken by magistrates includes a promise that they will 'do justice according to the law.' The juror's oath is to 'give a true verdict according to the evidence', i.e. what he or she believes is true. Auld was correct in arguing that giving merciful verdicts was not in accordance with this oath. Nonetheless, it is hardly likely that the general public would like to see the opportunity juries have of showing their disapproval of oppressive conduct by the police or the judiciary destroyed. After all, they are the ones on the jury who so act. And how much more likely might such aggressive conduct be if the jury system did not exist?

In some trials the evidence for the prosecution is overwhelming and the jury act upon it. In other trials the evidence may be slight and again it is not difficult to reach a verdict of acquittal. But what when the evidence is complicated or entirely circumstantial? Here the jurors will bring in their subjective assessments of the demeanour of the defendant and act intuitively in making up their minds, and why should this be baulked at? In one case a salesman was provoked by a number of thugs and wounded one of them. The judge expressly directed the jury that provocation was no defence but they returned a verdict of not guilty.[44] One area in which it can be said the jury plays an important role is in accepting provocation over time in certain cases as a reason for reducing a charge of murder to a finding of manslaughter. Indeed, it may be that legislation on the point is not needed precisely because of this power of the jury.

At least, the Government have decided against juries having to give reasons for their decisions. Although this may be challenged as not in keeping with the Human Rights Act 1998, it has been the view of the Court of Appeal that it ensures that decisions are final and prevents undue pressure on jurors.[45] Furthermore, both the trial and the verdict are open to full scrutiny. Although Darbyshire considers that juries should give reasons she also says that if they are to be asked to do so they 'must surely be told of their power to acquit in the face of condemnatory evidence, as an exercise of jury equity.'[46]

As we have seen, the Government have also sensibly determined not to undertake the almost impossible task of legislating to prevent juries returning perverse verdicts. But proposals to abolish the double jeopardy rule and allow previous convictions and hearsay evidence to be admissible in certain circumstances can be seen to undermine the function of trial by jury. In response to the present trend to diminish the role of the jury our legislators should remember the words of Lord John Russell and Blackstone:

Russell wrote:

> It is to trial by jury, more than even by representation (as it at present exists) that the people owe the share they have in the government of the country; it is to trial by jury also that the government mainly owes the attachment of the people to the laws; a consideration which ought to make our legislators very cautious how they take away this mode of trial by new, trifling, and vexatious enactments.[47]

And Blackstone:

> So that the liberties of England cannot but subsist so long as this palladium remains sacred and inviolate; not only from all open attacks (which none will be so hardy as to make), but also from all secret machinations, which may sap and undermine it; by introducing new and arbitrary methods of trial ... And however convenient these may appear at first (as doubtless all arbitrary powers, well executed, are the most convenient), yet let it be again remembered, that delays and little inconveniences in the forms of justice, are the price that all free nations must pay for their liberty in more substantial matters; that these inroads upon this sacred bulwark of the nation are fundamentally opposite to the spirit of our constitution; and that, though begun in trifles, the precedent may gradually increase and spread, to the utter disuse of juries in questions of the most momentous concern.[48]

A UNIQUE CONTRIBUTION

One of the most potent arguments against seeing the jury as a bulwark of liberty is that until modern times, it has been based upon a property qualification and women were excluded altogether. This has meant that it was largely unrepresentative and likely to support the prosecution in many cases. This has been powerfully expressed by Hay who, in relation to the eighteenth century, and using his researches in Northampton, draws the general conclusion that:

> The fact that the English jury was moulded to sustain the structure of power in eighteenth-century England through a complex of still imperfectly understood decisions under the terms of a very complicated body of law has helped to obscure from historians the extent of the inequality it protected and embodied. The evident independence of jurymen to decide, without appeal, to acquit the accused, as well as to convict, has seemed to some a powerful argument against the portrayal of juries as expressions of class power. It is, of course, no such thing. Probably jurors rarely decided entirely against the evidence, rarely perverted the course of English justice in overtly class-biased ways in the eighteenth century. They had no need to do so. The criminal law of England also shaped, and was shaped by, carefully structured class

inequality. The juries so carefully created by Parliament, sheriffs, constables, and wealth were the procedural corollary to the inequality embodied in the substantive criminal law and in English society itself.[49]

Although not dealing specifically with the class issue, as a contrast to Hay's view should be considered the arguments of Thompson who has written,

> The place of the jury in our constitutional history does not rest on a naïve belief that every jury verdict must be true, rational and humane. It rests upon a total view of the relation between the legislature, judiciary and the people; upon a notion of justice in which the law must be made to seem rational and even humane to lay jurors (hence inhibiting a thousand oppressive processes before they are even commenced, through the knowledge that no jury would convict); and upon a particular national history of contests between 'the people' and the Crown or state, in which the jury has won and reserved for itself, in its verdict, a final power.[50]

It appears to be clear that English people hold criminal trial by jury in high esteem despite its acknowledged defects. The jury is not perfect, but what institution is and what is the alternative? Trial by judge alone, or with assessors, does not win popular support and it is to be feared that if trial by jury were to disappear trust in the rule of law would be undermined.

Yet, a long historical background could not save assizes and quarter sessions from being replaced by the Crown Court. Equally, tradition has not prevented the curtailment of many of the former evidential protections for defendants. Even the ancient office of Lord Chancellor risks extinction, and against this swell of measures, many of which are aimed at producing more convictions and cutting costs, it may well be asked if the criminal jury has a certain future?

Undoubtedly, trial by jury retains the faith of the public and whilst that is so the public trust the fairness of the criminal courts, which is a prize worth holding on to. According to Lloyd-Bostock and Thomas, 'the jury has great symbolic significance and is still highly prized, not least because it continues to exercise its longstanding right to reach a verdict based on conscience, against the letter of the law, and occasionally in defiance of government.'[51]

Despite juries, until modern times, having been drawn from a small proportion of the population as a consequence of the property qualification they have always, to a greater or lesser extent at different periods, exercised nullification, and still do today. At first, this was continuing the Anglo-Saxon tradition of compensation rather than death for most crimes. The infliction of the death penalty came largely with the growth of royal justice under the Angevins and the manner in which the criminal trial jury originated after the ordeal was a continuation of the concept of justice based upon mercy and group harmony.[52]

This lasted a long time. The high percentage of acquittals in the Middle Ages, the Levellers' 'jury right', the seditious libel trials, the treason trials of the late eighteenth century, pious perjury to defeat the ubiquitous death penalty and nullification today are all part of the process. It is also the dialogue between formal legality and the intuitive power of the jury that has signally represented the unique contribution of the criminal trial jury to jurisprudence throughout the world.

CULTURAL SIGNIFICANCE

In modern times governments of the main political parties have continued the process of reducing the number of people who can avail themselves of jury trial in criminal cases. They appear to fear that juries allow too many criminals to go free. But there is no proof of this and it seems wrong that people whose careers and futures may be at risk should be denied the traditional right to choose trial by jury if they so wish. The jury system has strong support amongst the general public and many senior members of the legal profession despite their being well aware of its failings and drawbacks.

Sir Robin Auld quoted from E.P. Thompson but if the quotation is completed what Thompson wrote was:

> When the jurors enter the box, they enter also upon a role which has certain inherited expectations; and these expectations are inherited as much from our culture and our history as from books of law ... The English common law rests upon a bargain between the Law and the People. The jury box is where people come into the court; the judge watches them and the jury watches back. A jury is the place where the bargain is struck. The jury attends in judgment, not only upon the accused, but also upon the justice and humanity of the law ... Justice is not a set of rules to be 'administered' to a people. Verdicts are not 'administered'; they are *found*. And the findings, as matters of 'public importance', cannot yet be done by microchip. Men and women must consult their reasons and their consciences, their precedents and their sense of who we are and who we have been.[53]

Auld, and to some extent the Government, seem to go against any such acceptance of the importance of the cultural significance of the jury in our society and seriously to underestimate, and undermine, the jury as a safeguard of liberty. As Auld himself admitted juries have already been reduced to dealing with only one per cent of criminal trials. Experience in the courts shows that judges today are generally much more fair-minded than 50 years ago, and certainly exhibit nothing of the judicial tyranny of many in earlier times.[54] But, there appears to be a desire that they should act alone more than is justified. And is that what they themselves want? After all, the majority of the judges praise the jury system, although Auld suggested that this does not represent their true feelings when he referred to 'judges' lack of confidence in the competence of juries for their task, despite their tradition of eulogy of the jury system.'[55] How many people really think that a judge sitting alone or with a couple of laymen is better than the combination of a judge and jury? As Lord Devlin said,

> What makes juries worthwhile is that they see things differently from the judges, that they can water the law, and that the function which they filled two centuries ago as a corrective to the corruption and partiality of the judges requires essentially the same qualities as the function they perform today as an organ of the disestablishment ... Perversity is just a lawyer's word for a jury which applies its own standards instead of those recommended by lawyers ... The smear of perversity is applied by judges but erased by time. It is not the disobedient jurors whom history has reprobated, but the judges who called them perverse.[56]

And, on another occasion, when he declared, 'some of the verdicts which juries have as a matter of conscience returned have founded the liberties we now enjoy.'[57]

This is not the same, however, as saying that the jury can decide the law. Legally, at least since the seventeenth century, there has been a clear acceptance of the distinction drawn between the role of the judge and that of the jury. This is that the jury decides the facts of the case and the judge decides the law that will be applied to them. It was well put by one judge when he said to the jury in a trial in Australia,

> I cannot stress too strongly that the decision in this case on all questions of fact, the inferences to be drawn from the facts and the ultimate verdict to be returned, is yours and yours alone; and so much is that so that if in the course of summing up I appear to indicate that I have a view of the facts ... you are bound to disregard that apparent indication, because you have one function and I have another. You do not intrude into mine and I do not intrude into yours. [58]

Nevertheless, the jury is, and has always been, the keeper of the conscience of the community and it is a barrier to manipulation, oppression and abuse of authority. That is why totalitarian regimes can never accept free and independent juries. The criminal trial jury is an integral part of liberty and we must not allow it to be airbrushed out of the fabric of democracy in the UK. Without juries there would be no protection for people wrongly accused of crimes. That is why trial by jury is known as trial by the country or, in other words, by the people.

What it comes down to is that maintaining a balance between law and common morality, and reconciling legal practice with contemporary opinion, have always been essential elements of English criminal trial by jury and long may they remain so.

ENDNOTES for *Chapter 9*

[1] Nicholas Blake. (1988) 'The Case for the Jury.' In Findlay and Duff (eds) *The Jury Under Attack*. London, Butterworths. p. 142.

[2] Steven M. Warshawsky. (1996) 'Opposing Jury Nullification, Law, Policy and Prosecutorial Strategy.' Washington, 85 *Georgetown Law Journal*. p. 224.

[3] Neil Vidmar. (2000) 'A Historical and Comparative Perspective on the Common Law Jury.' In Vidmar (ed.) *World Jury Systems*. Oxford, Oxford University Press. p.1.

[4] Thomas Andrew Green. (1985) *Verdict According to Conscience: Perspectives on the English Criminal Trial Jury 1200-1800. Chicago, Chicago University Press*. pp. 35 and 61.

[5] Sir Patrick Devlin. (1966) *Trial by Jury*. London, Methuen & Co. p. 160.

[6] The Auld Report. (2001) *Review of the Criminal Courts of England and Wales*. HMSO. Cm. 5563. p. 173.

[7] Ibid. p. 176.

[8] [1935] AC. 462.

[9] Devlin. Op. cit. p. 84.

[10] M.D.A. Freeman. (1981) 'The Jury on Trial'. 34 *Current Legal Problems*. London, Stevens & Sons. p. 89.

[11] Andrew D. Leipold. (1996) 'Rethinking Jury Nullification.' Virginia, 82 *Virginia Law Review*. pp. 253-4.

[12] Ibid. pp. 257-8.

[13] Ibid. pp. 304-5.

[14] Ibid. pp. 312-15.

[15] Glanville Williams. (1963) *The Proof of Guilt. A Study of the English Criminal Trial.* 3rd edition. London, Stevens & Sons. pp. 259-60.

[16] Ibid. p. 259.

[17] [1979] AC 617.

[18] These trials were described by Lord Devlin as 'the greatest disasters that have shaken British justice in my time. (1991) 'The Conscience of the Jury.' *The Law Quarterly Review.* London, Stevens & Sons. p. 398.

[19] W.R. Cornish. (1968) *The Jury.* London, Allen Lane The Penguin Press. p.138.

[20] Warshawsky. 'Opposing Jury Nullification,' Op. cit. p. 215.

[21] 'M.D.A. Freeman. 'Why Not a Jury Nullification Statute Here Too? '(19 March 1981a) *New Law Journal* .London, pp. 304-6.

[22] Ibid. p. 304.

[23] Devlin. *Trial by Jury.* p. 89.

[24] Alan Scheflin and Jon Van Dyke. (1980) 'Jury Nullification: The Contours of a Controversy.' 43 *Law and Contemporary Problems.* Durham, Carolina, Duke University. p. 68.

[25] Ibid. p. 111.

[26] Ibid. p. 115.

[27] Sir Alfred Denning. (1949) *Freedom under the Law.* London, Stevens and Sons Limited. pp. 63-4.

[28] Ibid. p. 59.

[29] Lord John Russell. (1823) *On the English Government.* London, p. 393. Quoted by W. Forsyth. Op. cit. p. 420.

[30] Sally Lloyd-Bostock and Cheryl Thomas. (2000a) 'The Continuing Decline of the English Jury.' In Neil Vidmar. *World Jury Systems.* Op. cit. p. 56.

[31] Freeman. 'The Jury on Trial.' Op. cit. p. 92.

[32] Ibid. p. 65.

[33] Sir William Blackstone. (1830) *Commentaries on the Law of England.* London, Thomas Tegg. vol. iv. p. 344.

[34] *Ford v. Blurton.* [1922] 38 TLR 801, 805.

[35] Green. *Verdict.* Op. cit. p. xx.

[36] *Bruce Grobbelaar v. News Group Newspapers Ltd & Anor.* [2002] 1 WLR. 3024.

[37] Auld Report. Op. cit. p. 172.

[38] Devlin. *Trial by Jury.* Op. cit. pp. 89-90.

[39] *White Paper.* (2002) *Justice for All.* Cm. 5563. para. 4.50.

[40] Penny Darbyshire. (1997) 'An Essay on the Importance and Neglect of the Magistracy.' *The Criminal Law Review.* London, Sweet & Maxwell. p. 627.

[41] Ibid. p. 629.

[42] Ibid.

[43] Ibid. p. 643.

[44] Freeman. 'The Jury on Trial. Op. cit. pp. 92-3.

[45] *R. v. Qureshi.* [2001] *The Times* 11 September 2001.

[46] Darbyshire *et al.* (2001) 'What Can the English Legal System Learn from Jury Research published up to 2001?' www.kingston.ac.uk/~ku00596.elsres01.pdf p. 61.

[47] Lord John Russell. (1823) *On the English Government.* London, p. 394. Quoted by W. Forsyth. Op. cit. p. 432.

[48] Blackstone. Op. cit. iv. pp. 349-50.

[49] Douglas Hay. (1988) 'The Class Composition of the Palladium of Liberty: Trial Jurors in the Eighteenth Century.' In Cockburn and Green (eds.) *Twelve Good Men and True: The Criminal Trial Jury in England, 1200-1800.* New Haven, Princeton University Press. p. 356.

[50] Thompson. *Writing by Candlelight.* Op. cit. p. 232.

[51] Lloyd-Bostock and Thomas. 'The Continuing Decline of the English Jury.' Op. cit. p. 91.

[52] Trisha Olsen. (2000) 'Of Enchantment: The Passing of the Ordeals and the Rise of the Jury Trial. New York. Syracuse Law Review. pp 130-31.

[53] E.P. Thompson. (1980) *Writing by Candlelight.* London, The Merlin Press. p. 108.

[54] For examples see John Hostettler. (1998) *At the Mercy of the State: A Study in Judicial Tyranny.* Chichester, England. Barry Rose Law Publishers.

[55] The Auld Report. Op. cit. p. 137.

[56] Sir Patrick Devlin. *Blackstone Lecture.* Oxford. 18 November 1978.

[57] Devlin. 'The Conscience of the Jury.' Op. cit. p. 400.

[58] *R. v. Ali Ali* [1981] 6 A Crim R 161.

Bibliography

A. Primary sources

Bentham, Jeremy. 1821. *Elements in the Art of Packing as Applied to Special Juries etc.* London, Effingham Wilson.

    1843. *Principles of Judicial Procedure, Works.* vol. ii. Edinburgh, William Tait.

Blackstone, William. 1830. *Commentaries on the Law of England.* London, Thomas Tegg.

British Library:

    Hardwicke Papers. *Add. MSS.* 35863.

    Lambarde, William. 1569. *The Justice of the Peace.* BL. 516. a. 5.

    Lilburne, John. 1646. *The Just Man's Justification.* London. E 340 (12).

    Penn, William. 1671. *Truth Rescued from Imposture.* London, BL. T.407.(17)

    Somers *Tracts.* 1809-15 edn.

    Starling, Sir Samuel. 1671. *An Answer to the Seditious and Scandalous Pamphlet, entitled, The Trial of W. Penn and W. Mead.* London, BL. C110e. 3. (6).

    Thomason Collection. (Wm. Walwyn). E. 618 (9), and (J. Jones), E. 1414(1), and E. 1414(2).

Britton, J. c. 1291. (ed. F.M. Nicholls) 1865. Oxford University Press.

Campbell, Lord John. 1847. *Lives of the Chancellors.* London, John Murray.

Care, Henry. 1682. *English Liberties: Or, The Free-born Subject's Inheritance.* London, G. Larkin.

Coke, Sir Edward. 1797a *Second Institute.* London, E. & R. Brooke.

    1797b *Third Institute.* London, E. & R. Brooke.

Fortescue, Sir John. 1468. *On the Laws and Governance of England.* (ed. Shelley Lockwood) 1997. Cambridge, Cambridge University Press.

Hale, Sir Matthew. 1713. *The History of the Common Law of England.* London.

    1736. *The History of the Pleas of the Crown.* 2 vols. London, E. & R. Nutt and Others.

Hawkins, William. 1716. *Treatise of the Pleas of the Crown.* London, John Walthoe.

Hawles, John. 1680. *The English-Man's Right.* London, Richard Janeway.

Jefferson, Thomas. 1789. *The Papers of Thomas Jefferson.* vol. xv. [Julian P. Boyd. (ed) 1958] Princeton, Princeton University Press.

Madan, Martin. 1785. *Thoughts on Executive Justice, with Respect to our Criminal Laws.* London, J. Dodsley.

Old Bailey Proceedings. 1784. www.oldbaileyonline.org/

Paley, W. 1785. *The Principles of Moral and Political Philosophy.* In *The Works of W. Paley,* 1825. Edinburgh, Peter Brown and T & W Nelson.

Ridgway, James. 1847. *Speeches of the Rt. Hon. Lord Erskine at the Bar and in Parliament.* London, J. Ridgway.

Romilly, Sir Samuel. 1786. *Memoirs of the Life of Sir Samuel Romilly.* London, John Murray.

    1810. *Observations on the Criminal Law of England.* London, *Monthly Review.*

Shipley, William. 1783. *A Dialogue between a Gentleman and a Farmer.* London, John Stockdale.

State Tryals. 1719. London, Timothy Goodwin & Ors.

State Trials. 1816. London, Thomas Howell.

Walker, C. 1649. *The Trial of Lt. Col. John Lilburne.* London, Theodorus Verax.

Year Books. 1367. London, Selden Society.

B. Official documents

Auld, Sir Robin. 2001. *Review of the Criminal Courts of England and Wales.* Cm. 5563.

Hansard. 1816, 1837.

Home Office. 1999. *Research Findings.* No. 102.

House of Commons Journals. 1667, 1830.

House of Lords Journals. 1830-1831.

James Committee. 1975. *The Distribution of Criminal Business between the Crown Court and the Magistrates' Courts.* Cmnd. 6323.

Lord Morris Committee on Jury Service. 1965. Cmnd. 2627.

Narey Report. 1997. *Review of Delay in the Criminal Justice System.*

Parliamentary History. 1791.

Parliamentary Papers. Criminal Law Commissioners' Reports:

    First Report 1834 xiv. 1.

    Second Report. 1836 xxiv. 107.

    Eighth Report 1845 xiv. 161.

    Patent Rolls. 1219.

Public Record Office. JUST. 3.
Royal Commission on Criminal Justice. 1993. Cm. 2263. (The Runciman Commission)
White Paper: *Justice for All*. 2002.

C. Journals and newspapers
American Criminal Law Review. 1993, 1996.
American Journal of Legal History. 1973, 1974, 1982, 1983.
Cambridge Law Journal. 1999.
Criminal Law Review. 1991, 1997, 2000.
Current Legal Problems. 1981.
Edinburgh Review. 1838.
English Historical Review. 1941.
Harvard Law Review. 1935.
History Today. 1982
Insurance Law Journal. 1965.
Justice of the Peace. 2002
Law and Contemporary Problems. 1980, 1999.
Law and History Review.1991, 1997.
Law Magazine. 1844
Law Quarterly Review. 1950, 1953, 1988.
Law Society's Gazette. 1976.
London and Westminster Review. 1838.
Michigan Law Review. 1986.
Modern Law Review. 1937, 2003.
Monthly Review. 1810.
New Law Journal. 1981, 2000.
Past & Present. 1983, 1985.
Southern Methodist University School of Law. 2001.
The Times 1791, 1819, 1967, 1977, 1978, 2002.
University of Chicago Law Review. 1978, 1983.
Wayne Law Review. 1990.
Yale Law Journal. 1964, 2002.

D. Secondary sources
Asquith, H.H. 1928. *Memories and Reflections 1852-1927*. London, Cassell.
Aylmer, G.E. 1971. *The Struggle for the Constitution. 1603-1689 England in the Seventeenth Century*. London, Blandford Press.
    1975. (ed.) *The Levellers in the English Revolution*. London, Thames and Hudson.
Baldwin, John and McConville, Michael. 1979. *Jury Trials*. Oxford Clarendon Press.
Bartlett, Robert. 1986. *Trial by Fire and Water: the Medieval Judicial Ordeal*. Oxford, Clarendon Press.
Beattie, J.M. 1977. 'Crime and Courts in Surrey 1736-1753 In J.S. Cockburn. *Crime in England 1550-1800*. London, Methuen & Co. Ltd.
    1986. *Crime and the Courts in England 1660-1800*. Oxford, Clarendon Press.
    1988. 'London Juries in the 1690s'. In Cockburn and Green (eds) *Twelve Good Men And True: The Criminal Trial Jury in England 1200-1800*. New Jersey, Princeton University Press.
    1991 'Scales of Justice: Defense Counsel and the English Criminal Trial in the Eighteenth and Nineteenth Centuries. *Law and History Review. University of Illinois Press.*
Bellamy, John. 1973. *Crime and Public Order in the Later Middle Ages*. London, Routledge & Kegan Paul.
    1979. *The Tudor Law of Treason: An Introduction*. London, Routledge & Kegan Paul.
    1984. *Criminal Law and Society in Late Medieval and Tudor England*. Gloucester, Alan Sutton.
    1998. *The Criminal Trial in Later Medieval England*. Stroud, Sutton Publishing.
Black, J.B. 1959. *The Reign of Elizabeth 1558-1603*. Oxford, The Clarendon Press.
Blake, Nicholas. 1988. 'The Case for the Jury.' In Findlay and Duff (eds) *The Jury Under Attack*. London, Butterworths.
Brailsford, H.N. 1976. *The Levellers and the English Revolution*. London, Spokerman Books.
Brewer and Styles. 1980. *An Ungovernable People: The English and their Law in the Seventeenth and Eighteenth Centuries*. London, Hutchinson.
Bryant, Arthur. 1984. *Set in a Silver Sea*. London, Collins.
Cairns, David J.A. 1998. *Advocacy and the Making of the Adversarial Criminal Trial 1800-1865*. Oxford, Clarendon Press.

Cairns and McLeod (eds). 2002. *The Dearest Birthright of the People of England: The Jury in the History of the Common Law*. Oxford. Hart Publishing.

Cockburn, J.S. 1972. *A History of English Assizes 1558-1714*. Cambridge, Cambridge University Press.

1977. *Crime in England.1550-1800*. London, Methuen & Co. Ltd.

1985. *Introduction to Calendar of Assize Records: Home Circuit Indictments: Elizabeth I and James I*. London, H.M.S.O.

1988. (with T.A. Green, eds) *Twelve Good Men and True: The Criminal Trial Jury in England 1200-1800*. New Jersey, Princeton University Press.

Cole, G.D.H. 1966. *A Short History of the British Working-Class Movement: 1789-1947*. London, George Allen & Unwin Ltd.

Cornish, W.R. 1968. *The Jury*. London, Allen Lane The Penguin Press.

1978a. 'Criminal Justice and Punishment.' In *Crime and Law in Nineteenth Century Britain*. Dublin, Irish University Press.

1978b. 'Defects in Prosecuting – Professional Views in 1845.' In Glazebrook, P.R. (ed) *Reshaping the Criminal Law: Essays in honour of Glanville Williams*. London, Stevens & Sons.

Darbyshire, Penny. 1991. 'The Lamp That Shows That Freedom Lives – is it Worth the Candle?' *The Criminal Law Review*. London, Sweet & Maxwell.

1997. 'An Essay on the Importance and Neglect of the Magistracy.' *The Criminal Law Review*. London, Sweet & Maxwell.

Darbyshire, P. and others. 2001 *What Can the English Legal System Learn From Jury Research Published up to 2001?* www.kingston.ac.uk/~ku00596.elsres01.pdf

Denning, Sir Alfred. 1949. *Freedom Under The Law*. London, Stevens & Sons Ltd.

Devlin, Sir Patrick. 1960. *Trial by Jury*. London, Methuen & Co. Ltd.

1991. 'The Conscience of the Jury.' *The Law Quarterly Review*. London, Stevens & Sons.

Duff, Peter. 2000. 'The Defendant's Right to Trial by Jury: A Neighbour's View.' *The Criminal Law Review*. London, Sweet & Maxwell.

Dwyer, Déirdre M. 2003 'Review of Langbein's *The Origins of Adversary Criminal Trial*.' 66 *The Modern Law Review*. Oxford, Blackwell Publishing.

Elton, G.R. 1972. *Policy and Police. The* Enforcement *of the Reformation in the Age of Thomas Cromwell*. Cambridge, Cambridge University Press.

Enright, SE. & Morton, J. 1990. *Taking Liberties: The Criminal Jury in the 1990s*. London, Weidenfeld and Nicolson.

Epstein, James. 1996. *'Our Real Constitution': Trial Defence and Radical Memory in the Age of Revolution*. In James Vernon (ed.) *Re-reading the Constitution: New Narratives in the Political History of England's Long Nineteenth Century*. Cambridge, Cambridge University Press.

Fielding, Henry. 1751. *An Enquiry into the Causes of the Late Increase in Robbers*. London, A. Millar.

Fisher, George. 1997. 'The Jury's Rise as Lie Detector.' 107 *Yale Law Journal*.

Forsyth, William. 1852. *History of Trial by Jury*. London, John Parker.

Fraser, Antonia. 1996. *The Gunpowder Plot: Terror and Faith in 1605*. London, Weidenfeld & Nicolson.

Freeman, M.D.A. 1981a. 'Why Not a Jury Nullification Statute Here Too?' London, *New Law Journal*.

1981b. 'The Jury on Trial.' 34 *Current Legal Problems*. London, Stevens & Sons.

Friedman, Richard D. 2002. 'No Link: the Jury and the Origins of the Confrontation Right and the Hearsay Rule.' In Cairns and McLeod. '*The Dearest Birth Right of the People of England': The Jury in the History of the Common Law* . Oxford, Hart Publishing.

Garmonsway, G.N. 1977. *The Anglo-Saxon Chronicle*. London, J.M. Dent & Sons.

Glazebrook, (ed) P.R. 1978. *Reshaping the Criminal Law: Essays in Honour of Glanville Williams*. London, Stevens & Sons.

Green, J.R. 1974. *A Short History of the English People*. London, Folio Society.

Green, T.A. 1985. *Verdict According to Conscience. Perspectives on the English Criminal Jury Trial 1200-1800*. Chicago, University of Chicago Press.

1988. (with J.S. Cockburn eds.) *Twelve Good Men and True: The Criminal Trial Jury in England, 1200-1800*. New Jersey, Princeton University Press.

Gregg, Pauline. 1986. *Freeborn John: A Biography of John Lilburne*. London, J.M. Dent & Sons Ltd.

Groot, Roger D. 1982. 'The Jury of Presentment Before 1215.' 26 *The American Journal of Legal History*. North Carolina University Press.

1983. 'The Jury in Private Criminal Prosecutions Before 1215.' *The American Journal of Legal History. Ibid*.

1988. 'The Early-Thirteenth-Century Criminal Jury.' In Cockburn and Green (eds) *Twelve Good Men and True: The Criminal Trial Jury in England, 1200-1800*. New Jersey, Princeton University Press.

2002. 'Petit Larceny, Jury Lenity and Parliament.' In *'The Dearest Birthright of the People of England': The Jury in the History of the Common Law*. Oxford, Hart Publishing.

Hall, Jerome. 1935. *Theft, Law and Society*. Boston, Little Brown & Co.

Haller, W. 1944. *The Leveller Tracts 1647-1653*. New York, Columbia University Press.

Halsbury, Lord. 1911. *The Laws of England*. London, Butterworths.

Hamilton, Dick. 1979. *Foul Bills and Dagger Money. 88 Years of Lawyers and Lawbreakers*. London, Book Club Associates.

Handler, Philip. 2002. 'The Limits of Discretion: Forgery and the Jury at the Old Bailey, 1818-21.' In Cairns and McLeod. (eds) *The Dearest Birthright of the People of England: The Jury in the History of the Common Law*. Oxford, Hart Publishing.

Hardy, Thomas. 1832. *Memoir*. London, James Ridgway.

Harman, Harriet and Griffith, John. 1979. *Justice Deserted: The Subversion of the Jury*. London, National Council for Civil Liberties.

Havighurst, A.F. 1950. 'The Judiciary and Politics in the Reign of Charles II'. 66 *The Law Quarterly Review*. London, Stevens and Sons.

1953. 'James II and the Twelve Men in Scarlet'. 69 *The Law Quarterly Review*. London, Stevens and Sons.

Hay, Douglas. 1975a. 'Property, Authority and the Criminal Law.' In *Albion's Fatal Tree: Crime and Society in Eighteenth-Century England*. London, Allen Lane.

1975b. 'Poaching and the Game Laws on Cannock Chase.' *Ibid*.

1988.'The Class Composition of the Palladium of Liberty'. In Cockburn and Green, *Twelve Good Men and True*. New Jersey, Princeton University Press.

Heath, James. 1982. *Torture and English Law: An Administrative and Legal History from the Plantagenets to the Stuarts*. Westport, Connecticut.

Herrup, Cynthia B. 1985. 'Law and Morality in Seventeenth-Century England.' *Past & Present*. Oxford. The Past and Present Society.

1987. *The Common Peace: Participation and the Criminal Law in Seventeenth-century England*. Cambridge, Cambridge University Press.

Hill, Christopher. 1966. *The Century of Revolution 1603-1714*. London, Thomas Nelson & Sons.

1972. *The World Turned Upside Down: Radical Ideas during the English Revolution*. London, Temple Smith.

Hoffheimer, Michael H. 1987. 'Review of Green's *Verdict According to Conscience*. 56 *University of Cincinnati Law Review*.

Holdsworth, Sir William. 1966. *A History of English Law*. vols. i, viii, x. London, Methuen & Co. Ltd. And Sweet & Maxwell.

Hostettler, John. 1992. *The Politics of Criminal Law: Reform in the Nineteenth Century*. Chichester, England. Barry Rose Law Publishers.

1996. *Thomas Erskine and Trial by Jury*. Chichester, Barry Rose.

1998. *At the Mercy of the State: A Study in Judicial Tyranny*. Chichester, Barry Rose.

Houlder, Bruce. 1997. 'The Importance of Preserving the Jury System and the Right of Election for Trial.' *The Criminal Law Review*. London, Sweet & Maxwell.

Hurnard, Naomi D. 1941. 'The Jury of Presentment and the Assize of Clarendon.' *The English Historical Review*. London, Longman's Green and Co.

Hyams, Paul R. 1981. *Trial by Ordeal: The Key to Proof in the Early Common Law*. In Arnold, Morris S. and others, *On the Laws and Customs of England*. Chapel Hill, The University of North Carolina Press.

Inderwick, F.A. 1891. *The Interregnum 1648-1660: Studies of the Commonwealth, Legislative, Social and Legal*. London, Sampson Low, Marston, Searl & Rivington.

Ives, E.W. and Manchester A.H. (eds) 1983. *Law, Litigants and the Legal Profession*. London, The Royal Historical Society.

Jackson, R.M. 1937. 'The Incidence of Jury Trial During the Past Century.' *The Modern Law Review*. London, Stevens and Sons Limited.

Jacob, E.F. 1997. *The Fifteenth Century*. Oxford. Clarendon Press.

Jardine, D. 1838. *A Reading on the Use of Torture. Edinburgh Review*.

Jones, George Hilton. 1990. *Convergent Forces: Immediate Causes of the Revolution of 1688 in England*. Iowa, State University Press.

Kerr, Margaret andothers. 1992. *Cold Water and Hot Iron: Trial by Ordeal in England*. 22 J. Interdisc. Hist.

Keeton, G.W. 1965 *Lord Chancellor Jeffreys and the Stuart Cause*. London, MacDonald.

Kenyon, J.P. 1986. *The Stuart Constitution 1603-1688*. Cambridge, Cambridge University Press.

King, Peter. 1988. 'Illiterate Plebeians, Easily Misled': Jury Composition, Experience and Behaviour in Essex, 1735-1815. In Cockburn and Green.(eds) *Twelve Good Men and True: The Criminal Trial Jury in England, 1200-1800*.

2000. *Crime,Justice, and Discretion in England 1740-1820*. Oxford, Oxford University Press.

Kiralfy, A.K.R. 1958. *Potter's Historical Introduction to English Law and its Institutions*. 4th edn. London, Sweet & Maxwell.

Landsman, Stephan. 1990. 'From Gilbert to Bentham: the Reconceptualization of Evidence Theory.' 36 *The Wayne Law Review.* University of Oregon School of Law.

Langbein, John H. 1973. 'The Origins of Public Prosecution at Common Law.' 17 *The American Journal of Legal History.* North Carolina University Press.

1974. *Prosecuting Crime in the Renaissance; England, Germany, France.* Cambridge, Mass. Harvard University Press.

1977. *Torture and the Law of Proof: Europe and England in the Ancien Regime.* Chicago, University of Chicago Press.

1978. 'The Criminal Trial before the Lawyers.' Chicago, *University of Chicago Law Review.'*

1983a. 'Albion's Fatal Flaws.' *Past & Present.* Oxford, The Past and Present Society.

1983b. 'The 18th Century Criminal Trial.' Chicago, 50 *University of Chicago Law Review.*

1983c. 'Shaping the Eighteenth-Century Criminal Trial: A View from the Ryder Sources. Chicago, 50 *University of Chicago Law Review.*

1987. 'The English Criminal Trial Jury on the Eve of the French Revolution.' In Padoa Schiappa, A. (ed) *The Trial Jury England, France, Germany: 1700-1900.* Berlin, Durcher & Humblot.

1999. 'The Prosecutorial Origins of Defence Counsel in the Eighteenth Century: The Appearance of Solicitors.' Cambridge, 58 *The Cambridge Law Journal.*

2003. *The Origins of Adversary Criminal Trial.* Oxford University Press.

Lawson, P.G. 1988. 'Lawless Juries? Composition and Behaviour of Hertfordshire Juries, 1573-1624'. In Cockburn and Green. *Twelve Good Men and True: The Criminal Trial Jury in England, 1200-1800.* New Jersey, Princeton University Press.

Leipold, Andrew D. 1996. 'Rethinking Jury Nullification.' Virginia, 82 *Virginia Law Review.*

Levy, Leonard W. 1999. *The Palladium of Justice: Origins of Trial by Jury.* Chicago, Ivan R. Dee.

Lilburne, John. 1648a. 'The Humble Petition.' In G.E. Aylmer (ed.) 1975. *The Levellers in the English Revolution.* London, Thames and Hudson.

1648b. 'England's New Chains Discovered.' In W. Haller. 1944 *The Leveller Tracts, 1647-1653.* New York, Columbia University Press.

Lloyd-Bostock, Sally. and Thomas, Cheryl. 1999. 'Decline of the "Little Parliament": Juries and Jury Reform in England and Wales.' *Law and Contemporary Problems.* Durham, North Carolina, Duke University.

Lloyd-Bostock, Sally. 2000a. 'The Effects on Juries of Hearing About the Defendant's Criminal Record: A Simulation Study'. London, *Criminal Law Review.*

2000b. 'The Continuing Decline of the English Jury.' In Neil Vidmar, (ed.) *World Jury Systems.* Oxford, Oxford University Press.

Lobban, Michael. 2002. 'The Strange Life of the English Civil Jury, 1837-1914.' In Cairns and McLeod (eds) *'The Dearest Birthright of the People of England': The Jury in the History of the Common Law.* Oxford, Hart Publishing.

Mackie, J.D. 1992. *The Earlier Tudors 1485-1558.* Oxford, Clarendon Press.

McLane, Bernard William. 1988. 'Juror Attitudes to Local Disorder: The Evidence of the 1328 Lincolnshire Trailbaston Proceedings'. New Jersey, Princeton University Press.

Macnair, Mike. 1999.' The Origins of the Jury: Vicinage and the Antecedents of the Jury.' Illinois, 17 *Law & History Review.*

Maitland, F.W. 1888. *Select Pleas of the Crown.* London, Selden Society.

1908. *The Constitutional History of England.* Cambridge, Cambridge University Press.

Manchester, A.H. 1980. *A Modern Legal History of England and Wales.* London, Butterworth & Co. Ltd.

Milsom, S.F.C. 1969. *Historical Foundations of the Common Law.* London, Butterworth & Co. Ltd.

Musson, Anthony. 1997. 'Twelve Good Men and True? The Character of Early Fourteenth-Century Juries.' 15 *University of Illinois Law and History Review.*

Nichols, F.M. 1865. *Britton.* Oxford, Oxford University Press.

Odgers, Blake. 1901. *A Century of Law Reform.* London, Macmillan.

Ogg, David. 1969. *England in the Reigns of James II and William III.* Oxford, Oxford University Press.

Oldham, J.C. 1983. 'The Origins of the Special Jury'. Chicago, University Press.

Olson, Trisha. 2000. 'Of Enchantment: The Passing of the Ordeals and the Rise of the Jury Trials.' New York. 50 *Syracuse Law Review.*

Peters, Edward. 1986. *Torture.* Oxford, Basil Blackwell Ltd.

Pike, L.O. 1876. *A History of Crime in England.* London, Smith, Elder & Co.

Platt, Colin. 1978. *Medieval England.* London, Routledge & Kegan Paul.

Ploscowe, Morris. 1935. 'The Development of Present-Day Criminal Procedures in Europe and America.' 48 Harvard Law Review. Cambridge, Mass.

Plucknett, Theodore F.T. 1956. *A Concise History of the Common Law*. London, Butterworth & Co. (Publishers) Ltd.
1960. *Edward I and Criminal Law*. Cambridge, Cambridge University Press.
Pollock & Maitland. 1895. *The History of English Law*. 2 vols. Cambridge University Press.
Post, J.B. 1988. 'Jury Lists and Juries in the Late Fourteenth Century'. In Cockburn and Green (eds) *Twelve Good Men and True: The Criminal Trial Jury in England, 1200-1800*. New Jersey. Princeton University Press.
Postgate, Raymond. 1956. *That Devil Wilkes*. London, Dennis Dobson.
Powell, E. 1988. 'Jury Trial at Gaol Delivery in the Late Middle Ages'. In Cockburn and Green (eds.) *Twelve Good Men and True: The Criminal Trial Jury in England, 1200-1800*. New Jersey, Princeton University Press.
Prall, Stuart E. 1966. *The Agitation for Law Reform during the Puritan Revolution, 1640-60*. The Hague, Nijhoff.
Pugh, Martin. 1980. *Women's Suffrage in Britain 1867-1928*. London, The Historical Association.
2001. *The Pankhursts*. London, Allen Lane.
Pugh, Ralph B. 1975. *Calendar of London Trailbaston Trials under Commissions of 1305 and 1306*. London, HMSO.
Radcliffe and Cross. 1964. *The English Legal System*. London, Butterworths.
Radzinowicz, Leon. 1948. *A History of English Criminal Law and its Administration from 1750*. vol. i. *The Movement for Reform*. London, Stevens and Sons Ltd.
Randle and Pottle. 1989. *The Blake Escape: How We Freed George Blake and Why*. London, Harrap.
Read, Conyers. 1962. *William Lambarde and Local Government. His 'Ephemeris' and Twenty-nine Charges to Juries and Commissions*. Ithaca, New York, Cornell University Press.
Reynolds, Susan. 1997. *Kingdoms and Communities in Western Europe, 900 -1300*. Oxford, Clarendon Press.
Roberts, Clayton. 1966. *The Growth of Responsible Government in Stuart England*. Cambridge, Cambridge University Press.
Roberts, S.K. 1982. 'Jury Vetting in the 17th Century.' *History Today*. London, Trueword Ltd.
1988. 'Juries and the Middling Sort'. In Cockburn and Green (eds). *Twelve Good Men and True: The Criminal Trial Jury in England, 1200-1800*. New Jersey, Princeton University Press.
Rudé, George. 1962. *Wilkes and Liberty. A Social Study of 1763 to 1774*. Oxford, Clarendon Press.
Russell, Lord John. 1823. *On the English Government*. London.
Sabine, G.H. (ed.) 1941. *The Works of Gerard Winstanley*. Cornell University Press.
Sayles, G. 1938. *Select Cases in the Court of King's Bench under Edward I*. London, Barnard Quaritch.
Scheflin, A. and Van Dyke, J. 1980. 'Jury Nullification: The Contours of a Controversy.' 43 *Law and Contemporary Problems*. Durham, North Carolina, Duke University.
Seipp, David J. 2002 'Jurors, Evidences and the Tempest of 1499.' In Cairns and McLeod. *'The Dearest Birthright of the People of England': The Jury in the History of the Common Law*. Oxford, Hart Publishing.
Shapiro, Barbara J. 1983. *Probability and Certainty in Seventeenth-Century England: A Study of the Relationships Between Natural Science, Religion, History, Law, and Literature*. New Jersey, Princeton University Press.
1991. *Reasonable Doubt and Probable Cause*. Berkeley, University of California Press.
Skyrme, Sir Thomas. 1979. *The Changing Image of the Magistracy*. London, The Macmillan Press Limited.
1991. *History of the Justices of the Peace*. Chichester, Barry Rose Publishers.
Stanley, Eric Gerald. 2000. *Imagining the Anglo-Saxon Past. The Search for Anglo-Saxon Paganism and Anglo-Saxon Trial by Jury*. Woodbridge, England, Boydell and Brewer Ltd.
Stenton, Sir Frank. 1985. *Anglo-Saxon England*. Oxford, The Clarendon Press.
Stephen, James Fitzjames. 1883. *A History of the Criminal Law of England*. London, Macmillan.
Stephen, Leslie. 1991. *Hours in a Library*. London,The Folio Society.
Stern, Simon. 2002. 'Between Local Knowledge and National Politics: Debating Rationales for Jury Nullification After Bushell's Case.' Hartford. *Yale Law Journal.*
Stryker, Lloyd Paul. 1947. *For the Defense. Thomas Erskine the most Enlightened Liberal of his Times, 1750-1823*. New York, Doubleday & Co.
Thayer, J.B. 1898. *A Preliminary Treatise on Evidence at the Common Law*. Boston, Little, Brown and Company.
Thompson, E.P. 1968. *The Making of the English Working Class*. London, Penguin Books.
1975. *Whigs and Hunters: The Origin of the Black Act*. London, Allen Lane.
1980. *Writing by Candlelight*. London, Merlin Press. Thorne, S.E. 1957. Selden Society Lecture on Coke.
Van Caenegem, R.C. 1991. 'Public Prosecution of Crime in Twelfth-Century England'. In *Legal History: A European Perspective*. London, Hambledon Press.
Veall, Donald. 1970. *The Popular Movement for Law Reform 1640-1660*. Oxford, Clarendon Press.
Vennard, J. 1985. 'The Outcome of Contested Trials.' In D. Moxon (ed.) *Managing Criminal Justice*. London, HMSO.

Vidmar, Neil. 2000. 'A Historical and Comparative Perspective on the Common Law Jury.' In Vidmar (ed.) *World Jury Systems*. Oxford, Oxford University Press.

Vogler, Richard. (1991) *Reading the Riot Act: The Magistracy, the Police and the Army in Civil Disorder*. Milton Keynes, Open University Press.
  Unpublished comparative study of the jury.

Warren, W.L. 1973. *Henry II*. London, Eyre Methuen.

Warshawsky, Steven M. 1996. 'Opposing Jury Nullification: Law, Policy and Prosecutorial Strategy', Washington, 85 *Georgetown Law Journal*.

Watson, J. Steven, 1960. *The Reign of George III 1760-1815*. Oxford, The Clarendon Press.

Weinstein, Jack B. 1993. 'Considering Jury "Nullification": When May and Should a Jury Reject the Law to do Justice.' 30 *American Criminal Law Review*.

Wells, Charles L. 1911. 'The Origin of the Petty Jury.' cvii. *The Law Quarterly Review*. London, Sweet and Maxwell.
  1914. 'Early Opposition to the Petty Jury in Criminal Cases'. cxvii. *The Law Quarterly Review*. London, Sweet & Maxwell.

Wharam, Alan. 1992. *The Treason Trials, 1794*. London, Leicester University Press.

Williams, Glanville. 1963. *The Proof of Guilt: A Study of the English Criminal Trial*. London, Stevens & Sons.

Winslow, Cal. 1975. 'Sussex Smugglers.' In D. Hay and Others. *Albion's Fatal Tree, Crime and Society In Eighteenth-Century England*. London, Allen Lane.

Wolfe, Don M. 1967. *Leveller Manifestoes and the Puritan Revolution*. London, Frank Cass.

Zander, Michael. 2000. 'The Criminal Standard of Proof—How Sure is Sure?' London, 150 *New Law Journal*.

Index

The Criminal Justice Act 2003
A GUIDE TO THE NEW PROCEDURES AND SENTENCING
Bryan Gibson (with Michael Watkins)

The ideal all-round treatment of the CJA 2003 and its impact across the criminal process. **Whatever else you read, you will value this clear and accessible introduction** which covers all the key aspects of the 2003 Act in a readable and accessible way. All the essentials: the keys to decoding 500 pages of statutory provisions - In just 172 pages! **Another Waterside Press 'best-seller'!** 2004 ISBN 1 904380 07 7. Outstanding value at just £16.50 (Direct mail price).

Policing a Safe, Just and Tolerant Society
AN INTERNATIONAL MODEL FOR POLICING
Peter Villiers and Robert Adlam

This book bases its title on the UK Home Office motto: **'Building a Safe, Just an Tolerant Society'.** To build and sustain a society that is tolerant safe and respec other fundamental principles is a key challenge of the modern era: and the theme this book. From the authors of the acclaimed *Police Leadership in the 21st Centur* (Waterside Press, 2003). With a **Foreword by Professor Conor Gearty** plus oth highly expert contributions. 2004 ISBN 1 904380 09 3 160pp. Direct mail price £16.50

Images of Incarceration
REPRESENTATIONS OF PRISON IN FILM AND TV DRAMA
David Wilson and Sean O'Sullivan

A thought-provoking work that examines fictional portrayals of imprisonment in order t provide challenging insights into **how popular culture affects public understandin of penal issues and hence influences penal policy via the democratic proces** *'Images of Incarceration* will appeal to criminologists, sociologists, penal reformer media students and academics [etc.] . . . Recommended': *Scolag Legal Journal*. 200 ISBN 1 904380 08 5 172pp. Direct mail price. £16.50.

In Place of Rage and Violence
POEMS AND STORIES FROM WELFORD ROAD
Edited by Tim Reeves

Edited by HM Prison Leicester writer in residence **Tim Reeves.** Prisoners communicat their thoughts, experiences and feelings in their own words in a unique collectio amassed by the editor during his two year stint at Welford Road. 2004 ISBN 1 90438 14 X. 80pp. Direct mail price £8.50.

Punishments of Former Days Ernest Pettifer

An absorbing account of the origins and development of punishments in England. Found in the archives. Published in 1937: reprinted 1992 ISBN 1 872 870 05 8 £12.

Also by **John Hostettler**: *Famous Cases* and *Hanging in th Balance* (with Brian P Block) - Visit www.watersidepress.co.uk